Salman Rushdie's Cities

Continuum Studies in the City
Series Editors: Lawrence Phillips, Reader in English Literature, University of Northampton, UK; Matthew Beaumont, Senior Lecturer in English, University College London, UK.

Editorial Board: Professor Rachel Bowlby (University College London, UK); Brycchan Carey, Reader in English Literature (Kingston University London, UK); Professor Susan Alice Fischer (City University of New York, USA); Professor Pamela Gilbert (University of Florida, USA); Professor Richard Lehan (University of California, USA); Professor John McLeod (University of Leeds, UK); Alex Murray, Lecturer (University of Exeter, UK); Professor Deborah Epstein Nord (Princeton University, USA); Professor Douglas Tallack (University of Leicester, UK); Professor Philip Tew (Brunel University, UK); Professor David Trotter (University of Cambridge, UK); Professor Judith Walkowitz (Johns Hopkins University, USA); Professor Julian Wolfreys (Loughborough University, UK).

The history of literature is tied to the city. From Aeschylus to Addison, Baudelaire to Balzac, Conrad to Coetzee and Dickens to Dostoevsky, writers make sense of the city and shape modern understandings through their reflections and depictions. The urban is a fundamental aspect of a substantial part of the literary canon that is frequently not considered in and of it self because it is so prevalent.

Continuum Studies in the City **captures the best contemporary criticism on urban literature. Reading literature, drama and poetry in their historical and social context and alongside urban and spatial theory, this series explores the impact of the city on writers and their work.**

Titles in the Series:
The Contemporary New York Novel
Mark Brown

Irish Writing London: Volumes 1 and 2
Edited by Tom Herron

London in Contemporary British Literature
Edited by Nick Hubble, Philip Tew and Lynn Wells

Salman Rushdie's Cities
Vassilena Parashkevova

Salman Rushdie's Cities

Reconfigurational Politics and the Contemporary Urban Imagination

Vassilena Parashkevova

Continuum Studies in the City

continuum

Continuum International Publishing Group

The Tower Building	80 Maiden Lane
11 York Road	Suite 704
London, SE1 7NX	New York, NY 10038

www.continuumbooks.com

British Library Cataloguing-in-Publication Data
A catalogue record for this book is available from the British Library.

ISBN: HB: 978-1-4411-4850-6

Library of Congress Cataloguing-in-Publication Data
Parashkevova, Vassilena.
Salman Rushdie's cities: reconfigurational politics and the contemporary urban
imagination/Vassilena Parashkevova.
   p. cm. – (Continuum studies in the city)
Includes bibliographical references and index.
ISBN 978-1-4411-4850-6 (hardcover: alk. paper) – ISBN 978-1-4411-9256-1 (pdf) –
ISBN 978-1-4411-4864-3 (epub) 1. Rushdie, Salman–Criticism and interpretation.
2. Cities and towns in literature. I. Title. II. Series.
PR6068.U757Z797 2012
823'.914–dc23   2011049514

Typeset by Deanta Global Publishing Services, Chennai, India
Printed and bound in Great Britain

For Ivanichka and Neil

Contents

Acknowledgements

I am indebted to John Thieme and Geraldine Stoneham for their kind support and advice from the very inception of this project and to Claire Chambers who commented on parts of the work in progress at a very short notice. Thanks are due to Muneeza Shamsie for her helpful suggestions on Pakistani fiction in English and to Sara Upstone for her practical advice on copyright. I am particularly grateful to Beverley Goring, Michal Lyons and Suzanne Scafe for their timely (and ingenious) assistance in broadening my access to research resources in the face of unexpected but formidable adversities. To all those closest to me – my mother and brother, Ivanichka and Milen Parashkevov, my partner, Neil Leslie, and my dear friend, Maria Barrett, I am eternally obliged for their unfailing moral (and, sometimes, financial) support and for 'living in' my project with me.

Earlier versions of some of the discussions in this book appeared previously in the following publications, material from which is reprinted with kind permission. The discussion of catoptric urban configurations in the introduction and of *The Satanic Verses* in Chapter 3 was first published in '"Turn your watch upside down in Bombay and you see the time in London": catoptric urban configurations in Salman Rushdie's *The Satanic Verses*', *The Journal of Commonwealth* Literature 42(3), September 2007, and is reprinted by kind permission of SAGE Publications Ltd. Discussion of warring urban fictions in *The Moor's Last Sigh* was first published in '"Falling off" the urban map: cartographic divisions and travel in Salman Rushdie's *The Moor's Last Sigh*', *Commonwealth Essays and Studies* 31(2), 2009 and I am grateful to the editor, Marta Dvorak, for her kind permission to reprint it here. Part of the discussion of catoptric urban configurations in *The Ground beneath Her Feet* first appeared in 'Catoptric echoes and reversals: urban old/new bi-vocalities in Salman Rushdie's *The Ground beneath Her Feet*', *Journal of Postcolonial Writing* 45(4), 2009 and is reprinted by permission of

Taylor & Francis Group. Discussion of visual art in *The Moor's Last Sigh* will be first published as part of '"Living art": artistic and intertextual re-envisionings of the urban trope in *The Moor's Last Sigh*' in ed. Ana Mendes, *Salman Rushdie and Visual Culture: Celebrating Impurity, Disrupting Borders* (Routledge, 2011).

Abbreviations

Salman Rushdie's works and collected interviews:

CSR	*Conversations with Salman Rushdie*, Michael R. Reder (ed.)
EF	*The Enchantress of Florence*
EW	*East, West*
F	*Fury*
GBHF	*The Ground beneath Her Feet*
HSS	*Haroun and the Sea of Stories*
IH	*Imaginary Homelands*
LFL	*Luka and the Fire of Life*
MC	*Midnight's Children*
MLS	*The Moor's Last Sigh*
SATL	*Step across This Line*
S	*Shame*
SC	*Shalimar the Clown*
SV	*The Satanic Verses*
WO	*The Wizard of Oz*

An Alphabet of Rushdie's Cities

Historical, literary, 'lost' and 'new' - and works in which they appear:

Agra	MC
Amritsar	MC
Amsterdam	F, SC
Baghdad	MC (*passim*)
Belgrade	F (*passim*)
Benares/Varanasi	MC
Bombay/Mumbai	**MC, MLS, SV, GBHF**, F
Cambridge	'The Harmony of the Spheres' (EW, 125-46), F
'City beneath the postcard mountain'	SV
Delhi/New Delhi	**MC**, SC
Dacca/Dhaka	MC
Fatehpur Sikri	EF
Florence	EF
Gup City and Chup City	HSS
Genoa	EF
Granada	**MLS**, 'Christopher Columbus and Queen Isabella of Spain Consummate Their Relationship' (EW, 107-19)
Guadalajara	GBHF
Herat	EF
Islamabad	S
Jahilia	SV
Jerusalem	SV (*passim*)
Kabul	EF
Kahani	HSS, LFL
Karachi	MC, S
London	S, **SV, GBHF**, F, SC
Las Vegas	GBHF (figurative use)
Los Angeles	SC

Tabriz	EF
Mecca	SV
Medina	SV
Mexico City	GBHF
Mildendo	F
New York City	SV, **GBHF**, **F**
Paris	SC (*passim*)
Q./Quetta	S
Rawalpindi	MC, S
Rome	GBHF, F (figurative use)
'Saddest of cities'	HSS
Samarkand	EF
Srinagar	MC, 'The Prophet's Hair' (EW, 35-58), SC
Strasbourg	SC (*passim*)
Stamboul (Istanbul)	EF
Targoviste	EF
Troy	GBHF (figurative use)

Chapter 1

Introduction: Salman Rushdie's Cities and Reconfigurational Politics

When Osama Bin Laden was 'discovered' and killed by U.S. forces on 2 May 2011, the whole world learned of the Pakistani city of Abbottabad. Prior to this newsworthy event, it appeared to have shared its unknown whereabouts with the Al-Qaeda leader, though for very different reasons. Yet, the two will now be forever, and in complex ways, connected to each other. Location became, once again, an event – as much an event in the efforts of pinpointing an abstract, invisible, and elusive 'terror' as a forceful *cartographic* event. Bin Laden's unearthing put Abbottabad on the world map – at once, as a peaceful holiday town, the victim of a 'resident evil' from which it was explosively liberated; a garrison city accused of being criminally unaware of the alien presence close by and, now, almost a tourist attraction. Abbottabad was violently born into conflicting geopolitical configurations and with 'links' to other locations caught in them. Notably, these other locations included two cities, strategic points of reference already 'established' on the world map – the Pakistani capital of Islamabad, the proximity to which was recurrently cited and illustrated with maps, satellite images and computer graphics, and New York as the 'ground zero' of 9/11, to which Abbottabad was a response and to which New York, in turn, was shown responding live. Madrid and London were then added to this map, followed by the Tora Bora caves in the mountains of Afghanistan and the Arabian Sea, where Bin Laden's body was laid to rest. As a result, Abbottabad is now part of the stories of these places as well as of religious extremism, of the limits of Pakistan's national sovereignty in the context of the 'war on terror' and Western aid to the country, of the pain and suffering afflicted by terrorism and of the injustices that gave rise to it in the first place. Put in a different way, this developing configuration of stories has laid mutually antagonistic claims on Abbottabad, which attempt to give meaning to it and which now effectively constitute it within the continuing metanarrative of 'Third World newsworthiness'.

In a related context, Salman Rushdie makes a similar point in his essay on *The Baburnama*, the autobiography of the first Mughal Emperor, Zahiruddin Muhammad Babur (1483–1530). He comments on the shift of Western interest in this book, from its Indian part, with its first-hand account of the birth of the Mughal Empire, supplanted centuries later by the British, to its 'Afghan' part, with its descriptions of cities such as Konduz or Kabul, now part of a newly intriguing cartography (SATL, 188–92).

All these cities can be described as 'contemporary' in the sense that this book adopts, that is, not merely as existing in the present, but in and through the ways they have been brought into, and that they participate in, present cultural and political configurations. Employing Rushdie, more broadly, as a guide to a historicized contemporary through a postcolonial emphasis on the political worldliness of literature has been one of the main strategies of reading his work. Rushdie has himself recurrently stressed that such a positioning 'outside the whale' or 'in a world without hiding places' (IH, 99) is the political responsibility of contemporary novelists. In recent interviews, he repeatedly contrasts his work with that of Jane Austen, who could live and write, he points out, during the Napoleonic wars, but barely make a reference to them in her novels (see Rushdie 2008a, 19).

That Rushdie has acquired an almost cult status as a cultural commentator, however, is evinced in statements such as the following: Ruvani Ranasinha ends her piece on events since the 'Rushdie Affair', in the *Cambridge Companion to Salman Rushdie* (2007a), with a nearly devotional plea: 'we await our foremost commentator's response' (56). Indeed, Rushdie and his writing have been called upon not only to comment on the contemporary but also to suggest remedies for present conflicts.

At the other extreme of the reception of Rushdie's work, Timothy Brennan (1989) and Aijaz Ahmad (1992) have taken issue with the implications of the 'Third World cosmopolitan' position from which the author offers his assessment of the contemporary. In a paraphrase of the opening sentence of L.P. Hartley's 1953 novel, *The Go-Between*, Rushdie famously wrote that 'it may be that the past is a country from which we have all emigrated, that its loss is part of our common humanity' (IH, 12). In response, Ahmad argued that such an articulation of migrancy as an 'ontological condition of all human beings' (127) posits an 'ideological location', which enables him to borrow themes and issues from the counter-canon of 'Third-World Literature', thereby validating the idea of 'the availability of all cultures of the world for consumption' (128), while masking his 'moorings in the High Culture of the modern metropolitan bourgeoisie' (127). In particular, he found the conditions of Rushdie's production rooted in and mimicking the modernist trope of 'self-exile':

> . . . that predominant image of the modern artist who lives as a *literal* stranger in a foreign and impersonal city and who, on the one hand, uses the condition of exile as the basic metaphor for modernity and even for the human condition itself, while, on the other, writing obsessively, copiously, of that very land which had been declared 'suffocating'. (134)

While this image of the modernist city of exile can hardly do justice to the cities inhabited by Rushdie's protagonists, it is reminiscent of an urban location that he critiques in the figure of the Imam, who attempts to close himself off London's realities in his Kensington flat in *The Satanic Verses*. The cosmopolitanism of Rushdie's cities is modelled, in particular, on the precedent of Bombay, whose secular mixture of faiths and cultures has an archetypal status in his work. Although an idealization, as historian Thomas Blom Hansen (2002) has pointed out, this archetype nevertheless posits a useful, dynamic and itself reconfigurable point of critique against which Rushdie judges cities across a vast historical and geographical range, including Delhi, Karachi, Islamabad, Mecca, London, Florence, Mexico City, New York, Los Angeles, and Suva, as well as Bombay's own deviations from the ideal it has engendered.

An important aspect of employing Rushdie as a guide to the contemporary, however, involves tracing the specificities and complexities of its configurations. These configurations include, most prominently, the interurban trajectory Bombay–London–New York and, particularly, the idea of America as the final destination and culmination of postcolonial diasporas, what Michelle Keown *et al.* refer to as the 'unidirectional migratory model privileging the US' (2009, 9). A related development within which Rushdie's writing should be seen is the global circulation and institutionalized visibility of the Indian novel in English as opposed to those written in the many vernacular languages of India or those translated into English. His writing favours a multiply mediated over a straightforward, source-to-target translation. In his now notorious 1997 *New Yorker* essay on Indian writing (versions of which also appeared in the co-edited anthologies *Mirrorwork* and *The Vintage Book of Indian Writing*, published in the same year), he argued that Indian fiction in English constitutes a 'stronger and more important body of work' than vernacular writing and thus the 'most valuable contribution India has yet made to the world of books' (1997, viii). While such a sweeping statement points to the hegemonic role of English in global

publishing as well as Rushdie's privileged place in it, Sarah Brouillette draws
attention to the similarly dangerous claims that have emerged in defence of
an 'authentic' vernacular:

> Transnational firms now commit to publishing the same vernacular lan-
> guages they were once engaged in marginalizing, as they recognise that
> English is not the only globalisable South Asian language. . . . A cele-
> brated and romanticised localism is just as marketable as an ostensibly
> delocalized cosmopolitan English-language writing. (2007a, 37)

Whereas in Ahmad's accusations, we can recognize a similar localist claim,
they were aimed more specifically at Rushdie's indictment of Pakistan.
Indeed, as we shall see in both *Midnight's Children* and *Shame*, Pakistani cities
are given little potential for reconfiguration in their own right. They even
figure within the terms of a characteristically antipodean imagination, as
the inversion of the Bombay ideal. In response to Ahmad's argument, critics
such as Andrew Teverson have risen to Rushdie's defence in order to justify
the limits of his political commentary. Teverson argued that Rushdie's
politics should be seen as 'reactive', or in response to existing situations,
rather than 'transformative' (2004, 50–3). I would argue, however, that such
a distinction cannot address the complexity of Rushdie's politics. His writing
often crosses, and purposefully so, the fine line between a 'reactive' (or
what could be termed 'diagnostic') and a 'transformative' politics. One of
the central claims in this book is that Rushdie's urban politics is constituted
precisely in this passage between the two, a passage that is sometimes
explosive and frequently creative, regardless of whether this process tends
in a utopian or a dystopian direction. Utopia and dystopia have been
conceptualized as related, rather than diametrically opposed 'histories of
the present', which 'seek to alter the social order' not only by attending to
causes but also by offering 'revolutionary solutions' (Gordin *et al.*, 2010,
1–2). In Rushdie's writing, urban dystopias such as Bombay in *The Moor's
Last Sigh*, Islamabad in *Shame*, or Mildendo in *Fury* are shown as utopias
'gone wrong', or exclusive utopias, planned for a specific part of a community
(ibid.). *Fury* rehearses, as we shall see, a cycle of urban utopias and dystopias
that initially respond to an existing situation but then develop further into
an apocalyptic nightmare. This development is also creative or transformative, and it offers a solution – a Galilean choice between facing and
dismissing reality. If Thomas More's Utopia, originally connected to the
mainland by an isthmus, was transformed into an island by King Utopos,
Rushdie's urban utopias and dystopias never sever their links to the

'mainland' of the contemporary and its historical and cultural specificity. The term *Rushdiesque* has been coined to describe the creative aspect of these links, what we have conceptualized as the passage from 'reactive' to 'transformative' in his writing, involving the processes of cultural hybridity, translation and re-description. Despite the ways in which cities are disciplined, fixed or already configured, this study demonstrates that they are constantly in the process of reconfiguration.

Bombay's Place on Rushdie's Interurban Map: Cultural and Historical Coordinates

Most of Rushdie's novels establish configurations of two 'types' of cities: 'real' or named ones, which exist on the map, and coded, phantasmal, utopian or dystopian cities or places. These two urban types, however, engender and interact with each other in complicated and diverse ways. Bombay, Mecca and London generate Islam's precedent and other, Jahilia, as much as Jahilia generates them in *The Satanic Verses*. Granada and Bombay, on the one hand, and the Cervantes-indebted Benengeli, on the other, similarly produce each other in *The Moor's Last Sigh*. The recognizable Delhi, Cambridge, London, Amsterdam and New York interact with the Swiftian Mildendo in *Fury*. Exceptions to or variations on this rule are also significant. In *Midnight's Children*, *The Ground*, *Shalimar* and *The Enchantress*, all the cities are geographically identifiable but they can give rise to parallel versions of themselves or contain other cities. *Shame* alternates between a reluctance to name its cities and an overemphasis on clarifying their 'real' referents. While, as Jane Jacobs reminds us in her study on the postcolonial city, 'material and imagined geographies constitute each other' (1996, 3), in Rushdie's writing, this process is frequently and self-consciously pushed to an extreme. His work teems with cities, which multiply in a manner reminiscent of the arithmetical progression in which babies come out of Naveed Hyder's womb in *Shame*. This progression figures, on the one hand, in Marina Warner's sense of 'organic metamorphosis', as a process of positive, rejuvenating and creative shape-shifting (2002, 37). On the other hand, the 'natural' effect of this organic quality is repeatedly unsettled by the many urban dystopias that Rushdie's writing generates. Islamabad, for instance, is created out of 'Rawalpindi's rib' in *Shame* (200) in an ironic biblical allusion.

This book's main concerns are the complexity and diversity of this regeneration and proliferation of cities, seen within the materiality of the places in which the artistic production of cities is rooted and the lives of their inhabitants. While the following chapters will attend to the relevant cultural and historical contexts of Rushdie's many cities, in this Introduction, it is imperative to zoom in on Bombay as a city of a unique status in his writing.

Bombay has emerged and negotiated its place within a number of developing cultural, geopolitical and economic configurations. Home to the Koli fishermen, the seven islands that later formed the city were ruled by a succession of Hindu and Mughal dynasties until they were ceded to Portugal by the Sultan of Gujarat in the sixteenth century. The name 'Bombay' may have been a corruption of the Portuguese 'buan bahia' ('good harbour') and/or of the name of the local goddess Mumbadevi. In 1661, the islands were secured by the East India Company in a manner reminiscent of the matrimonial alliances forged by Mughal Emperor Akbar (1542–1605) with the Rajputs – as part of the dowry of a Portuguese princess, Catherine of Braganza, when she married Charles II (Metcalf *et al.*, 46). Bombay was born as a colonial city, a 'gateway to India' and India's gateway to the West, a trading port that attracted merchants, artisans and capital, and grew from 'the Cinderella' of English settlements in India, considered 'noxious and pestilential' by seventeenth-century European visitors, to a modern industrial city and a commercial capital of British India 200 years later. The Company's China trade, in cotton and opium, was instrumental to this development as it integrated Bombay into the imperial economy as well as established its connection to the hinterland (Chandavarkar 2009, 31–6). Gradually, however, the city redefined itself in contradistinction to the countryside, despite the fact that this was where most of its citizens had come from (Thorner 1995, xviii). By the nineteenth century, it had become selective in its openness to migrants by rejecting, for instance, famine refugees from rural areas (Masselos 1995, 51–2). Growth was paralleled by the intensification of social divisions. Kosambi compares this period's British perceptions of Bombay with those of its Maratha community, at opposite ends of the social hierarchy. Whereas the former associated it simultaneously with prosperity and poverty (the familiar dichotomy buttressing the civilizing mission of British colonialism) and considered it an exotic melting pot, the latter saw the city as a power centre of military might and economic wealth, a parasite exploiter that had produced extreme economic inequalities and that posed threats to purity and tradition (1995, 13–21). In these early articulations of Bombay by its Marathi-speaking poor, we can recognize the omens of what was to trigger the city's radical transformation in the 1990s.

The city's twentieth-century claim of representing modern India because of containing its multiplicities (Patel and Thorner 1995a) can be traced back to a particular historical development. In the context of India, the opposition city-village intersected that of city-nation in anti-colonial struggles and rhetoric. As Vinay Dharwadker notes, the Indian village and the Indian city 'deployed distinct antimetropolitan strategies and also opposed each other intransigently' (2001, 8). The opposition village-city is apparent in the contrast between Mahatma Gandhi's and Jawaharlal Nehru's political locations. Gandhi identified with the Indian village and excluded cities as materially and ideologically imperial constructions. Returning from South Africa in 1915, he expressed his dislike for Bombay: 'it looks as though it were the slum of London. I see here all the shortcomings of London but none of the amenities' (cited in Shukla, 94). Conversely, Nehru, an urban modernist and an 'unapologetically westernized Indian', identified with the city. This massive discursive and demographical shift from village to city, notes Dharwadker, is rendered in much of twentieth-century Indian literature, where the spatial axis from village to city intersects the temporal axis from colonial domination to Independence and Partition (10). The identification of modern India with the cosmopolitan city, however, silences the village or the countryside, which indeed is sometimes equated with a vast expanse of nothingness in Rushdie's novels. For instance, on his journey through Madhya Pradesh, the narrator in *The Ground* compares himself to a 'Cabot or Magellan of the land', exploring the 'sheer unchartedness' of rural India (GBHF, 238) in a manner reminiscent of the colonial homogenizing constructions of the land as blank or empty (Ryan, 12).

In an interview on his book, *A Journey to the City* (2007), tracing the implications of the rural–urban trajectory in India, Ashis Nandy laments the loss of the village as a crucial critical counterpart of the city: if the colonial city 'broke the dyad' and it now returns to the village mainly as a 'developer, planner, ruler, marauder, and functionary of the law-and-order machinery', the nostalgia for it survives in the discourse of globalization's trope of the global village, he reminds us (n. pag). While Rushdie critiques the pastoral nostalgia of the 'global village' in *The Moor*, as we shall see, his arrogance towards the countryside's inhabitants, whether in India or in America, for instance, can be seen in the way he describes his protagonist in *Fury*: a 'born-and-bred metropolitan of the countryside-is-for-cows persuasion' (6). At the same time, the region of Kashmir, which figures in the more mythic than urban topos of Srinagar in *Midnight's Children*, and in the village of Pachigan in *Shalimar*, offers a certain corrective to his urban preoccupations.

To return to the story of Bombay, Rushdie's urban ideal is associated with an image of 1950s–1960s' Bombay or the 'Bombay *classique*', as Hansen puts it (2008, 93), as a city that had drawn, from the start, on its open, secular and cosmopolitan mix of ethnicities, languages and cultural traditions. Undoubtedly, this post-Independence image of the city – of tolerance and chic – was exclusive to its elites. It was based, to a degree, on the profit its commercial and banking elites had made during the colonial era and that expanded to a global scale after Independence, as demonstrated by the growth of Bombay's cotton textile industry. Rather than being an effect of the enabling violations of colonialism, however, the specificity of Bombay's modernity, its diversity and hybridity, was drawn from its local experience; according to historian Rajnarayan Chandavarkar, it was specifically enabled by the autonomy of the city's elite from the colonial state. As early as the final decades of the nineteenth century,

> [Bombay's] public life was marked by its secularism, its equidistance from the particularisms of caste and religious community and often its transcendence of their differences. In the Indian imagination, the city had acquired [. . .] an almost mythic significance as a major metropolis. . . . In the decades after independence, . . . Bombay's residents took it for granted that they were a part of the vanguard that would pull India kicking and screaming into the modern world. . . . Religious or communal conflict was deemed alien to the city. (16–7)

Bombayites' confidence and pride in this resilience of their city's secular, eclectic ethos survived both the Partition of the subcontinent on 15 August 1947 and the partition of the state of Bombay along linguistic boundaries in 1960. Rushdie says in an interview that while 'a lot of Muslim families knew that Delhi was going to be difficult', in Bombay, 'essentially nothing happened at partition'; riots in Bombay 'were language riots', and religion was 'not a contentious issue' (2008a, 17–8). Bombay's cinema, specifically its 'masala (mixed spice) films' (Gangar 1995, 210), is often evoked as a cultural medium that both reflected and enhanced this spirit of the city as well as its long-standing traditions of street theatre. Cinema emerged precisely as an allegory of urban experience (Mazumdar, 2007).

This Bombay, as we suggested earlier, is posited in Rushdie's fiction as the urban ideal in relation to which all other cities are viewed – specifically, in the extent to which they are capable of accommodating this ideal or of developing it further, and in the extent to which they depart from it. It is important, however, to note that Bombay is never envisaged as a point of origin. Rushdie's novels trace a variety of ways of arriving in Bombay from a plural and already liminal elsewhere, whether that be Kashmir, the airspace above Britain, the port of Cochin, or America. *Midnight*, Rushdie's first 'Bombay novel', traces a journey *towards* Bombay as a city of multiple beginnings.

The Moor, however, raises questions about the extent to which this ideal was an exclusive utopia, a hybrid cosmopolitan melange reserved for the city's elite and middle classes, from which the urban poor were increasingly excluded. Hansen notes that *The Moor* reveals a Janus-faced Bombay in which upper-class life is intimately dependent on 'the underworld, on sectarian violence, and on brutal exploitation' (2002, 5). Yet, whereas Rushdie locates a rupture in the image of the city with the 'arrival of Hindu nationalist politics' (2008b, 18) – where the choice of 'arrival', pointing to an outside/alien influence, is perhaps not accidental – for Hansen, this ideal pre-Shiv Sena Bombay is 'a historical fantasy that conceals the fact that Bombay was always fundamentally divided by class, caste and religion' (2002, 5).

This change of Bombay, whether merely an intensification of long-standing tensions or a radical rupture from a previously existing cosmopolitan ethos, has been the object of much discussion and debate. The change is linked to the violent 1992–1993 riots in the city when thousands of Muslims were killed, following the earlier destruction of the Babri Masjid mosque in Ayodhya by Hindu fanatics in 1992, and to the growth of the Shiv Sena (founded in 1966) into a dominant political power. The Shiv Sena's 'pro-native' or 'sons-of-the soil' platform combines 'language chauvinism (Marathi), regional primordialism (a cult of the regional state of Maharashtra), and a commitment to a Hinduized India (Hindutva, the land of Hinduness)' (Appadurai 2000, 629). In November 1995, Bombay was officially renamed Mumbai (after the goddess Mumbadevi) in an attempt at reclaiming a pre-colonial urban identity, or at a 'vernacularization', as it was claimed (Hansen 2002, 1), as well as in an attempt at imposing on it a Maratha identity. While for Arjun Appadurai, this change is symptomatic of the city's 'decosmopolitanization' (649), Rashmi Varma refers to it as a 'provincialization', based more broadly on 'historically sedimented notions of particularisms (regional or local), homogeneity, and anticosmopolitanism' (2004, 66). Hansen traces back this regionalism to a seventeenth-century 'Deccan pastoral' mythology and describes it as a phenomenon with much deeper roots in Maharashtrian culture (20).

For Rushdie, the Bombay–Mumbai reformulation has become a veritable rupture in the history of the city, which has inaugurated a dark urban age and from which he has increasingly distanced himself. While in Hansen's view, 'the iconoclasm and unashamed enjoyment of difference and cultural impurities' is not extinct in Mumbai but is rather in the process of 'trying to find a new language in which to express itself and maybe produce a new set of urban utopias' (2008, 110), Rushdie has effectively abandoned imagining contemporary Mumbai.

Bombay, as an idea and an ideal, however, 'travels' in Rushdie's work, interacts with and is tested by other cities and places along his transnational East–West continuum. The broader interurban trajectory Bombay–London–New York in his fiction highlights the development of his political engagement with the processes of India's decolonization and the exclusions performed by South Asian nationalisms; the rise of ethnic/religious fundamentalism as a result of these exclusions and of the lingering effects of colonialism and the shift of the imperial centre from the British metropolis (as a metonymic articulation of British colonialism) to the seductive American metropolis, particularly New York City, as symbolic of the US's hegemonic leadership of a global liberal order in a post-Cold War world.

Urban Configurations

This book, then, foregrounds and investigates the location of Rushdie's cities at the dynamic intersections of colonial, postcolonial and global contexts. Each of these contexts contaminates, illuminates or interrogates the others, often resulting in contestatory geographical and historical configurations. Whereas explorations of Rushdie's work that foreground the urban problematic tend to focus on a particular city (usually, either London or Bombay), which is generally viewed in isolation from other urban topoi in the texts, the perspective of this study is urgently broader. In contrast to those investigations of cities that 'stay within the place', as Doreen Massey puts it (2007, 13), the discussion here offers an exploration of cities within their wider and constantly shifting interconnections with other cities and places. Rushdie's cities rarely stay within themselves.

The city is understood here as an arrangement of heterogeneous, shapeshifting and open-ended trajectories, of journeys, stories and histories, which intersect and interact with each other. *Urban configurations* refer to the temporary and uneven patterns achieved through or imposed on such arrangements and their potential to disturb hegemonic cultural and political orders or hierarchies. This conceptualization of cities is indebted to the work of cultural geographer Doreen Massey, specifically her idea of space as constituted through 'happenstance positionings-in-relation-to-each-other' (2005, 116). Space should be recognized, she argues, as being always under construction, as being predicated upon the existence of a plurality of stories and histories and as being constituted through interactions, 'from the immensity of the global to the intimately tiny' (ibid., 9). The term *urban configurations* seeks further to dissociate the city from its understanding as a delimited entity and from such theories that define cities exclusively in terms of types. Urban configurations spill over what are assumed to be the various boundaries of a city, criss-crossing the urban geographies beneath and within which they arise and unfold.

As a sobering reminder of the failures of urban reconfigurations, however, remains the possibility that they can lead to a conformity with existing power relations or to a mere reshuffling that replaces old with new structures of domination. Whereas cities can have a 'different relationship to global processes than the visions and policies of their nation states may admit or endorse', they are also crucial nodes in the development of neoliberalism and privileged sites for citizenship (Holsen and Appadurai, 1996, 189). B. S. A. Yeoh draws attention to the contemporary 'upsurge of urban image making' within the global economy, where 'place wars' are staged between cities to attract investors in a process of jostling for a share in a 'new urban utopia' (2005, 946). Reconfigurational politics is thus a contested politics of constant negotiation that is not immune to exclusions but that also, importantly, takes account of the ways in which hegemonic fictions and materialities of place are also capable of regroupings, realignments and adaptations.

Tectonic Urban Configurations

In *The Ground beneath Her Feet*, Rushdie posits tectonic instability as one of the defining aspects of life:

> Earthquakes, scientists say, are common phenomena. Globally speaking, there are around fifteen thousand tremors a decade. Stability is what's rare. The abnormal, the extreme, the operatic, the unnatural: these rule. There is no such thing as normal life. (GBHF, 500)

When in 1915, the German climatologist and geophysicist, Alfred Wegener, proposed his theory of continental drift, his ideas were met with considerable resistance by a scientific community entrenched in the belief of the permanence of the earth's crust. Later, this model was developed by the American geophysicist W. Jason Morgan into the theory of plate tectonics, widely accepted today, which argues that the earth's surface is divided into rigid plates that move in relation to each other and that folding, faulting and earthquakes take place mainly at the *margins* of these plates (Seyfert and Sirkin 1979, vii; 87). Plate tectonics hypothesizes the inherent dynamics of the earth's lithosphere, adopting a vocabulary of movement, instability and violence: floating, travelling, transformation, sliding, forcing, compression, tension, displacement and collision, where all these processes produce highly visible surface effects and can have global repercussions. For instance, the 2004 Indian Ocean tsunami, the earthquakes in China's south-western Sichuan province in 2008, in Italy's historic city of L'Aquila in 2009 and, most recently, the 'mega-thrust' earthquake in Japan on 11 March 2011 tragically demonstrated not only the rapidity of movement, the instability and the violent dynamics of tectonic activity, but also the ways in which a *discourse* of tectonic instability, particularly, a sudden and dramatic sense of *before* and *after*, can enter world consciousness and language. BBC's *Japan Earthquake: A Horizon Special* sensationally announced that the Japanese earthquake had shifted Earth's axis, affecting the speed of its rotation, which had, as a result, made each day slightly shorter for all of us. As Graham Huggan reminds us, the role of the global media is simultaneously 'constitutive' and 'distortive' in 'constructing the latest, highly visible human/ecological catastrophe as a newsworthy "event"' (2004, 705). The vivid vocabulary of tectonic science, in this case, is only further reinforced by the dramatic tropes of journalism. Here, emphasis was placed on the global implications of the events in Japan, and the viewer was invited to share in a scientifically inspired awe, paradoxically both for the power of nature and for the degree to which Japan, a country with extensive experience of seismic activity, but also, crucially, a 'developed' one, was technologically and economically 'prepared' to deal with such an emergency. By contrast, the coverage of the Indian Ocean or 'Boxing Day' tsunami in 2004 highlighted the poverty of the affected areas and the civil conflicts in Sri Lanka and Indonesia as the 'hardest hit' countries and focused on the worldwide humanitarian response in the spirit of (Western) Christmas giving. Seismic eruptions continue to occur as much along political and economic fault lines as they do along 'natural' ones.

The development of tectonic urban configurations in Rushdie's novels, as the following chapters demonstrate, draws on the full range of seismic processes, whether on literal or metaphorical levels, and lays bare the competing claims to their interpretation. These processes include the slow, gradual build-up of stress underground to the point where no more tension can be absorbed and where the smallest amount of pressure added can trigger an eruption; the eruption itself as the sudden release of pent-up energy, which can rip urban ground and send shock waves of destruction radiating outwards; the terror that ensues as the result not only of the earthquake's devastating effects but also of its unpredictability, of the very invisibility of underground activity until the point of tremor; the divisions and fault lines that the tremor reveals or deepens; the monolithic constructions it assaults; the regroupings it triggers and the human attempts to, variously, explain, forecast, suppress or appropriate it. These processes are often geared towards a politics of forceful, even explosive reconfiguration, but they are, at the same time, geographically, historically and politically contextualized. For instance, in *Midnight's Children*, cracks appear in the earth of the city that both presage and follow the partitioning of the Indian subcontinent in 1947; in *Shame*, urban earthquakes are interpreted as acts of tribal and migrant varieties of separatism in a politics of 'shaking into place'; *The Ground beneath Her Feet* demonstrates how seismic activity generates global divisions along both economic and discursive lines, and *The Enchantress of Florence* engages in remoulding the boundaries of 'continental' thought. Urban tectonics accumulates an extraordinary breadth of political significations in the form of anti-colonial resistance, postcolonial coup d'états, revolution, insurgencies of terror and secular/ ecological apocalypse. In this respect, it is important to note that the tectonic, like the catoptric and the specular, as we shall see, is necessarily ambiguous – it can be described as both a hegemonially situated movement and a liberating one. This study engages in exploring the conflictual configurations it assumes in and between the cities along the axis between critique and potential. 'Fault lines', for instance, figure in Samuel P. Huntington's neoliberal thesis of the 'clash of civilizations' (1993) as the 'battle lines' of post-Cold War global politics posited between Western and Islamic 'civilizations' or, more broadly, between 'the West and the rest' (23–27), which have since been used in the discourse justifying the 'war on terror'. The fault lines in Rushdie's novels often shift, but they also tend to form along older lines of tension brought about by the geomorphic exercises of colonialism or in the name of national sovereignty.

The term *tectonics* also appears in theories of architecture as it derives from the Greek *tekton*, meaning 'carpenter' or 'builder'. Kenneth Frampton traces the historical development of the term's usage, noting that in Homer, it refers to construction in general; in Sappho, the *tekton*, or carpenter, assumes the role of the poet; and in Aristophanes, it is associated with 'machination and the creation of false things' (1996, 3–40). A renewed architectural interest in the tectonic has come in response to the modern commodification and standardization of building production, which it aims to challenge. Annette LeCuyer speaks of 'radical tectonics', which undertakes to restore the balance of technique and art, and construction and poetry. She argues that radical tectonic built-forms 'grow out of the land', blurring the boundaries between the site and the building and connecting in this way the architectural with the geological definition of the tectonic. LeCuyer posits radical tectonic projects as deeply contextual, revealing 'intrinsic, invisible energies', 'imprints, rhythms, traces and tendencies' latent in the site (2001, p. 15–8). Such articulations of the tectonic are useful in exploring *Midnight*'s critique of Partition in the Pakistani city of Karachi, where stunted, deformed or grotesque houses 'grow out of the land' or of an attempt at national modernization in *Shame*'s Pakistan, during Zia-ul-Haq's Islamization programme, as manifested in the buildings of Islamabad. There, the 'alien gods of Greece and Rome' meet overcompensatory Mughal architectural forms and reveal this 'modernism', in Rushdie's assessment, as a form of 'pre-stressed nostalgia' (S, 204–05).

Ecocriticism has also attended to tectonic processes and tropes – broadly, as part of its engagement with the 'relationship between literature and the physical environment' or the interactions between the human and the non-human (Glotfelty 1996, xviii–xix) and, more specifically, under the rubrics of ecological catastrophe or secular apocalypse (see Garrard 2004, 85–107). While ecocriticism and postcolonial criticism have often been seen as divergent, even antagonistic schools of thought and ways of reading, work by Susie O'Brien (2001), Graham Huggan (2004) and Rob Nixon (2005), for instance, have helped pave the way for the emergent area of postcolonial ecocriticism not by merely bridging the two fields but by suggesting ways in which they can offer correctives to each other's biases. Nixon points out some of the schisms between postcolonialism and environmentalism. These include the former's emphasis on cross-culturation, displacement, transnationalism and the excavation of marginalized histories as opposed to the latter's commitment to discourses of purity, preservation and an ethics of place within a national (predominantly American) framework as well as its tendency to bury precisely those histories that postcolonialism has sought to unearth in an act of 'spatial amnesia' (235–36). Where environmental visions open out beyond a spiritualized or naturalized national frame, he argues, they often do so into transcendental abstraction (236). Instead, Nixon urges towards a 'transnational ethics of place', entailing a movement from the local to the specificities of the international

(236–39). Conversely, in its refusal of 'natural' belonging as a form of neo/colonialist essentialism, postcolonialism has tended to favour unhomeliness or 'cosmopolitan restlessness' (O'Brien, 140), to focus on 'social justice' (Huggan, 702) and to shy away, as a result, from environmental concerns (Nixon, 234). While postcolonialism may appear anthropocentric, Huggan argues that it has 'effectively renewed, rather than belatedly discovered, its commitment to the environment' and its 'insistence on the inseparability of current crises of ecological mismanagement from historical legacies of imperialistic exploitation and authoritarian abuse' (702). In his recent book, *Slow Violence and the Environmentalism of the Poor* (2011), Nixon draws attention precisely to the historical processes of the accumulation of environmental violence in the global South, where the long-drawn eroding effects of war, for instance, are often ignored by a public activism more readily responding to sensationalist constructions of ecological catastrophe. The response to the Japan earthquake only too well demonstrates the urgency of Nixon's study.

In its postcolonial inflection, ecocriticism offers conceptual angles for a productive exploration of Rushdie's political re-positioning of cities in the context of environmental processes, their construction as 'events' and their polyphonic, yet often essentialist or hegemonic interpretations. Rejecting pastoral nostalgia in its mythic varieties of Mother India and of England as a 'green and pleasant land', his writing offers an engagement with 'urban nature'. *Midnight's Children*, as we mentioned above, records speculations on 'natural' signs and omens, which are simultaneously critiqued and constituted as a subversive text, alternative to public discourses of history. Here, animals appear to be an urban under-class and as much the victims of, and protestors against, postcolonial state policies as the citizens of Bombay. In the novel, there is a cat invasion of Methwold's Estate, seen as presaging the division of the state of Bombay, while a group escape of cobras from the Shaapsteker Institute is interpreted as a response to India's secularization.

Earthquakes in *Shame* and *The Ground beneath Her Feet* offer Rushdie the opportunity not only to critique the brutality of Zia-ul-Haq's regime in Pakistan in the former novel, and global North–South divisions, nuclear armament as well as millenarian discourse in the latter, but also to suggest earth's contingency, indeterminacy and dynamism. The exploration of tectonic processes is also an engagement with the underground urban earth, posited in the latter novel as the origin of music and reminiscent of the pastoral trope of the weather as 'subterraneous music', which communicates meaning to Wordsworth's shepherd in his poem, 'Michael'

(1800). The urban–pastoral configuration in this novel is indebted to Virgil's *Aeneid* – charting out an epic interurban route from Troy through Carthage to Rome – and to the fourth book of his *Georgics*, a practical handbook on the bee-keeping aspect of work on a farm. Such urban–rural interactions owe, in the context of Indian history, to the Gandhi–Nehru debate that we noted earlier. In Rushdie's view, India chose Gandhi 'with its heart' and Nehru 'in terms of practical politics' (IH, 104–05). Gandhi's rural, spiritually intuitive, home-spun India often figures as the suppressed subterranean realm of the city that, nevertheless, makes its presence known, through omens and signs, in the modern, industrialized Nehruvian urban overground.

Tectonic urban configurations develop, in this way, from almost imperceptible cracks in the earth to seismic activity along global fault lines, to environmental apocalypse and the remoulding of continents in a critique of the violent earthographies brought about by colonialism, ethnic and communal conflict, globalization and the naturalization of national and continental boundaries.

The term *tectonics*, then, partaking of geological, architectural and eco-critical discourses, is adopted in this study to conceptualize the simultaneous instability and contextual dynamics of the urban condition. Composed of dialogic or conflicting trajectories and stories, Rushdie's cities are situated at the intersection of tectonic discourses – of empire, of history and the map – that constantly collide, shift, slide under each other and regroup, while re-articulating urban spatialities and temporalities, itineraries, subjectivities and bodies.

Tectonics needs to be further situated in relation to the concept of the palimpsest. David Punter, for instance, notes that there are 'clear parallels between [the] world of tectonic plates and geological formations and the inhumanity of colonisation', but proceeds to render the geopolitical violence of colonialism in the terms of the palimpsest: resistance is signalled by residual traces 'whose unreadable marks and signs come to signify the only possibility for the unravelling of a contorted history' (2000, 31). The eruption of the suppressed voices and stories of the other, however, cannot be articulated through the notion of the palimpsest alone. It is through the tectonic model of the city that such subterranean insurgence, its 'slowness' and invisibility, as we saw in Nixon's analysis, and its 'radical contemporaneity' (Massey 2005, 110), can be conceptualized. As the architectural radical tectonics suggests, tectonic insurgence 'grows out of the land'. Like the palimpsestic, the tectonic imagination gestures towards the inescapable accumulation of historical traces, the simultaneous rigidity and fragility of hegemonic discursive constructions, the dynamic overwriting or imperfect erasure of previous urban texts and identities and the incestuous/palimpsestuous interaction between cultures. Yet, the tectonic also accounts for the expansion and retraction, the impact and the redistribution of geo-historical accretions; the subversive activity of the subterranean and its seemingly spontaneous, but not accidental, volcanic eruption. Counter-discursive urban reconfigurations are initiated at the *margins* of dominant discourses, thus suggesting that resistance is as much *of* as it is *against* them. Tectonic tensions and processes reveal these discourses' own gaps, absurdities and contradictions, as well as the uneven distribution of *visibility* around the globe. Specifically, tectonic processes – explosions, collisions and various other cataclysms and mobilizations – cause the eruption of the suppressed, alternative and frequently subterranean stories of the other onto the visible urban surface, destabilizing, in this way, the epistemological ground of the Same and reconfiguring existing urban narratives.

The process of creative unearthing, however, is sometimes (if much less often in Rushdie's work) balanced against by that of a forceful uprooting. *The Enchantress of Florence* employs a botanical metaphor, the mandrake root (a reference to Niccolò Machiavelli's play, *La Mandragola* or *The Mandrake*, 1518), which cries when it is being pulled out into the air. The tectonic potential for resistance is further problematized by such extreme antagonisms that lead to the destruction of the city. This is the case in *The Moor*, where rivalling claims to place produce an urban geography of exclusion. The rise of Hindu fundamentalism points to the relative stability and rigidity of essentialist notions of place. Such notions, as Pat Jess and Doreen Massey remind us, are based on representations that are like snapshots of a place, frozen at a particular point in time and space and usually associated with the nostalgic wish to return to a golden past or a moment of origins that posits the idea of the singularity of spatiality and temporality and effectively deprives others of their stories or histories (1995, 172). The tectonic, therefore, seeks to take account of the interactions between the rigidity and the dynamics of the *understanding* of urban histories and geographies. Tectonic eruptions resist romanticizing in this way and point both to the necessarily ambiguous nature of urban tensions and to Rushdie's even-handed critique of essentialist urban fictions.

The ambiguity of urban tectonics should also be seen in relation to discourses on, and manifestations of, 'terror'. Elleke Boehmer discusses two main interrelated inflections of postcolonialism by referring to Rushdie's writing as exemplary of the former: a 'globalized', 'hybridizing', 'Rushdiesque' inflection and a 'resistance' inflection (2007, 5). Under the

heading of the latter, she argues, postcolonialism 'aligns itself more closely
with some of the theories and significations of "terror"' as struggle against,
or subversion of, 'the global status quo, whether capitalist-driven colonialism or neo-imperial globalization' (ibid.). While what she conceptualizes as
the Rushdiesque category *par excellence* is related to what I designate the
catoptric aspect of his politics, examined in the next section, it cannot
encompass the breadth of Rushdie's reconfigurational politics. The tectonic reconfigurational movement in his work partakes of this explosive/
slowly eroding dynamic of resistance as a process of a forcible modification
in Boehmer's second postcolonial inflection, less explored in relation to
Rushdie. In particular, urban tectonics demonstrates that violence and terror may appear as the 'sudden' manifestations of an invisible force but are
historically conditioned; that terror has also been 'the medium of the modern state and the modern imperium'; that the 'terror' on which eternal war
is declared has been solicited and that it provides the 'modern and imperialist state' with a strategy of constituting its authority and that rather than
either denouncing terror or sidestepping the suffering it has caused, it is
necessary to explore 'what is at stake subjectively and sequentially for the
different parties involved' (5–7). If the tectonic reconfigurational movement in Rushdie's novels is less prominent than the catoptric or the specular, their continuing relevance to the contemporary moment is in the
interactions between the three dynamics.

Catoptric Urban Configurations

In postcolonial theory, the mirror figures most prominently in the
conceptualization of the Other/other, othering and mimicry, as informed
by Lacanian psychoanalysis. These concepts refer to those aspects of the
mirror as a cultural phenomenon that concern the formation of subjectivity,
particularly colonial subjectivity, and the relationship between the original
and the mirror image – here, the ambivalent relationship between the
colonizer and the colonized – where the mirror image is *'almost the same but
not quite'*, 'at once resemblance and menace' (Bhabha 1994, 86, original
emphasis). Mirror reflections in postcolonial mimicry are different in kind,
since they involve asymmetrical binaries. The colonized subject is invariably
the 'poor relation' in such mirrorings, but is also invariably more aware of
the colonizer's *modus operandi* and psychology, than vice versa.

   In relation to the concept of the Other/other, the mirror is perhaps less
explicitly discussed in its involvement in the colonial discursive production

of such notions as *antipodality*, where 'Australia is positioned as a repository of all that is perverse, odd, unexpected', the projected image of an inverted Europe (Ryan 1996, 10; 107), or what Anne McClintock terms the *porno-tropics* of the European imagination, a zone of sexual aberration and anomaly, the perverse, negative image of Europe (1995, 22). Various inversions also form a large part of the vocabulary of postcolonial criticism, as in discussions of the re-visioning of colonial maps, epistemologies and Manichean oppositions. Mirrors thus both underlie the articulation of colonial hierarchies and asymmetries and offer a variety of strategies for their destabilization that are yet to be assessed.

Since the mirror is an ancient artefact and not exclusive to Western cultures, it has pervaded both fictional and theoretical writing and is subversive in its border-crossings. Mediating between science and magic, truth and illusion, and knowledge and speculation, mirrors occupy an ambivalent, unstable conceptual position. Michel Foucault defines the mirror as a cultural space of indefinite status that functions both as a utopia and a heterotopia (1984, 178–79), while Umberto Eco describes it as a threshold phenomenon, situated between perception and signification (1986, 216). Mirrors presuppose a speculative mode of thinking, as the etymology of the word *speculative* (from the Latin for *mirror, speculum*) would also seem to suggest.

Mirrors and mirroring, as this book demonstrates, have a central role in the representation of the city in Rushdie's novels, where they invite interurban reflections and inform the dynamics of travelling, physical and metaphorical, within and between cities. In order to address the problematics of figuring the variety of mirror effects, reflections, optical illusions and perspectives in these novels and assess their counter-discursive significance, I employ the term *catoptrics*. Catoptrics, like the mirror, is necessarily speculative, associated with magic rather than science, with illusion rather than truth.

The term *catoptrics* originated in Greco-Roman antiquity, where it denoted a branch of optics concerned with the theory and applications of mirrors and light, as well as with the so-called 'theory of images', as in the writings of Euclid (fl. 300 CE); Geminus (first century CE); and Hero of Alexandria (fl. 62 BCE). These works dealt with the problems of vision, reflection and perspective, particularly in their relation to the eye as the active participant in the visual process, reaching out to apprehend its object (Lindberg 1976, 220). In the Middle Ages, Roger Bacon, in particular, popularized catoptri-cal science, which influenced the alchemist, astrologer and mathematician John Dee. Dee's optical and astronomical treatise, *Propaedeumata Aphoristica*

(1558), explains that by means of optical instruments, it was possible to collect the occult virtues of the stellar radiations. According to Dee, mirrors could imitate planetary influences, increasing and decreasing the intensity of their radiations catoptrically and imprinting their influences on matter. Further on, late Renaissance alchemists created a number of catoptric devices whose names contain the methods of their production: multiplication, substitution, inversion, shrinkage, enlargement, dispersion and narrowing of forms (Szulakowska 2000). For instance, in the seventeenth century, Athanasius Kircher and Johannes Zahn described various catoptric machines, including the catoptric box, or *camera obscura*, which would employ different configurations of mirror-lined spaces, multiplying, in this way, various scenes (gardens or architectural compositions) to display fantastical microcosmic landscapes. Gilles Deleuze notes that in the Baroque imagination of space, such catoptrical devices stood for the understanding of the mind's capacity to represent and imagine the whole world at once (Teyssot 2000, 79). Umberto Eco provides a list of some catoptric contrivances, known across the centuries as *Theatrum Catoptricum, Theatron Polydictum, Speculum Heterodicticum,* and *Speculum Multiplex* (1986, 232–33).

In the discussions of the literature, catoptrics has been employed almost exclusively in relation to poetry, either as a metaphor or as a critical paradigm for the exploration of mirror imagery and symbolism (see LaBossiere 1983; Chardin 1989). Most relevant to this study is Kleo Protohristova's examination of what she refers to as 'literary catoptrics' in her monograph on the mirror metaphor in poetry and fiction. She discusses three dominant epistemic paradigms that have successively governed this metaphor. The first paradigm, the *unitary or harmonious mirror*, most characteristic of the Middle Ages, when *Speculum* is also a marker of genre, reflects the Universe and bridges God and man. Humankind is only allowed to look upon the Creator in his image reflected in the material world. Here, the mirror reflects simultaneously the real and the ideal. The second paradigm, the *broken mirror*, signals the collapse of the theocentric universe and governs late Renaissance thinking. For instance, French poetry of the seventeenth century foregrounds imagery to do with reflections in the water's surface, which is in turn related to the idea of life as an illusion, a dream or a deceptive hall of mirrors. The third paradigm, the *mirror reflected in another mirror*, corresponds, in Protohristova's view, to the shift from the classical to the modern era, in Foucauldian terms, and is associated with the crisis of representation. Here, Protohristova cites the works of Jorge Luis Borges, Umberto Eco and Lewis Carroll, where the mirror becomes analogous to the book, the library, the labyrinth, chess and the dream (21–41). The work of Italo

Calvino should also be added to this literary genealogy as a major catoptric influence, in its combinatorics, on Rushdie's work. Calvino's *Invisible Cities* (1972) includes, for instance, Valdrada, a city partitioned by its mirror-like lake into an upper half and a lower, upside-down, half, but there the mirror informs the twin cities' relationship of radical asymmetry, inversion and hostility (53–4). Contemporary Indian author, Githa Hariharan, imagines in her novel, *When Dreams Travel* (1999), a similarly split dystopian urban landscape – the suggestively named Eternal City – which is eternally divided into 'eastwallas' and 'westwallas'. There, however, it is symmetry that imprisons the inhabitants and the 'lopsided but acute vision' of a one-eyed visitor that temporarily unsettles mirror binarisms (139–40). Catoptric boundaries and transgressions pervade, as we shall see, the literary imagination of the Indian subcontinent's multiple colonial, communal and religious partitions.

Protohristova's conceptual history of the mirror is part of an enormous body of writing on this subject that tends to favour European material and cultural histories over indigenous or pre-colonial forms of mirroring (see, for instance, Melchoir-Bonnet, 2001, and Anderson, 2007), whereas work in the scientific field known as 'archaeological optics' (exploring the early material histories of mirrors and lenses) has revealed a trajectory of mirror technology that begins in Stone-Age Anatolia, at the cross-roads of what are to become 'East' and 'West' and spreads to Mesopotamia, Egypt, the Levant and, later, Europe (Enoch 2007, p. 1237). J. M. Enoch hypothesizes the existence of two parallel 'mirror styles', 'Western' (along the previously mentioned trajectory) and 'Eastern' (popular among Siberian and Chinese peoples), and notes the need to explore the early history of mirrors in India so as to establish how these two influences interacted there (ibid.).

The development of mirror symbolism includes, too, the genre of the 'mirror-for-princes', which also has a history of multiple origins, strands and mutual reflections. This genre was especially popular in Arabic and Persian literature, influenced by classical Greek and Hellenistic elements and is represented by numerous medieval European texts. It is significantly indebted to Indian sources in its early history. Conveying 'examples of correct conduct for rulers, statesmen and other officials', mirror-for-princes books 'educate by employing a mixture of admonition and entertainment' (Marzolph and van Leeuwen 2004, 647). Such tales were subsequently incorporated into the *Thousand and One Nights* – a text that has itself been seen as a 'manual for royal instruction' because of Sheherazade's didactic project in the frame narrative (ibid.). Here, the mirror is associated with the ideas of proliferating narratives and cultural hybridity that have informed contemporary re-appropriations of the *Nights* in various contexts, including works by Borges, Franz Kafka, John Barth, M.G. Vassanji, and Rushdie (Jones 2005, 116).

Mirrors imported into colonized lands have interacted with local forms of mirroring in ways that have not been investigated. As 'objects of exchange' between the explorers and the 'natives', they reveal, as Marina Warner notes, 'more than the patronizing trifles they seem' (2006, 172). As a space of both encounter/violence and resistance, the mirror offers a fresh approach to well-worn ideas, such as mimicry. While, as objects and metaphors, mirrors have figured in colonial and postcolonial texts, both literary and theoretical, in an extraordinarily broad range of ways, a comprehensive study attuned to the postcolonial significance of mirrors does not exist. This book suggests ways in which this curious omission can be rectified by offering an exploration of the political ways in which Rushdie's cities refashion the mirror as a theme and a paradigm.

Whereas Fokkema and Bertens (1989) find that mirroring has a central role in postmodernist fiction, where one of the most frequent lexemes is mirror and some of the most active semantic fields are those of multiplication and permutation, also evident on the level of narrative structure, I argue that the catoptricity of Rushdie's cities is not a matter of a postmodernist hall-of-mirrors play. Rather, the catoptric urban configurations in the novels are orientated towards the critique of such notions as the colonial unidirectionality of travel; essentialist urban fictions or constructions of identity and political borders and communal divisions. Like Lewis Carroll's Alice, the characters frequently cross and thus subvert a number of looking-glass frontiers, which in turn have the 'home' and the destination city, the self and its double, and the city and its narrator reflect each other in new ways. The catoptric spectrum of Rushdie's novels includes doubles, twins, and shadows (elements that are also characteristic of Menippean satire); partings and partitions; journeys through the looking-glass; dreaming and self-dreaming; various *mise en abymes*, such as a story in the story or a city in the city; permutations; metamorphoses; translations; inversions; prophecies; and analepses and prolepses. Rushdie employs the term 'broken mirror' to illustrate the ways in which the postcolonial migrant envisions his 'imaginary homelands':

It may be that when the Indian writer who writes from outside India tries to reflect that world, he is obliged to deal in broken mirrors, some of whose fragments have been irretrievably lost. But there is a paradox here. The broken mirror may actually be as valuable as the one which is supposedly unflawed. (IH, 10–11)

Distorting mirrors, inverting mirrors and mirrors reflected in other mirrors recur in Rushdie's texts, pointing, for instance, to the fracturing of identity and the city by colonialism, to the exercise of power involved in the drawing of boundaries and to the violence perpetrated by notions of urban purity or imperial urban lineage. Motifs, self-reflexive patterns and intertextual routes function as catoptric devices, based on the paradigm of the mirror reflected in another mirror. For example, motifs (the perforated sheet in *Midnight's Children* or the parting of the sea in *The Satanic Verses*) invite parallels between all their contexts and usages in a novel and across texts.

Not only texts, but diverse literary traditions contemplate their reflections in each other's mirrors in Rushdie's texts. In his essay on mirrors and reflections, the Indian poet and scholar A. K. Ramanujan discusses the plural cultural traditions of India, listing the many forms reflexivity takes in Indian classical and folk literatures: awareness of self and other, mirroring, distorted mirroring, parody, family resemblances and rebels, and utopias and dystopias, among others. In a later edition of the *Ramayana*, the hero hears the story of his own adventures, recited to him by his children, and 'sees himself become a story' – a fate that is shared by the protagonist of *The Moor* – while the folk version of the *Mahabharata* is similarly a 'story that is itself about the way an oral text was converted into the written' (Ramanujan, 8; 22) – a tradition mirrored by *Midnight*. Rushdie's texts thus demonstrate and perform the contamination of Western texts by Indian literary traditions, pointing to the perforation not only of identity by colonialism, but also of the essentialist ideas of cultural purity and finitude. These forms of catoptric cosmopolitanism and intertextuality should be seen not merely as a celebration of cultural eclecticism and hybridity, but, as Stephen Baker argues, as a 'realistic portrayal of the construction of a postcolonial culture' (2000, 50). This impurity is best demonstrated in the context of translation as a colonial practice, where Indians were taught Persian literature in English, as evinced by the subsequent multiple translations into Hindi of Edward Fitzgerald's *Omar Khayyam* (Bassnett and Trivedi 1999, 8). Such translations of translations operate in terms analogous to the principle of a mirror reflected in another mirror, both testifying to the violence of the colonial translative encounter and enabling further, politically reconfiguring translations. Rushdie's characters often find that they have already been translated into racist categories or other stereotypes, but this awareness enables them to interact with and re-appropriate their English 'renditions' against the translators, rather than returning to an 'original' in an attempt at an unmediated translation. In this view of translation, Rushdie is indebted to Borges's celebration of the translator's creative infidelity, his/her 'charming meanderings' (42), for instance, or to Walter Benjamin's engagement with a translation as part of the 'afterlife' of an 'original' – the process through which it accumulates meanings (16) in its travels.

Specular Urban Configurations

In an essay on Rudyard Kipling, Rushdie devotes particular attention to one of his early short stories, 'On the City Wall' (1888), arguing that there 'the Indian Kipling manages to subvert what the English Kipling takes to be the meaning of the tale' (IH, 78). The story revolves around the brothel of the courtesan Lalun on the Lahore city wall. Her salon seems to assemble the whole city to 'smoke and talk' – Muslims, Hindus, Sikhs and Europeans, including the anonymous English narrator – without any conflicts. In the course of the story, the narrator is seduced by Lalun into unwittingly escorting an escaped revolutionary across the city. Afterwards, he realizes what has happened: 'Lalun had used me and my white face as even a better safeguard than Wali Dad' (350). Wali Dad, one of Lalun's 'native' visitors and a young intellectual Muslim, who has spent a long time experimenting with various religions, has found refuge and understanding at Lalun's. At this wall house, Lalun announces that she will be Queen and Wali Dad the King, while to the narrator she assigns the rank of Vizier. Whereas after this pronouncement, he has a dream in which 'Wali Dad had sacked the city and I was made Vizier' (341), in the wake of Lalun's deception at the end of the story, he admits that the dream has become reality, turning him into 'Lalun's Vizier after all' (355).

Kipling's story has been the object of considerable critical attention. While Benita Parry (1988) and David Sergeant (2009), for instance, argue that it ultimately reaffirms the colonial master/native hierarchy, Bart Moore-Gilbert joins Rushdie in contending that it contains 'ideological contradictions and psychic ambivalence' that reveal 'disabling resistances in the unconscious of imperial desire' (1996, 112).

It is not only the imperial/emasculation anxiety dreams of Kipling's narrator but also the focal point of his story, Lalun's salon, as a place of intercultural mingling and dialogue and contrasting with the rest of the city, that seems to have had a significant impact on Rushdie and that informs what I have termed the *specular* aspect of urban politics in his novels. It can be seen in his frequent representation of courtesans and brothels, most notably the controversial brothel in *The Satanic Verses*, where prostitutes adopt the names of the wives of Mahound (Rushdie's fictional Mohammed figure) in the city of Jahilia, but also as early as *Midnight's Children*, where the Karachi prostitute, Tai Bibi, becomes an avatar of history, and as late as *The Enchantress of Florence*, where the brothels of Florence and Fatehpur Sikri mirror each other. As Parry points out, Lalun's salon is 'neither a zone liberated from the Raj, nor one displacing the master/native positioning'; it appears 'out of bounds' for most Anglo-Indians, but only as far as it is 'licensed by the centre for the episodic transgression of colonial interdicts' (59). In this early Kipling story and its brothel on the city wall, however, Rushdie recognizes a potential for resistance that he develops, as I argue in this book, into a provocatively radical urban space. Brothels and temptresses are a similarly liminal, impermanent, carnivalesque feature of the city or of interurban space that interrupts and often threatens the dominant order by dramatizing what Parry refers to as a 'movement between Law and Desire' (59). Specifically, seduction 'on the city wall' is often staged in the form of various processes of mirroring, as in the brothel's duplication of the harem, for instance, or of the political structures (cliques and hierarchies) of the regime in power. Sometimes cities *as such* are symbolically ascribed the role of a prostitute: Karachi in *Shame* is described as a 'whore city' (S, 118), in contrast to the ideologically and religiously pure Islamabad, where the two cities mirror the political conflict between, respectively, Pakistan's Zulfikar Ali Bhutto and Muhammad Zia-ul-Haq. Such processes form a part of the specular movement of urban configurations.

The specular is therefore related to the catoptric insofar as it involves mirror effects, but its separation from the catoptric is necessary for conceptualizing and examining in detail the distinctive ways in which Rushdie's cities are informed by a specific property of the mirror – its ability to deceive by granting illusory wholeness or certitude and to allure, coerce or seduce. In the work of the French psychoanalyst Jacques Lacan, the formation of subjectivity involves the infant's passage from the Imaginary Order, associated with the mother, to the Symbolic Order, the realm of the father, language and representation, which fixes meaning and guarantees patriarchal structure. This passage entails the 'drama' of the Mirror Stage, whereby the child, upon identifying with its mirror image, loses it symbiotic relationship with the world and becomes established in the Symbolic (Lacan [1949] 2004, 1–8). In Frantz Fanon's development of Lacan's thought, the mirror offers a 'progressive infrastructure where the black man can find the path to [his] disalienation' (161) as the other of the white man, since the eye is 'not only a mirror, but a correcting mirror' of 'cultural mistakes'

(178). Stephanie Newell, however, poses questions about 'the extent to which Fanon's experience of race is refracted through his masculinity' and of the importance, in the post/colonial encounter, of the recognition of the black man *as a man*' (2009, 244).

In her critique of patriarchal thought, the French feminist theorist Luce Irigaray also resorts to the figure of the mirror, specifically, the gynaecological instrument, *speculum*, which comes to symbolize the patriarchal-mediated knowledge of women as based on the idea of lacks and absences. The speculum is 'an instrument to dilate the lips, the orifices, the walls, so that the eye can penetrate the interior', so that 'the eye can enter, to see, notably with speculative intent' (144–45). Metaphorically, the speculum and its use testify, in her view, to the ways in which women and female sexuality are seen as reflecting man's image. This specular (speculative and narcissistic) 'detour' or 'passage' through the non-space with which a woman is identified serves to reassure masculine wholeness.

In the writings of Jacques Derrida, the figure of the mirror informs the conceptualization of philosophical reflection. He employs the phrase 'the tain of the mirror', referring to its 'lustreless back', to suggest that reflection as a philosophical concept 'requires that the action of reproduction should also be thrown back upon itself' and that the mirror should be 'made to see itself' (Gasché, 1986, 16–7). Derrida explores, in this way, philosophy's own self-foundation, its unreflective back, in order to undermine the foundations and certitudes of metaphysical thinking, which has pervaded Western philosophy. This is an idea that Newell seems to echo in her questions on Fanon's optics of race.

The metaphorical relationship of the mirror with the issues to do with writing, identity, race and sexuality is useful for conceptualizing the city and inter-urban travel in Rushdie's novels. After Irigaray, I employ the term *specular* to refer to the instrumental role of female characters and specific constructions of femininity in urban representation in these texts in order to explore the ways in which Rushdie's cities accommodate postcolonial masculinities. Rushdie seeks to emancipate, as we shall see, the postcolonial male migrant from colonial discursive constructions of the Oriental male as an effeminate figure, as in Kipling's Wali Dad, the 'clean-bred young Muhammadan, with pencilled eyebrows, small-cut nostrils, little feet and hands', 323), or to subvert gendered notions of nation and empire. Women are given the power and agency, indeed often greater than that of men, to demystify hegemonic and patriarchal fictions. He has persistently been criticized, however, for his polarized representations of women – as in the specular duplication of wife and prostitute, for instance. Catherine Cundy observes that in most of Rushdie's texts, women and female sexuality stand for both 'the refuge and the abyss' (1997, 41), figuring as an important device in reconstructing postcolonial migrant identity.

Whereas postcolonial analysis has tended to concentrate on 'constructions of women rather than gender per se' (Newell, 244), the discussion here examines the libidinal economy of Rushdie's urban maps, specifically the ways in which gender and sexuality inform cartographic representation and inter-urban travel. Here, I draw on Anne McClintock and Marina Warner to investigate this cartographic dynamic. McClintock notes that on crossing 'the dangerous thresholds of their known worlds', colonial explorers 'ritualistically feminized borders and boundaries':

> Female figures were planted like fetishes at the ambiguous points of contact, at the borders and orifices of the contest zone. Sailors bound wooden female figures to their ships' prows and baptized their ships – as exemplary threshold objects – with female names. Cartographers filled the blank seas of their maps with mermaids and sirens. (24)

Whilst subverting the uni/directionality of colonial travel, Rushdie's itinerant narrators nevertheless frequently reinstate the gender metaphysics of colonial exploration and cartography, producing similarly feminized exotic urban margins in order to ward off masculine loss of boundary, particularly the loss of the 'home' city and, in the process, also betray a sense of anxiety associated with the anticipation of the danger of the Western, destination city. In Rushdie's novels, the inter-urban realm is not only frequently feminized, but also associated with a particular idea of femininity, of woman as standing for libidinal excess. This gesture can be seen as a response to Kipling's bewitching 'India-Lalun' (IH, 80), who succeeds in upturning the colonial hierarchy precisely through her powers of seduction. Yet, this specular reconfiguration is often emancipatory for Rushdie's male protagonists and not for his Laluns. The masculine imagination of the city is negotiated, for instance, through the figurative, and sometimes literal, inscription of cities or urban maps on the female body. Further, if the process of migration is envisaged as a form of positive metamorphosis in his work, the reverse – what Marina Warner refers to as *Dantean* or *infernal* metamorphosis, perceived as leading to a loss or dissolution of identity to a point of obliteration (2002, 37) – is often mediated through the female form. The otherwise celebrated concept of urban pluralism, for instance, is embodied by a woman, Uma Sarasvati, in *The Moor's Last Sigh*, when it acquires its extreme form of a chameleon-like adaptation to circumstances and beliefs for personal advantage. In this sense, the specular urban configurations in the texts often intersect the tectonic and the catoptric: women mediate across catoptric boundaries or manifest their 'citizenship' of the subterranean, which threatens to erupt and consume the male traveller.

Seduction, however, figures more broadly, and ambiguously, in Rushdie's novels. It is staged both in the form of essentialist or hegemonic fictions with which the male characters flirt, as in New York's seductions of capital and neoliberal discourse in *Fury*, as we shall see in Chapter 6, and as a subversive force, which can lead them astray, into doubt, by questioning monolithic constructions of Islam, as in Mahound's flirting with the possibility of including three of the goddesses of Jahilia as Allah's archangels in *The Satanic Verses*. Rushdie revels in this dissident sense of seduction as the temptation to hesitate, to err, to blaspheme and to lead astray – geographically, philosophically and politically. Such seductions contribute to his secular, cosmopolitan urban ideal by inviting specular/speculative reflections between the figure of the courtesan, on the one hand, and the various roles assigned to, or adopted by, women in the familial, domestic, religious and economic structures of urban life, as well as by revisiting their relationship with colonial norms and stereotypes, on the other.

The specular urban configurations in Rushdie's fiction seem largely, however, to ignore the dark nature of the sex trade, specifically, the coercive brothel and pimp sociologies of the city or the transnational scales of sex trafficking (a notable, though isolated exception being Angélique in *The Enchantress of Florence*), even as it engages with other, celebratory types of migration on such scales. In her work on *kothas* (brothels) in colonial Bombay, Ashwini Tambe draws attention to issues such as the racial stratification in the city's sex trade that served colonial purposes and the criminalization of prostitutes as a result of a nationalist attempt to fight Orientalist stereotypes of a backward Indian culture (2009, 78; 121). Prostitution, Tambe notes, was also experienced in ways that often furthered, rather than offering an alternative to, colonial and patriarchal forms of domination and protection of women (2006, 222). Such reminders belie both Kipling's and Rushdie's romanticized (if in very different ways) urban tropes of the brothel.

The ambiguous quality of the specular thus enables the otherwise methodologically challenging conceptualization of the gender/city interface in Rushdie's texts, accommodating, at once, patriarchal constructions of femininity, traditional dichotomies and objectifications, and active, radical subversion of idealized or essentialist gender paradigms.

Rushdie's Cities and Contemporary Fiction

Situating Rushdie's cities within the contemporary scene of urban writing would be a gargantuan undertaking, regardless of how narrowly we may delimit their 'contemporaneity', or indeed 'Rushdie's contemporary', in historical, geographical or literary-intertextual terms. Rushdie's literary production spans several decades (from the 1980s to the present day, if we take *Midnight's Children* as a starting point) and three continents and has been examined (often centrally) within the broad categories of the Indian/ South Asian novel in English, the British contemporary novel, the postcolonial novel, the magical realist novel, the postmodern novel, the self-conscious novel, the New Atheist novel and the global or transnational novel. He draws inspiration for his cities from an extraordinarily broad range of literary sources, which are not necessarily 'urban' but which highlight, in this way, the ability of novelistic cities to accommodate, uneasily, an infinite variety of discourses. In his essay, 'Influence' (1999), Rushdie stresses precisely this need for 'cross-cultural pollination without which literature becomes parochial and marginal' (SATL, 76).

Rushdie's acknowledged 'urban' influences, some of which are examined in this book, include Sheherazade's fictional Baghdad in the *Thousand and One Nights*; Emperor Babur's Kabul and Samarkand in his autobiographical *Baburnama*; Niccolò Machiavelli's Florence in his play, *La Mandragola/The Mandrake* (1519?); Shakespeare's Venice in *The Merchant of Venice* (1596?) and *Othello* (1604?); Jonathan Swift's Lilliputian capital Mildendo in *Gulliver's Travels* (1726); Dickensian London; the Vienna of Robert Musil's *The Man without Qualities* (1930); James Joyce's Dublin; the Danzig-become-Gdansk of Günter Grass's *The Tin Drum* (1959); Mikhail Bulgakov's Moscow and Jerusalem in *The Master and Margarita* (1966); Italo Calvino's *Invisible Cities* (1972); Milan Kundera's Prague in *The Unbearable Lightness of Being* (1984); E.L. Doctorow's New York (specifically, the Bronx) in *Billy Bathgate* (1989); Saul Bellow's Chicago and Bucharest in *The Dean's December* (1982); Kurt Vonnegut's post-Vietnam New York in *Hocus Pocus* (1990); Don DeLillo's New York in *Underworld* (1997) and many more. Rather than evincing a mere heterogeneity of cities or a technique of postmodern pastiche, however, each of these intertexts is employed, in Rushdie's texts, in a reconfigurational engagement with their cultural specifics. There are, nevertheless, notable exceptions, such as Baghdad, for instance, which figures in Rushdie's work as a cipher for an urban paradigm that can best be described, in the terms of Michel de Certeau, as the street-level of the city's ordinary practitioners (in this case, the subjects of the Caliph) who live beneath the simulacrum of the Concept-city (the Caliph's regime, which structures and contains urban life), but whose stories can, if temporarily, negotiate against or undermine it (1988, 93–9).

Rushdie's writing has come to occupy a dominant position within the parallel, though rarely discussed together, categories of Bombay writing and London writing. Within the context of the 'Bombay novel', Rushdie's work has established its influence, shared with other diasporic re-imaginings of Bombay in English, such as Anita Desai's, Rohinton Mistry's, Amit Chaudhuri's or Vikram Chandra's, against fiction on the city in languages such as Marathi (Gopal 2009, 4). No discussion of the breadth of Bombay fiction fails to examine Rushdie's writing, and, even more indicatively, such discussions are often *centred* on his Bombay or employ it as their starting point. For Roshan G. Shahani, not only has Rushdie tapped into Bombay's 'infinite variety, its paradoxes and contradictions', but also this achievement as such becomes representative of the 'polyphonous voices' of 'Bombay writers', including Rushdie himself (1995, 104–05). Priyamvada Gopal, too, opens her discussion of the Bombay novel with a quotation from *Midnight's Children*, whose evocation of the city illustrates, for her, the appeal it has had to other writers in English as a 'port metropolis – with its self-conscious commingling of cultures and commodities, fabulous wealth and unimaginable poverty, and teeming tensions and contradictions' (2009, 116).

From its emergence in the nineteenth century and its development in the twentieth, A. K. Mehrotra notes of the Indian Anglophone novel that it is part of 'a literature whose writers have seldom acknowledged each other's presence'; that has 'no schools, literary movements, or even regional groups'; and whose history is 'scattered, discontinuous, and transnational' (2003, 24–5). Drawing on Mehrotra, Brennan and Bhabha, Gopal argues that despite the lack of a distinct tradition or genealogy, Indian English novels share the fundamental task of the narration of India and situates Rushdie within the Bombay novel as an inflection of this tradition. The city haunts the nation, she argues, exposing the failures of its claimed inclusivity through its disenfranchised, its minorities and its unvoiced (4–8). At the same time, for Sujata Patel *et al.*, (1995), Jon Dee (2003) and Gopal, Bombay's heterogeneity is paradigmatic of that of India. The city projects an image of urban modernity unrivalled by other Indian cities. This is the only category of specifically 'urban' writing examined in Gopal's discussion of the Indian novel in English. For example, she locates Esther David's *The Walled City* (1997), set in Ahmedabad, under the rubric of 'domesticity and gender', while Dee reveals a contrast in Amit Chaudhuri's treatment of a disorientatingly modern Bombay as opposed to a timeless Calcutta (324).

Dee describes Rushdie as a 'messiah' of the Indian novel in English in the 1980s, though obscuring parallel works such as I. Allan Sealy's *The Trotter-Nama* (1988), a chronicle of some 200 years of Anglo-Indian history leading up to Independence (12–13; 289). *The Trotter-Nama*, like *Midnight's Children*, offers a nomadic saga, but of an even broader scope: seven generations of Trotters, held together in the Persian *nama* (epic auto/biography) form, which Rushdie would evoke in *The Enchantress* in a reclamation of a hybrid Mughal heritage. In Sealy's playful names – Mik, a second-generation Trotter (a mirror image of Kipling's 'Kim') and the city of Nakhlau (an anagram of Lakhnau or Lucknow) – we can recognize a catoptric revision of Anglo-Indian liminality. Is home, the novel asks, 'the place where things were the right side up' (489)?

Shahani locates Rushdie's writing within a new 'city-centred' form, in contrast to earlier works, including Mulk Raj Anand's *Untouchable* (1935) or Raja Rao's *Kanthapura* (1938), which tend to posit city and countryside in binary opposition (99). It is this narrative of arrival (from the countryside) and survival in the city that also marks the beginnings of Bombay's film industry, as exemplified in Raj Kapoor's *Shri 420* (1955). There are, nevertheless, many ways of arriving and surviving in the city, as evinced by Bombay fiction. The middle-class heroines of Shashi Deshpande's *That Long Silence* (1988) and *The Dark Holds No Terror* (1990) arrive in a glamorous, seductive Bombay from provincial towns, but, although it can offer them 'successful careers', it also imposes patriarchal restrictions (Shahani, 106–07). Rohinton Mistry's first novel, *Such a Long Journey* (1991) and his earlier stories, *Tales from Firozsha Baag* (1987), focus on Bombay's Parsi communities, walled in the 'ethnic' apartment complexes of, respectively, Khodadat Mansions and the eponymous Firozsha Baag, both offering safety and imprisoning. Mistry's *A Fine Balance* (1996), set in a Bombay-reminiscent 'city by the sea', demonstrates the city's ability to weave new stories out of happenstance encounters, while revealing a different side of urban existence – life in the slums. Set in Central Works Department chawl No. 17 in Bombay, Kiran Nagarkar's *Ravan and Eddie* (1995) echoes Rushdie's catoptrically twinned protagonists, Saleem and Shiva, in its Hindu-Goan Catholic pair, respectively, Ravan and Eddie, in a layered and conflictual proximity. Although separated on different floors, the uneasily heterogeneous stories of the city's communities come to intersect each other in a not altogether pessimistic revision, in Dee's view, of the Nehruvian model of the nation as a 'mansion with many rooms' (324). This model is also echoed, however, in the more recent vision of London's multiculturalism, constituted in and through boxed-in communities, as evoked in Tower Hamlets' Dogwood

Estate in the opening chapters of Monica Ali's *Brick Lane* (2003), for instance.

The violent transformation of Bombay as a result of the rise of the Hindu right, culminating in the renaming of the city, can be seen in novels such as Rohinton Mistry's *Family Matters* (2002), where Mr Kapur, ironically a Hindu shop-owner, is killed after he refuses to change the name of his shop from Bombay to Mumbai Sporting Goods. The city's transformation has also been examined in non-fictional works – part-memoir, part urban *life-writing* and comparable to Peter Ackroyd's *London: The Biography* (2000) – such as Suketu Mehta's *Maximum City* (2004) and Gyan Prakash's *Mumbai Fables* (2010). Out of these three writers, Mehta seems to venture, most often, outside the city to discuss its relationship with other locations. In drawing parallels, for instance, between New York City and Bombay, it is reminiscent of earlier trans-urban non-fiction works such as Amitava Kumar's *Bombay, London, New York* (2002), which explores not only the diasporic capitals of the title but also their shifting connections with each other and with the village, the small town and suburbia.

Mehta has been criticized, however, for slipping into what have become readily summoned images of contemporary Mumbai: 'A city at war. Riots. Ethnic violence on an apocalyptic scale. Ruthless and barbaric politics and police' (Belliappa 2008, 350). Incidentally, this list echoes what Rushdie has recently described as one of the 'untold' stories of Bombay: 'the battle between the political gangs and the criminal gangs. The political gangs are all fundamentalist Hindus, and the criminal gangs are all Muslim. So you have Hindu–Muslim struggle at the level of the mafia' (2008b, 17). What Rushdie is describing here, however, is precisely the Bombay of *The Moor's Last Sigh*, as we shall see in Chapter 4. Gyan Prakash describes a similar urban landscape: Mumbai, he writes, pulsates 'to the throbbing beat of greed, ambition, jealousy, anger, communal passions, and underworld energies' (12). This Mumbai landscape figures, perhaps most prominently, in the fiction of Vikram Chandra, another cosmopolitan author, situated 'between' Bombay and Washington DC: *Love and Longing in Bombay* (1997); *Red Earth and Pouring Rain* (1995), and *Sacred Games* (2006). Mukund Belliappa draws parallels between Mehta's 'collaborators' in *Maximum City* and Chandra's fictional characters in *Sacred Games*, which have, themselves, been derived, he reminds us, from the urban-underground characters of Bollywood (346). The interplay of old and new in the idea of Mumbai that Rushdie, Mehta and Chandra repeatedly return to is summed up in Chandra's *Red Earth*: 'politics old and deep, alliances and betrayals', 'the old story, you've heard it before, but there was one new thing, one new idea that overwhelmed everything else, and this was simply that there should be only one idea, one voice, one thing, one, one, one' (615).

Rushdie's *Midnight* and *The Moor* form, what I discuss in this book, as a Bombay diptych, which can be seen as crossing the genre boundaries between fiction and urban biography. Both novels are first-person narratives, which invite a parallel with what can be termed *postcolonial urban life-writing*. There has been a continuing interest in this form, related not only to Bombay and London, but to cities such as Lahore on which Sara Suleri's memoir *Meatless Days* (1989) and Bapsi Sidhwa's *City of Sin and Splendour* (2006), an anthology including autobiography, essays, fiction, poetry and history, are based. In his recent book on postcolonial life-writing, Bart Moore-Gilbert examines the genre as a 'branch of autobiographical literature', which seeks to interrogate the assumptions of Western male autobiography, specifically the 'implicit, historical equation of the (theoretically ungendered) western Self with "the human"' (2009, xi–xvii). An exciting route of future critical exploration of works such as those listed above can be mapped out in the relationship of the contemporary urban condition with the genre of postcolonial life-writing as conceptualized in Moore-Gilbert's innovative study. Specifically, such an exploration (on which the present book can, sadly, only touch) could focus on the processes of interweaving of the stories of the postcolonial auto/biographical self with the stories of the city; on the city as a biographable self; on the relationship between the tropes of life and the city as journeys of personal exploration in a challenge of hegemonic conceptions of 'subjectivity as "real", singular and unified/"sovereign"' (89) and on non-Western precedents in which the lives of the self and the city converge, such as the *Ramayana* (the life of Rama and the city of Ayodhya, the mythical relationship between which has otherwise informed articulations of Hindu nationalism) or the 'namas' of the Mughal emperors Babur and Akbar, for instance (with their many cities: Samarkand, Kabul, Lahore, Delhi, Agra and Fatehpur Sikri).

Moving on along Rushdie's inter-urban trajectory would involve a journey into fiction on Karachi and Islamabad. Some indicative works on these cities can be noted that reveal, as in Rushdie's *Midnight, Shame* and *Shalimar*, the fraught nationalist cartographies of the subcontinent's India–Pakistan–Bangladesh triangle; cultural and political configurations across the Pakistan–Afghanistan border; the role of the military in Pakistani politics and the imagination of the Pakistani nation; the official censorship of West Pakistan's military actions in what was to become Bangladesh in 1971; the effects of U.S. involvement in the region during and after the

Cold War; gender politics in the context of the regime of Pakistan's General Muhammad Zia-ul-Haq and beyond and migration. The work of Pakistani author, Kamila Shamsie, has been credited with putting Karachi on the literary map of South Asian fiction in English (King 2011, 157). All her novels to date engage with the city and the historical configurations in which it has entered with other cities and places, such as London, New York, Afghanistan and Japan: *In the City by the Sea* (1998); *Salt and Saffron* (2000); *Kartography* (2002); *Broken Verses* (2005) and *Burnt Shadows* (2009). Shamsie's fiction offers an important counterpart to Rushdie's Karachi in exploring, for instance, the legacy of Partition from the less discussed Pakistani side; in providing an intimate portrayal of the lives of Karachi's citizens as marked by social, linguistic and ethnic divisions and the production of alternative urban maps (drawing on Urdu literary traditions), which not only unsettle the linearity of nationalist narratives but also point towards a potential for reconciliation that embraces 'difference and discontinuity' (Herbert 2011, 160; 170). Against Rushdie's exclusively authoritarian Karachi in *Shame*, Aamer Hussain's portrait of the city in 1950s–1960s in the novella, *Another Gulmohar Tree* (2009), offers an insight into its artistic life, opening up avenues for a cross-cultural dialogue of Urdu, Russian, French and English traditions (Shamsie, M. 2010, 642). A different perspective on Karachi, the lives of its social underclasses, is revealed in Bina Shah's latest novel, *Slum Child* (2010), imbued with an emotional sympathy for the city's various minorities (Chambers and Faqir 2010, n. pag.), whereas Uzma Aslam Khan's novels, *Trespassing* (2003) and *The Geometry of God* (2008), set in, respectively, Karachi and Islamabad, delve into what has been described as the land's 'deep topographies', challenging 'contemporary stereotypes of Pakistan as a nearfailed, inward-oriented, Islamic state' and gesturing towards a 'mode of imagining an inherent cosmopolitanism for this nation' (Kabir, 174).

To arrive, with Rushdie, in London, we need to return to the 1980s' 'simultaneously more disreputable and more politicized' metropolis, marked by the superior morality of its overground, by racist political institutions, by a Thatcherite distrust of local government and a limitless faith in laissez-faire economics, but also by the explosive 'sub-cultural capital' produced by the postcolonial migrant inhabitants of run-down inner city neighbourhoods (Sandhu, 369–71). Rushdie's intervention in writing on the city, based more or less purely on *The Satanic Verses*, has received vast critical attention. In 1990, Homi Bhabha heralded the advent of a 'novel metropolis', the 'metropolitan novel of the nineties'. Commenting on *The Satanic Verses*, he wrote that the 'metropolitan histories of *civitas* cannot now be conceived without evoking the savage colonial antecedents of the ideals of civility' (16). Fourteen years later, however, John McLeod noted *The Satanic Verses*' privileged status in postcolonial representations of London:

> Rushdie's novel has been considered the quintessential celebration of the city's migrant foundations and cosmopolitan melange, while his poly-vocal fictional style – drawing upon Latin American magic realism, film and cartoons, Indian traditions of storytelling, postmodernist experimentation, Dickensian caricature and so much more – is often understood as capturing rhetorically the heterogeneity, diversity, bewildering change and rapid speed of city life. (147)

Sukhdev Sandhu and John McLeod have situated Rushdie within a tradition of black and Asian writing on London, but, whereas McLeod groups him, thematically, with writers such as Hanif Kureishi (in an exploration of their engagement with popular revolt in 1980s' London), Ruvani Ranasinha and Sara Upstone place Rushdie in a position in-between and bridging first- and second-generation migrants. Ranasinha sees Rushdie and Kureishi as cultural translators or mediators between, respectively, countries (India and Britain) and communities (majorities and minorities within Britain). Such an argument, however, sits uneasily with both Rushdie's and Kureishi's emphasis on the impurity of cultures and identities. Rushdie's writing, she argues, forms a bridge between a politics of 'writing back' and 're-writing Britain', paving the way for Kureishi's and subsequent generations of British South Asian writers' increasing withdrawal from the politics of a collective 'ethnic' identity (2007b, 13–4). This generational perspective is further problematized by the specific place from which Kureishi speaks as a mixed-race, Indian Muslim/Pakistani English 'migrant' from suburbia to London. It is this specific situatedness, perhaps, that could account, to some extent, for the general development of Kureishi's work away from a collective ethnic politics in works such as *Intimacy* (1998). However, as Stuart Hall and Ranasinha have shown, Kureishi has sought to move away specifically from *prescribed* ethnic politics, a move that constitutes a re-politicization or reconfiguration of identity as responding to developing stereotypes and essentialist appropriations of cultural difference.

McLeod, too, has taken issue with Ranasinha's generational framework. He finds parallels between Kureishi's romantic imagination of London, as seen from Bromley, in *The Buddha of Suburbia* (1990) and that of first-generation 1950s' migrants as a result of the author's suburban early life

(138). *The Buddha* reveals a development in the protagonist Karim's attitude towards London as he gathers insights into the hierarchies of the city's artistic life and sexual relationships, and, in the process, becomes attuned, himself, to exploring and manipulating his own exoticization in the metropolis, sometimes to political ends, sometimes (and self-admittedly) as a means to furthering his own career. This marketability of 'ethnic' identities' perceived authenticity is a continuing theme explored in subsequent generations' writings on London, as we shall see.

Some interesting variations can be noted in Rushdie's and Kureishi's treatment of cities as related to their protagonists. Rushdie approaches London, for instance, through the catoptric pair of Saladin and Gibreel, whose contrasting, respectively, Anglophile and Anglophobe, attitudes allow him to reveal the city's various polarizations and to then complicate these polarizations towards interrogating them. Kureishi, by contrast, views London (in *The Buddha*) mainly through the eyes of a single protagonist and first-person narrator, which allows him a broader introspection of London's realities and also, importantly, the possibility to explore the multitude of ways – micro- as well as macro-political – in which identity is formed and develops in interaction with other identities. This reactive concept of identity can be termed, in a biochemical metaphor, its *polyvalence*, reflective of a multi-connectivity. An alternative metaphor has been offered by Sandhu in what he describes as Kureishi's 'urban messthetics' (246), which undermines monolithic ideas of urban experience, as Bart Moore-Gilbert (2001) has shown. Both Sandhu and Moore-Gilbert, however, refer to the range of characters who make up, together, Kureishi's London, rather than this radical constitutive characteristic of the identity of a particular character like Karim (although Moore-Gilbert notes Karim's slippage in and out of normative categories of race and sexuality). This is an aspect of postcolonial identity less explored in Rushdie and it could be said to have prefigured what becomes a tendency towards a schematicity of urban representation in his later work, specifically, *The Enchantress*. These two types of configurations – a catoptric dialectics as opposed to a centred polyvalence – otherwise appear in both Kureishi's and Rushdie's other works, for instance, in Rushdie's Malik Solanka in *Fury* and in Kureishi's Omar and Johnny in his film *My Beautiful Launderette* (1985). Overall, however, Rushdie and Kureishi's divergence along these lines reveals a difference in their reconfigurational politics.

Upstone, too, situates Rushdie, ambiguously, between a 'conventional migrant positioning' and a 'newly emerging, as yet unrealized, British Asian sensibility' (31). The latter is exemplified, as becomes evident in her discussion, in the gender-polarized 'post-ethnic' Londons of Atima Srivastava's *Transmission* (1992) and *Looking for Maya* (1999), on the one hand, where the city enables the unfolding of women's 'romantic dilemmas' in the form of a universal romance (83), and, on the other, in Gautam Malkani's *Londonstani* (2006), marked by the 'hyper-masculine bravado' of a street gang whose members feel no need to either claim an ethnic authenticity or to reclaim Britain, according to Upstone (210–11). Sara Brouillette, however, has complicated Upstone's argument by examining *Londonstani*'s relationship with the contemporary culture industries and its attempt to parallel the success of London authors such as Zadie Smith and Monica Ali. *Londonstani*'s 'street thugs or self-professed Desi rude boys' can be seen, she argues, as the result of a conspiracy between 'arts funding and corporate blending', which identifies gaps in the market (particular, less well represented communities) in order to market a new 'popular and saleable authenticity' (2010, 8). Malkani's text evinces, for Brouillette, both Malkani's own apprenticeship to such a marketable urban anthropology and an embarrassment about the ethnic affiliations that he has drawn upon 'in order to produce a text that he could then circulate as his unique, brand-worthy cultural property' (8–16).

While it is unclear what Upstone means by a 'conventional migrant position', her argument seems to prefigure the cultural marketability of which Brouillette speaks. Insofar as the British Asian sensibility that Ranasinha and Upstone conceptualize conveys, at least in geographical terms, a sort of settling down, Rushdie appears to have moved on, partly in search of new in-between places to sit in uncomfortably and partly in response to the ever-changing configurations in which cities, old and new, find themselves. Chapter 6 explores some of the transformations in the later development of his position as well as the problematics of his claim of 'unbelonging' to which Brouillette (2007b) and others have drawn attention.

The remainder of this chapter offers a more detailed exploration of three novels by Indian-born transnational authors whose interurban trajectories converge with Rushdie's. In shuttling between cities, each of these texts reveals a specific configurational dynamic comparable to his, while also containing significant differences from it. In juxtaposing texts by Anita Desai and her daughter, Kiran Desai, I hope to demonstrate the development of urban representation across generations of diasporic Indian writers who belong, historically, to the contours of Rushdie's oeuvre.

Anita Desai's *Baumgartner's Bombay* **(1988):**
Berlin–Venice–Calcutta–Bombay

Drawing upon her mixed Bengali and German heritage, Desai's novel traces
a less explored arrival in Bombay, which offers an unusual perspective on
the city, on India and on the encounters of East and West. The protagonist,
Hugo Baumgartner, a German Jewish refugee from Nazi Berlin, flees, via
Venice, to colonial India, imagined as a benevolent British haven from pre-
World War II Europe and full of business possibilities. When war is declared,
Baumgartner is arrested in Calcutta as a 'German citizen' and sent to an
internment camp, along with other 'hostile aliens' (106) to the colonial
government, only to emerge, after the war, into the pre-Partition violence
of Calcutta and another war, 'their war' (173), which he does not understand.
In comparison, he observes, the city 'made the internment camp seem
privileged, an area of order and comfort' (162). Advised by a Muslim
tradesman, Baumgartner flees, again, to Bombay, where 'you can do
business and not be stabbed in the back when you go home at night' (169).
Independence Day finds him, yet again, 'on the fringe', observing
celebrations from a distance, but glad, nonetheless, that Bombay has 'settled
back into its familiar activities of trade and commerce' and 'the possibilities,
the opportunities, the sanguine nature of a port' (191). This fringe stability,
however, proves, once more, illusory, as Baumgartner's kindness to the
needy and downtrodden and his lingering fondness for a lost, if alienating,
Germany leads him to his death at the hands of a young fellow countryman,
the 'Aryan' Kurt, representative of a new Western generation in India, the
rich 'hip-py' (216) back-packers from Europe and America who arrive in
the East in search of a mystical experience and end up in a perpetual drug-
induced stupor.

   Baumgartner's Bombay, then, is, on the one hand, an abstract location
encapsulated in the archetypal homelessness of the wandering Jew, of the
'*Firanghi*, foreigner' (19). Baumgartner's Bombay is as much Bombay as it
is Nazi Berlin, the internment camp, and riot-torn Calcutta. (Venice, as we
shall see, is positioned more ambiguously.) In this respect, Baumgartner
is reminiscent of Rushdie's narrowly liminal Bombayite, the 'Cathjew'
protagonist in *The Moor*. On the other hand, however, the novel offers a
specific, defamiliarizing perspective on the city and on India's post-
Independence history. Gopal rightly points out the Orientalist undertones
of the text – Baumgartner's first impression of Bombay is reminiscent of
Mrs Moore's India as 'a mystical yet recalcitrant trickster', and his experience in a cave somewhere in the barren dusty countryside expels him like

Adela Quested from the Marabar caves in *A Passage to India* (127–28). However, I wonder whether the choice of such a protagonist is intended to expose rather than embrace this attitude. Baumgartner allows Desai a double interrogation – of the exclusions of both European/global history and of national narratives of Indian history. In Calcutta, Baumgartner casts off 'the thick heavy clothing of Europe' and feels 'lighter', 'physically unburdened', but wonders, nevertheless, if Calcutta is 'a mirage, a dream' (91; 93). In all his suffering, dangerously verging, in Desai's representation, on a (perhaps intended) romantic sentimentality, we risk being tricked into sympathizing with him to the extent that we may overlook his own unwitting share in others' marginalization. Such an ambivalence of representation is also present in Kiran Desai's novel and sharing in the polyvalence of identity characteristic of Kureishi's Londoners. Baumgartner's perspective on Bombay plays off those of other 'citizens'. One of these is Zoroastrian Farrokh, the owner of the European-aspiring Café de Paris, a 'high-class two-star Irani restaurant for good families' (141), which Baumgartner helps 'cleanse' of Kurt to his own demise. Farrokh insists that he has served Kurt only because he is a compatriot of 'Bommgarter': 'I know your country must be good country' (139). Despite all his protests, in principle, against the likes of Kurt and what damage they are doing to India, Farrokh is motivated by self-preservation and is instantly satisfied when the problem has been removed, if only out of his sight. Baumgartner's Bombay is governed by such chain reactions of intersecting and clashing stories and social hierarchies – the tragic urban causality of life on the ground that reveals a very different image of the city from the post-Independence middle-class Bombay of *Midnight's Children*. The life of a family of pavement dwellers is shown in naturalistic detail, as part of, and in a judgemental response to, Baumgartner's daily routine of walking guiltily past, having just emerged out of his slightly more dignified level of habitation:

The woman, washing, automatically edged her sari over her face with a twitch of her wet hand as she did in the presence of any male; actually she hardly thought of Baumgartner, a lump in grey pants, as one . . . . The child that had the straw-coloured and straw-textured hair of the famine-struck . . . sat on its haunches, straining to defecate. It looked up at Baumgartner as it looked at all passers-by, its face clenched with the problem: should it sing out for money, for *baksheesh*, or not waste its small, painfully hoarded energy? In the case of Baumgartner, the problem was easily solved: he clearly had nothing to give, they all knew that . . . . So she drew the snot on her upper lip back into her nostrils with a contemptuous snort and began to wail for her mother who cursed her casually, simply as a comment on life, on all their lives. (7)

This passage offers an intricate interplay of the generic and the specific Baumgartner's Bombays in the mother's and her daughter's adjustment of perspective upon seeing him. He is forced to occupy this position in between anonymity and national, racial and gender recognizability and instinctively seeks it as his familiar, comfort zone. Thus, whereas the city that comes closest in corresponding to his sense of self, Venice, is 'that magic boundary' where East and West 'met and blended', 'where they became one land of which he himself felt the natural citizen' (63), it is also a city whose 'easternness' disturbs him and in which he gets lost in his search for the Jewish quarter (60; 64).

That Berlin, Venice, Calcutta and Bombay are connected by the forces of history's repetitive effect of loss is demonstrated not only in the travels of the protagonist but also in the way the novel constantly veers between episodic locations, so that the Holocaust to which Baumgartner loses both of his parents is mirrored by the communal bloodshed in Calcutta, and the wars merge. If Baumgartner's Bombay appears to offer him refuge, it also contains and traps him in a perpetual statelessness as the account of his life is enveloped by the opening and closing Bombay chapters. At the same time as Baumgartner's life allows Desai a perspective on both World War II and Partition, however, her protagonist remains largely ignorant of the latter or of the link between the two. Indian history continues to play out for him 'on the other side of the mirror' (85). Bombay is, in this respect, also a hiding place for what appears to be a most marginalized, multiply displaced figure.

Amitav Ghosh's *The Shadow Lines* (1988): Calcutta–Dhaka–London

Despite its multiple flashbacks and non-linear chronology, Desai's novel traces a more or less straightforward West–East journey with a clear starting and a clear end point. The cities on Baumgartner's route do no interact with each other but merely take turns in dispossessing and evicting him – a pattern that continues even after his death, when the police take away his belongings and memorabilia. Ironically, his death is the event that stirs the greatest response from his fellow citizens, who gather round his flat hungry for scandal. Although Ghosh's novel also explores the relationship between the histories of the subcontinent's partitions and World War II through inter-urban links, his protagonist and the reader experience the cities as multiple, converging, yet often conflicting, spatialities and temporalities. The book is divided into two parts – 'Going Away' and 'Coming Home' – but by the end of the narrative, this distinction has been revealed as absurd and irrelevant, a linguistic convenience that cannot account for the geopolitical 'shadow lines' governing the lives of the characters. 'Home' and 'away' are unstable, yet repeatedly rehearsed, points of reference for each of which several locations compete along the novel's reciprocal Calcutta–London and Calcutta–Dhaka continuums. These locations include the various Calcuttas experienced by the unnamed narrator (born in 1952), of his childhood and his adolescence as remembered in and intertwined with his contemporary moment of the early 1980s; the various Londons, merging with his own experience of the city, that he comes across in others' stories, such as those of his cousins, Tridib (who witnesses the city at the outbreak of World War II) and Ila (for whom London is one of the many places around the world between which she spends her childhood as a daughter of a U.N. official); and the twin Dhakas of his grandmother (Tha'mma) separated, once, by the Partition of India and Pakistan in 1947; for the second time, by Tridib's death in the 1964 Hindu–Muslim riots following the theft of the Mi-Mubarak (the sacred relic of the Prophet Mohammed's hair) in Srinagar; and, again, beyond her life-time, by the secession of Bangladesh from Pakistan in 1971.

The novel traces a multitude of catoptric itineraries that bridge and divide cities in this complex, ever-shifting and turbulent cartographic mosaic of the world between 1939 and 1981. As a child in Calcutta, the narrator travels in his mind to London by piecing it together from his cousins' stories and photographs that he receives 'in instalments' (13). This fragmented journey parallels the method in which the narrator's grandfather shipped a table from London to Calcutta in the 1890s – 'in sections' (59). The awkwardness of this unusually large piece of English furniture in India is one of the novel's many Alice-in-Wonderland echoes that project Calcutta as the inverted image of London and that multiply in the incessant national, communal, religious and social borderlines in and between cities. The table had been bought at a Crystal Palace exhibition, itself, it can be argued, an ambiguous point of origin, given these exhibitions' celebratory display of the profitability of the cultures brought together under the auspices of empire. If Crystal Palace exhibitions brought to the Victorians the world situated on the other side of empire's hegemonic mirror 'in sections', more than half a century later, the citizens of their decolonized territories continue to be bound by its fragmentary optics.

In the process of assembling London's fragments, however, the narrator acquires such an intimate knowledge of this landscape that when he travels to London years later, he can find his way around the city, recognize its streets, houses and tube stations and cite details of their histories with a precision that not only rivals but also surpasses that of the Prices, the English family (Mrs Price and her children, Nick and May) with whom Tridib and Ila stay, successively, in North London. Such a familiarity with the British metropolis from a distance is dictated by the desire to emulate the superior Other across the shadow line that separates the colonized from the colonizer. The narrator imagines himself as the mirror image of Londoner Nick Price, whom he had never seen: he 'became a spectral presence beside me in my looking glass; growing with me, but always bigger and better, and in some ways more desirable' (61). This lop-sided mirroring also characterizes the relationship between Calcutta and London. In the decades after Independence, the protagonist's social life in Calcutta revolves around the paan-shop at Gole Park, where young people gather to exchange news and gossip and where they collectively dream of the London in Tridib's fantastic tales. That London never reciprocates this desire produces a 'special quality of loneliness' for the people on the subcontinent (250).

A similar catoptric boundary, however, informs Calcutta's own, social divisions. The (literally) 'poor relation' the narrator's family visit on the 'wrong' side of the city turns out to know everything about them – a knowledge they fail to replicate. This scene is, ironically, the inverted image of the narrator's and Nick Price's first meeting in London. Calcutta's social divisions are carried over from the familial partitions of Dhaka which, in turn, prefigure the Partition of India and Pakistan. As a child in Dhaka, Tha'mma lives in one part of a house, bisected by a wooden wall by the two feuding sides of the family, where she speculates and fantasizes, with her sister Mayadebi, about the 'other' family, across the wall: 'Everything's upside-down over there'; 'at their meals they start with the sweets and end with the dal; their books go backwards and end at the beginning'; 'I'll drop you over the courtyard wall,' she threatens her sister, 'and then you'll have to become upside-down too'; but equally, sometimes it 'seemed a better place . . . and we wished we could escape into it too' (154).

Such cognitive asymmetries highlight the divergent ways in which politics figures in Britain and in India. The narrator's mother religiously follows the news on the radio, not because she is interested in politics for its own sake but because her life and those of her relatives depend on it: for her, it is 'a simple rule of survival' (243). Conversely, in London, Ila claims centrality of experience in being part of global history in the making – in this part of the world, in her view, 'revolutions or anti-fascist wars' take place, which set a 'political example to the world' as opposed to the 'local things', the famines, riots and disasters of the subcontinent (128). While Anglophile Ila lives in this powerful delusion, she plays the 'bit role' of a 'decoration' in the quiet, intellectual political discussions of her Marxist friends in the house she shares with them in Stockwell (120). She also seems to remain largely oblivious to her greater role in the politics of the local – her readiness, for instance, to confront 'a gang of jack-booted racists armed with bicycle chains' in Brixton (129). May Price is similarly convinced in the global significance of her political endeavours – she collects Russian novels and cushions decorated with Gujarati mirror-work; she fasts one day a week in the name of 'the human race', in general, and in solidarity with those who starve in the Third World, in particular. While capable of recognizing the violence of colonialism – she is outraged at the sight of the enormous statue of Queen Victoria in Calcutta (a visual rhyme with the large table shipped from the same location) – she comes to occupy the same role of maternal imperial benevolence in London. As the narrator joins her on one of her fasting, money-collecting days amid the shopping crowds at the intersection of Oxford and Regent Streets, she informs him that the proceeds are for 'famine relief . . . . In Africa mainly. But who knows? Even you might benefit from it some day' (198).

If shadow lines breaking apart subjectivities, cities and histories cannot be erased, they can be reconfigured as connecting lines – in the 'meeting' of London and Calcutta in the protagonist's mind, in the 'symmetrical accusations' (282) the Indian and Pakistani governments aim at each other during the 1964 riots or in the reciprocal flows of refugees north and south as if reflecting each other in a mirror. This form of catoptric inter-urban connectivity transcends the fixity of the nation form as illustrated in the narrator's experiment at an alternative cartography. He employs the logic of Euclidean space to interrogate the boundaries of national politics and discovers that 'Khulna is about as far from Srinagar as Tokyo is from Beijing; or Moscow from Venice; or Washington from Havana; or Cairo from Naples' (284). Since what bridges Khulna to Srinagar is a communal riot, the experiment proves that what could most effectively connect any pair of cities at the same Euclidean distance from each other is none other than conflict. While the narrator laments the victims of the riots, including the personal loss of his cousin, he recognizes in the riot a form of interpersonal connectivity that contradicts the nation-state and its interests. The riot is a manifestation of 'indivisible insanity', an 'independent relationship', and 'the natural enemy of the government' (283).

Ghosh's novel posits an interplay of catoptric and tectonic reconfigurations comparable to Rushdie's. The violence of the riot mimics and transforms the violence of the state. Both are described in seismic metaphors: the fear of the former is like the fear of an earthquake (250) and the latter causes cities to 'sail away from each other like the shifting tectonic plates of Gondwanaland' (286). However, such tectonic partitionings ironically bind cities catoptrically even more closely to each other, 'so closely', the narrator writes, 'that I, in Calcutta, had only to look into the mirror to be in Dhaka; a moment when each city was the inverted image of the other, locked into an irreversible symmetry by the line that was to set us free – our looking-glass border' (286). Cities, then, offer a space for the imagination of, and interaction with, the other in the mirror across post/colonial centre–periphery and religious, communal and national shadow lines. In the Euclidean experiment, nations disintegrate while cities remain intact as the smallest, multilayered but indivisible, units of space. Herein lies the difference between Rushdie's and Ghosh's reconfigurational politics. In addition to its rejection of the possibility that the nation might stand for a form of empowering filiation, the *Shadow Lines* offers little more than catoptric equivalence as a strategy of resistance against hegemonic divides. By contrast, *The Satanic Verses*, for instance, pushes its mirror re-envisioning of cities a step further, through a transformative or translational politics, into the articulation of something new.

Kiran Desai's *The Inheritance of Loss* (2006): Darjeeling–New York City

As in Rushdie's *Fury*, as we shall see, Desai's novel explores the status of contemporary New York as a global city, by tracing some of the hegemonic 'shadow lines' that lead to and stretch outwards from it. Specifically, the American city is shown in its connection to the politically, economically and territorially fraught region of Darjeeling, including the town of Darjeeling, and the hill station of Kalimpong, situated in the northern part of the Indian state of West Bengal, in the lower range of the Himalayas. A considerable portion of the narrative is set in a house near Kalimpong, named 'Cho Oyu', after a mountain range in the Himalayas and of a similar symbolic significance in its border location between China and Nepal.

The events of the novel are based on the 1980s' ethnic uprisings of the minoritized Indian–Nepalese community pushing for a separate homeland under the leadership of the increasingly militant Gorkha National Liberation Front (GNLF). Desai traces the effects of the Front's statehood agitation and its violent clashes with Indian security forces in the Darjeeling region and its inhabitants. The story moves back and forth between two narratives. The first one, the Darjeeling narrative, is centred around the lives of Cho Oyu's owner, the Cambridge-educated and now retired from the Indian Civil Service judge, Jemubhai Patel; his teenage granddaughter, Sai, and his cook, Panna Lal. The second narrative is set in a Third World, social underground New York, where the cook's son, Biju, works in a series of restaurants as an illegal immigrant. *The Inheritance of Loss*, then, juxtaposes and explores the complex interrelations between, on the one hand, the processes of political mobilization of South Asian ethnic minorities, trapped in their linguistic and cultural difference and their politically and economically subordinate position as the result of a long and tortured history of colonial drawing and redrawing of territorial and political boundaries and of the postcolonial state's hegemonic territorial reorganization policies and, on the other, narratives of the contemporary South Asian diaspora in a similarly entrapping and disturbing, global-underclass New York, its interaction with the products of other histories of migration and its links with the 'homeland'. These two locations are shown in a reciprocal, yet historically consequential, relationship based on the common legacy and the contemporary experience of loss, humiliation and violence.

The text foregrounds the various losses and dislocations that occur with travel and diaspora in an unevenly 'globalized' world through failures in communication and the seeping of meaning between languages and cultures. These obstacles are shown as part of an Indian historical legacy that is projected into New York. For instance, although Sai and the cook are close, he speaks Hindi, whereas she speaks English (19); when talking to the local chemist, the cook invents his own medical terms, which always leaves the chemist bewildered; the judge hears cases in Hindi, which are then recorded in Urdu by the stenographer, before translating them into English – 'nobody could be sure how much of the truth had fallen between languages, between languages and illiteracy' (62). Gyan, Sai's Gorkha maths teacher and, later, boyfriend, who is increasingly drawn to the GNLF, nevertheless cannot understand the different languages that the protestors speak all at once, but feels instead only 'the vibrations of what was being said' (157). When Lola (an upper-class Anglicized widow) complains to the head of the Kalimpong wing of the GNLF, Pradham, about their invasion of her vegetable patch, he teases her, in turn, about the French name of her house, 'Mon Ami': 'I didn't know we live in France, do we? Tell me why don't I speak in French then?' (243–44). This is a political, and sarcastic, comment, in that Pradham is very well aware of the incongruence of languages, nationalities and locations, especially given the very GNLF demand for the teaching of Nepali at school. In a telephone conversation between the cook and his son, the novel poignantly demonstrates the hierarchical connectedness of Darjeeling and New York in the cook's comic attempt to project his voice all the way to America by shouting. More is left unsaid and implied than spoken. Others interfere in the conversation, prompting questions and repeating what they have heard. There are, importantly, technical problems on the Indian side, where the weather seems to reject the possibility of Western technological developments. Such is the distance, geographical and economical, between them that, later in the novel, the cook is led to doubt the existence of his son.

Like *Baumgartner's Bombay*, *The Inheritance* reinforces the idea of the domino effect of history's inevitability against which the characters seem powerless, but such chain reactions often involve accidental historicities and random violence. When Swiss-born Father Booty takes an innocent photograph of a butterfly, his camera is confiscated by the Gorkha soldiers; they find the photograph of a bridge with a sentry post, accuse him of being a spy, and ransack his house to discover that he is illegally residing in India and force him to leave the country, where he has lived for 45 years. The judge is racially abused in England; bitter on his return to India, he becomes estranged, a violated being who in turn commits violence against his own wife and his subordinates in the Indian Civil Service. A street drunk (who cannot work and make a living because of the Gorkhas' road blocks) is taken in by the police at random, beaten almost to death and blinded in the process; his family beg the judge for help, but he sends them away; in an act of revenge, they steal and sell his dog, whose new owners then tie it to a tree and kick it.

This knock-on movement is codified in tectonic terms, which share with Rushdie's urban configurations an ecocritical concern. The narrative continuously refers to the cracks in houses and on roads, to crumbling, sloping and landslides. Such references serve, in turn, to challenge the rigidity of borders and communal divisions. All boundaries in the novel are impermanent and slippery: the mist charges 'down like a dragon, dissolving, undoing, making ridiculous the drawing of borders' (7). In this development, the novel approximates Ghosh's vision of boundaries as invisible lines that nevertheless violate lives. Here, however, the emphasis is on exposing catoptric illusions rather than establishing equivalence with others in the mirror. In the opening scene at Cho Oyu, when Sai looks back from the garden, the house is gone; when she climbs the steps back to the verandah, the garden has vanished; when she looks at the judge sleeping, she believes that this is 'exactly what he would look like if he were dead' (2). The house itself is enveloped in vapour, mist, a plume of snow, ocean shadows and depths (1), which combine to convey a sense of a precarious, vulnerable or relative existence. Even the Himalayas that have been part of the region's landscape for centuries and upon which the characters frequently look to reassure themselves of their world's stability and permanence are changeable and interpretable; they mislead by continually offering optical illusions of truth and enlightenment. In the final scene of the novel, when the cook embraces his son on his return from America, the reader is shown the mountain of Kanchenchunga turning 'golden with the kind of luminous light that made you feel, if briefly, that truth was apparent. All you needed to do was to reach out and pluck it' (324). Jill Didur discusses Desai's fluid poetics as a postcolonial ecological strategy of subverting the 'naturalized status' of the Himalayan landscape in 'British social, cultural, horticultural, architectural, and environmental experiences'. The Indian 'hill station', she points out, is a British creation brought about by 'fantasies of virgin landscapes and the possible recovery of or retreat to the Garden of Eden' (43). The novel's 'contingent sense of community' rejects this 'colonial aesthetic of the picturesque and the sublime' (43; 59).

Darjeeling and New York participate in and motor a complex network of historical, cultural and political consequentialities. The extensive interweaving of stories of migration suggests that individual and cultural identities are influenced by a global traffic of cultural forms (fictions and stereotypes), often informed by older hegemonic constructions. This is evident, for instance, in the novel's many references to the illusion of films, to actors and roles. A group of young Nepalese insurgents are described as 'unconvincing', 'screaming like a bunch of schoolgirls' (4) and 'shivering in camouflage' (7). Their aggression is portrayed as an adopted, mimicked film role or a fake posture: they laugh 'a movie laugh', that of the 'classic cinema' of 'pre-terrorist days' (5). When Gyan is 'gathered up accidentally' (160) by the Gorkha procession, he finds everyone behaving as if in 'a documentary of war' (157) and his pulse 'leap[s] to something that felt entirely authentic' (160). In the way in which he is subsumed into the larger narratives of history and the collective march of Gorkha identity, which give 'meaning and shape to his anger' (160), we see old truths, authenticities and films being violently replaced by new ones. The ethnic/political majority is not immune from such re-articulations either. When Sai and Gyan argue, Sai behaves and speaks 'as if she were on a stage; the role was

more powerful than herself' (261). Desai and her heroine Sai make little
effort, as Scanlan points out, to consider the claims of the GNLF (2010,
271). The novel's political message concerns more broadly the larger scripts
and power relations within which the characters find themselves and
attempt to negotiate their identities. This is satirically dramatized in two of
the Darjeeling characters' battle of pro-American versus pro-English
values.

Desai's New York is the diametrical opposite of Rushdie's, as it offers
almost no degree of creative cosmopolitan potential in its global economic
underbelly. While Schoene finds it a generic capitalist upstairs–downstairs
society that could have been set in any American metropolis (139), this
comment points precisely to the dislocated nature of this experience of
urban contemporaneity. Just because this experience has been recorded,
theorized and imagined, it should not suggest that the phenomenon has
ceased to exist and to govern many lives with its clichés. The strength of the
novel is in the way it historicizes the relationship between its two main
locations, as we have seen. Desai also shows that her Indian and African
immigrants in New York are not immune from essentializing others and in
this they mirror Darjeeling's socio-ethnic hierarchies. In New York,
Zanzibaran Saeed Saeed describes the incessant influx of African immigrants
(whom he has to help find work) as 'more tribes' (96). In Darjeeling, one
of the Indian residents complains that the Nepalese are 'multiplying like
Muslims' (129). Downstairs New York is itself revealed as a hierarchical
structure of exclusion, also evident in the 'national' floor levels of
restaurants, a French one above a Mexican or an Indian one. The wife of
the owner of Pinocchio's (a predictably Italian restaurant) dreams of being
able to hire Bulgarians and Czechoslovakians, with whom she feels she has
religion and skin colour in common (48).

While the complexity of these national and racial power hierarchies is
infinitesimal, they are also ambivalent. In *Mission London* (2001), a Bulgarian
novel set in contemporary London, for instance, a Bulgarian restaurant is,
at once, benevolently housed by, organically sprouting out of, and
unceremoniously suppressed into, the basement of a Russian one, named
'Borsht and Tears' in an ironically nostalgic and deliberate cliché. Such a
rearrangement of post-communist power relations in the British metropolis,
however, is unsettled further as 'Borsht and Tears' gathers a combined team
of Russian, Bulgarian and Serbian would-be entrepreneurs stealing ducks
from Richmond Park to sell them to Chinese restaurants in Soho via the
kitchen of the Bulgarian Embassy, whose chef is involved in the operation.
The Eastern European presence in contemporary London is also registered

in Kureishi's most recent novel, *Something to Tell You* (2008), where it is problematic not least for its polarization along gender lines. A vertical hierarchy emerges here that is the exact opposite of the dreams of Pinocchio's owners in *The Inheritance*. Vaguely Eastern European prostitutes and erotic dancers negotiate their space in the background of his twenty-first-century London, whereas the protagonist's (Jamal's) best friend, role model and, later, accomplice, in the 1970s, the Bulgarian Valentin, assumes a central role, associated with a romantic, unassailable yet sensitive, masculinity. An exotic relic of a bygone world and, after a fashion, Jamal's dark alter-ego, Valentin kills himself in what ultimately serves as an act of atonement for the 'crime' of the protagonist. Jamal, by contrast, cultivates himself, haunted by his crime and by (the suicide of) his Eastern European other, into a professional psychoanalyst.

The novels discussed earlier merely gesture towards the myriad of dis/connecting stories of and between the cities. In the chapters that follow, I explore individual texts or pairs of texts by Rushdie in relation to a specific idea of urban configurations that resonates across the three dynamics – the tectonic, the catoptric and the specular. I offer close examinations of his novels within their cultural contexts to reveal the interplay of their urban configurations. The triple approach of this study allows the conceptualization and analysis of Rushdie's cities as dynamic space-times, as tectonically unstable meeting-places of incomplete histories, as constituted through multiple catoptric and specular trajectories and as conditioned by what Doreen Massey terms *power-geometries* (2005, 130), but also as exercising the possibility of negotiating and subverting these power geometries.

Chapter 2

Partition and After: Bombay Re/beginnings and Subcontinental Twin Cities in *Midnight's Children* and *Shame*

In a recent article on Salman Rushdie's Bombay, Thomas B. Hansen argues that *Midnight's Children* is a 'story unfolding in Bombay, though not a story about Bombay' (2008, 91). This contention seems to not only gravely downplay the significance of the city by positing its purely allegorical role (or, worse, its irrelevance as a mere background to the story), but to also dangerously gloss over the intricacies of Bombay's relationship with India/ the subcontinent in the novel. At the same time, however, Hansen's statement points to the way in which the story of the city is inevitably caught up in, intertwined with and constituted through stories of other cities and places as well as being shaped by the larger historical and geopolitical narratives that contain it, such as those of the birth of the nation, of Partition and of postcolonial national modernity.

Crucially, Bombay itself dictates, to a large extent, Saleem's particular version of these narratives. Dictation/recitation and scripting as well as the creative passage between the two inform the novel's method of unreliable historiography and geography and draw, simultaneously, on Muslim (the *Qur'an*), Hindu (the *Ramayana* and the *Mahabharata*) and Western (radio) cultural traditions or technologies of oral transmission. For instance, the narrator Saleem and the narratee Padma are each compared to both the alleged author of the *Ramayana*, the poet Valmiki, and to his putative scribe, the elephant-headed god Ganesh, taking down Valmiki's dictation (MC, 149, 195). In his essay, 'Errata', Rushdie famously identified some of Saleem's mistakes, pointing out, for instance, that in Hindu mythology, Ganesh sat, 'in fact', 'at the feet of the bard Vyasa', taking down the *Mahabharata* rather than the *Ramayana* (IH, 22).

The necessarily suspect authority of Rushdie's narrator as a guide to the migrant's plural 'imaginary homelands' or 'Indias of the mind' (IH, 10) has been celebrated as advocating an anti-essentialist notion of place. What seems to have received less attention is the role of Bombay as the home of the narrative position and, thus, the prism through which the reader can view Saleem's India, specifically, the nature of this story as one in which Bombay has a central place, in terms of both form and content. The novel explores this idea of the 'plotted' birth – of the postcolonial self, city and nation – within the broader sense of historical emplotments. Saleem's and the nation's conjoined births are heralded in the *Times of India*'s 'Bombay edition' (MC, 119), so that through the protagonist, modern India is symbolically born in Bombay and articulated under Bombay dictation/recitation. In this respect, the novel self-consciously complicates the diegetic architecture of the *Thousand and One Nights* by dramatizing, for instance, the relationship between the narrative frame and the framed narrative as a metafictional journey. Saleem compares himself both to Scheherazade the storyteller (9) and to her character, the legendary Caliph Haroun al-Rashid, who 'enjoyed moving incognito amongst the people of Baghdad' (219).

Midnight's Children's Bombay presents a crucial duplicity – as a frame, it shapes Saleem's history of India, but as a framed narrative, it appears to be contained and claimed by this history. The imagination of Bombay as imprisoned within modern India is more explicitly developed in *The Moor's Last Sigh*. Chapter 4 attends to this Bombay diptych. Nevertheless, throughout Rushdie's work, cities are celebrated as inherently positive, pluralistic, cosmopolitan formations, vulnerable to manipulation from outside. When they do become the subject of hegemonic control, its origin is historically and conceptually traced to a context that is alien to the urban spirit. Cities are often plagued by communal, ethnic and linguistic conflicts that arise elsewhere, but rather than positing urban boundaries or purity, Rushdie's texts dramatize cities' constant and often turbulent negotiations and realignments in relation to essentialist and hegemonic narratives. *Midnight's Children*'s Bombay is iconic in this respect. It is multiply forged and multiply interpellated. It is claimed by a pastoral nostalgia, as an ancient place of 'natural', unspoilt romantic harmony: the Koli fishermen 'sailed in Arab dhows, spreading red sails against the setting sun' (MC, 92). Paradoxically, this vision is invoked by Saleem, the 'city boy', as Padma deprecatingly calls him, yet it serves to suggest that this vision has a hold on the imagination as strong as all the ones that follow it. It is also a nod to dung-named, illiterate, village Padma, a 'useful' counterpart to, and critic of, Saleem's urban imagination of India. Padma's role has been associated with historiographic erasure as she is both its victim and a device of its narrative dramatization in the novel. Her persistent 'what-happened-nextism' and her impatience with Saleem's self-conscious, unreliable narrative method, however, are eroticized in that Saleem both flirts with and feels restrained by the possibilities of conventional, linear narrative.

The romantic vision of Bombay's pre-colonial origins is then successively interrupted by the Portuguese 'christening' of the place ('Bom Bahia'), by the dream of the East India Company officer William Methwold of a 'British Bombay, fortified, defending India's West against all comers' (92), and, finally, by Saleem's and the nation's conjoined, multiply prophesied births. Each of these events is both rupturing and foundational.

Bombay as a frame, however, is the vantage point of Saleem's history of India and, therefore, simultaneously a narrative, geographical and political location. This history bears, specifically, the brand stamp of Braganza Pickles (Private) Ltd., allusive of Bombay's commercialism and entrepreneurial spirit as well as of the city's Portuguese and British histories of exploration and colonialism. Braganza Pickles, where Saleem writes his story, advertizes Bombay's aspirations as a city of national synthesis in its/Saleem's desire to mix, contain and preserve India's multitudinously hybrid traditions and in its mimicry/parody of Bombay's film industry as a factory for popular national imaginaries. The Bombay in which Saleem will be born and which will 'handcuff' his life to that of the nation has been paved for by the idealism of the era of Nehruvian nationalism (1950s–1960s), celebrated in the city's 1950s' cinema in the images of the modern Indian who places nation before self (Metcalf *et al.*, 2002, 233). As a result, Saleem's identity as a trope for the nation and his conscious responsibility for history both offer him and his city a purpose and deny them an ordinary life.

In an incident during his childhood in Bombay, for instance, Saleem is forced to act as a prop in a lesson in 'human geography'. His face is read like a map and, more specifically, like a political map of the subcontinent, where his nose is used by the geography master to illustrate the shape of the Deccan peninsula: the birthmark on his ear is compared to the East Wing of Pakistan (later Bangladesh); the 'drip from his nose' to Ceylon (later Sri Lanka); and the 'stains' on his face to Pakistan as a 'stain on the face of India' (MC, 231–32). Saleem's features, thus, both come to serve what Homi Bhabha terms the nation's 'pedagogical discourse' and are shown, literally, in the process of this pedagogy, as tools in affirming India's centrality and dominance over its neighbours. The fact that the geography master, Emil Zagallo, also teaches gymnastics, points to geopolitics' agility and the acrobatic lengths at which it is capable of stretching in order to justify its paradoxes – at once, its exclusions and its totalities.

Braganza Pickles also asserts Bombay's claim of a cosmopolitan identity as the laboratory for the 'chutnification' of larger than national – South Asian, diasporic and as Vilashini Cooppan contends, global – histories, not only for the novel's 'cosmopolitan intertextuality' but also for the way it shapes a 'global sense out of national signification' (2009, 47–50). The text, however, also moulds, as we shall see, national out of urban and, in turn, urban out of subjectival signification. This gradation of scales becomes a repetitive motif in the novel. It is evident in the four identical houses of Methwold's Estate, named after the palaces of Europe: Versailles Villa, Buckingham Villa, Escorial Villa and Sans Souci. For Cooppan, the idea of Methwold's Estate as a 'compound of faux-European mansions' points to the novel's strategy of expressing globalism through nationality (43). The European aspirations of these names, however, are also derived from Bombay's cultural and commercial openness to the West and the ambition of its post-Independence elite to keep with the imagination of an urban cosmo-politanism, albeit rooted, as it is, in the colonial past.

The gradation of scales becomes even more apparent in Saleem's interpretation of a painting in his childhood bedroom in Buckingham Villa, particularly of the significance of a detail in this painting – the fisherman's pointing finger, one of the novel's recurrent motifs. Neil Ten Kortenaar has pointed out that the painting, as described by Saleem, evokes Sir John Everett Millais's *The Boyhood of Raleigh*, painted in 1870, in which 'two aristocratic Elizabethan lads', one of whom is presumably the explorer Sir Walter Raleigh as a boy, sit by the sea, listening to an old sailor telling of his voyages as he points towards the horizon beyond the sea:

> The setting of the painting is presumably Raleigh's native Devon, and the sailor is pointing west to the New World. The painting depicts the moment when Raleigh first conceived the dream of making history: we understand that the old salt's stories of the New World will inspire the young Raleigh to go himself in search of El Dorado in the voyage he will later record in *The Discovery of Guiana*. (Kortenaar 1997, 232–33)

In the novel, Saleem attempts to make sense of this scene in its new Bombay surroundings and in relation to his own life: does the fisherman's finger point, within the room, to the framed letter of the Prime Minister in which Saleem is heralded as the nation's twin, or, through the window of his room, to the horizon and his future doom, or, closer, 'down the two-storey hillock, across Warden Road, beyond Breach Candy Pools, and out to another sea which was not the sea in the picture; . . . an accusing finger, then, which obliged us to look at the city's dispossessed' (MC, 122)? This re-contextualization of the painting in post-Independence Bombay is undoubtedly ironic in exposing the equal absurdity of the imperial vision and of Saleem's national significance. However, it also succinctly illustrates Bombay's positioning in relation to domestic, local/urban, national and global orders in Saleem's world, which figure as frames or concentric circles.

The role of Bombay as a narrative frame, then, is in its projection of a specific national imagination of India – urban, secular, Nehruvian – its critique of the failure of this ideal, and, to some extent, its self-reflexive diagnosis of the exclusions performed by such an imagination. Saleem's Bombay history of India – from 1915 to 1978 – is performed as a journey that takes the form of an interurban route: from Srinagar to Amritsar, Agra and Delhi to Bombay, from Bombay to Rawalpindi, Karachi, Dhaka, Delhi, Benares and back to Bombay. Although marked by nostalgia, this journey mobilizes the past in a stringent political critique of India's post-Independence realities. An exception to this urban story is the region of the Sundarbans, which figures in the novel's envisioning of Bangladesh's secession from Pakistan in 1971. The Sundarbans are imagined as an ahistorial place (reminiscent of Rama's exile in the forest in the Indian epic of the *Ramayana*) from which the protagonist needs to emerge into a city (Dacca/Dhaka) in order to regain his memory and identity as Saleem.

In an interview, Rushdie argued that the period between Independence and the Emergency (1947–1977) 'had a kind of shape to it', representing a 'closed period' in Indian history or 'a betrayal' of the nation's possibilities (CSR, 18; 46). In the novel, it is from Bombay where the narrative launches its critique of the imposition of geopolitical shapes and historiographical emplotments as it reclaims its own shape of urban and national histories – the journey – from narratives of colonial advance, historical progress and teleology and territorial nationalisms. As we noted in the Introduction, the transition from colonial domination to Independence and Partition was imagined in much of twentieth-century Indian literature as a journey from the countryside to the city. Rushdie's novel offers an alternative to this imagination in Saleem's history of India in the form of inter-urban travel and of travel within the boundaries of a city but across various urban divides. This vision articulates the idea of the city as continually unfolding routes or movements that adopt and undermine the linearity or uniformity of the national route, the 'national longing for form' or the 'belief that forms lie hidden in reality' (MC, 300). It is this idea of the city as a plurality of shape-shifting itineraries, alternative to and erosive of established cartographical and historical trajectories, that informs the conceptualization of urban configurations in all of Rushdie's texts in this book. The novel's play with 'historical shapes' can be seen as a poststructuralist gesture in subverting the historical imagination of templates, genres, periodizations and categories, but it is also a specific response to the historical closures of possibility in independent India that have been performed, in the novel's terms, by nationalist idealism at Independence as belied by the horrors of Partition, by communalist politics, by the discrepancy between 'Indian Muslim identity as consolidated during the period of British colonialism and the actual territorial and demographic reality of the Pakistani nation-state' (Toor 2005, 319) and by Indira Gandhi's politics of authoritarian centralization.

Midnight's Children and Rushdie's subsequent novel, *Shame*, have often been seen as contrasting postcolonial national fictions of, respectively, India and Pakistan. The 'India-idea', writes Rushdie, is based on plurality, tolerance, devolution and decentralization (IH, 44); it has 'multiple possibilities', whereas 'contemporary Pakistan seems to represent a closure of possibilities'; 'I had the feeling, with Pakistan, of claustrophobia, and in India of wide open landscapes' (CSR, 49; 66). In comparative critical assessments, *Shame* has often been regarded as a lesser fiction so that rehabilitations of the novel, such as Brendon Nicholls', are compelled to redeem its 'literary failure' by reconsidering it as a crucial part of the novel's conscious political strategy (2007, 110). In a recent tribute to Rushdie's work, Sara Suleri also emphasizes the point: '*Shame*'s plot is indeed embarrassingly dated: much as *Midnight's Children* enriches with each decade, *Shame* atrophies in its own journalistic allegoricalisism'. Nevertheless, she acknowledges that it 'plays as vitally' with 'what is and what is not available to historical forgetfulness' (2008, 116–17).

As we saw in the introductory discussion, the criticisms of *Shame*'s style and representations concern the issue of Rushdie's political location as an author. This issue is, in other words, relevant to an examination of any of his novels, including *Midnight's Children*, but it becomes particularly pertinent to *Shame* because its indictment of Pakistan is served from the position of an avowed outsider. The narrator's insistence on his migrant lens is more explicit, didactic or 'journalistic', as Suleri puts it, and perhaps even more forceful than that of the narrator in *The Satanic Verses*, Rushdie's most paradigmatic novel of migration. Whereas Saleem's story of India is told from a narrative location in a Bombay of memory, *Shame*'s narrator, a transparent Rushdie figure, looks upon his imagined Pakistan from an explicit positioning in a contemporary London and draws parallels between his observations on the events in his life in the British metropolis and his narration of the events in the lives of his Pakistani characters.

The overall urban maps of *Midnight's Children* and *Shame* contribute to the national antitheses that Rushdie associates with India and Pakistan. Whereas the former novel charts out an open-ended, multi-city cartography, the latter meanders in a circuitous fashion within what can be described as a maze of cities. The urban triangle of *Shame*'s Q./Quetta, Karachi and Islamabad indicates the contours of Pakistan – East, South and North – which is seen, in this way, as a national fiction that entraps its citizens. As this chapter demonstrates, however, that the two novels offer a continuity of urban critique – both texts are marked by the imagination of the 'failure' or 'atrophy' of the urban ideal. It is necessary, therefore, to move beyond a mere identification of the two novels' antithetical relationship and examine more closely the dynamics of urban configurations within and across these texts.

Josna Rege notes that Rushdie once reportedly kept on his desk a little sculpture of an unpartitioned India: 'Even as he wrote of the realities of a divided subcontinent, he couldn't help but persist in holding on to India's geopolitical wholeness as both an idea and an ideal' (1997, 361). An effect of this 'pan-Indian' vision (Teverson 2007, 136), however, is the imagination of Pakistan's cities in *Midnight's Children* – an imagination that prefigures, to some extent, the representation of Pakistan in *Shame*, as an 'insufficiently imagined' nation or a 'failure of the dreaming mind' (Rushdie 2008a, 16). In an interview, Rushdie suggestively claims that in *Shame*, he used 'the material that interested [him] that was left over from *Midnight's Children*' (CSR, 19), but it is as early as *Midnight's Children*, where Rawalpindi and Karachi figure as 'leftovers'. On the one hand, as geopolitical carvings off British India, they are the product of the drawing of territorial boundaries along necessarily imaginary ethnic/religious lines and carry the text's critique of such divisions – particularly, of the construction of the Indian Muslim as the 'residue' of Partition politics (Kabir 2002, 248). On the other hand, these cities are denied the political potential of Bombay and cast, symbolically, as its antipodean versions. Whereas, as we saw in the Introduction, Amitav Ghosh juxtaposes Dhaka and Calcutta across national boundaries as each other's mirror equivalents in *The Shadow Lines* (1988), Rushdie has his protagonist say: 'I won't deny it. I never forgave Karachi for not being Bombay' (MC, 307). Rawalpindi is, similarly, a city with 'not all human' a face (MC, 291) and denotes the absence of Bombay.

Discussing the development of the idea of 'South Asia', Ashis Nandy argues that it is 'the only region in the world where most states define

themselves not by what they are but what they are not' in an otherwise joint
pretence of being 'radically different from each other' (2005, 541). When
Saleem falls in love with his own sister, Jamila, as she gains fame as Pakistan's
national singer, its 'Nightingale-of-the-faith' (MC, 306), he describes her as
his 'subcontinental twin sister', only to realize later that his feelings are for
his 'true birth-sister, India herself' (MC, 385).

This episode illustrates cities' interplay of tectonic, catoptric and specular
configurations in *Midnight's Children*. Partition is imagined as a tectonic
fissure in the earth that breaks cities apart and one that will be continually
eroded and deepened, most prominently, through three Indo–Pakistani
wars. In a military camp near Rawalpindi, for instance, General Zulfikar
plans to 'mine the entire Indo-Pak border' (MC, 285) in the novel's
fictionalization of Pakistan's second military encounter with India over
Kashmir in 1965. Simultaneously, the line of Partition acts as a catoptric
boundary, not as in Ghosh's imagination of a connecting shadow line, but
as an invisible barrier that obstructs Saleem's communication with the
midnight children once he has crossed over it to Rawalpindi. Similarly, the
narrator in *Shame* would refer to the country he is narrating as his 'looking-
glass Pakistan' (S, 88).

The fact that the relationship between Bombay and the Pakistani cities
takes on a romantic/erotic twist points to an overall development of specular
configurations in Rushdie's works, where the male protagonists often find
themselves seduced by, and consciously flirting with, monolithic or
exclusivist fictions, which are frequently personified and gendered feminine
in this way. Equally, however, women are often given the role of the most
radical demystifiers of these fictions – they are capable of exposing, for
instance, what Srivastava terms, nationalism's 'mythopoesis' or its
de-politicizing tendencies (2008, 58). In Karachi, Saleem 'nose[s] out' the
prostitute Tai Bibi, the specular counterpart of the Kashmiri boatman Tai.
While Tai is as old as the mountains (MC, 14), Tai Bibi's age is of 'crackling
antiquity' (MC, 320) and while his face is compared to 'a sculpture of wind
on water' (MC, 14), she has no face. In the Karachi prostitute, reminiscent
of Lalun (the Lahore courtesan) in Kipling's 'On the City Wall', as we saw
in the Introduction, the novel offers a critique of the sequestration of
women as a policy of newly formed Pakistan's religious nationalism: 'no city
which locks women away is ever short of whores' (MC, 318). Tai Bibi,
however, possesses 'a mastery of her glands so total that she could alter her
bodily odours to match those of anyone on earth' (MC, 319). It is specifically
Saleem's 'sense of history' that is 'aroused' when he meets her. Tai Bibi,
then, becomes a cipher for the idea of history as a prostitute: history 'loves

only those who dominate her' in a 'relationship of mutual enslavement' (MC, 124). The Partition-created frontier is also a specular barrier, a dystopian, surreal and perverse rupture in the fabric of Indian history. As Toor points out, 'the contours of the new nation-state effectively cut the citizens of Pakistan adrift of some of the clearest manifestations of Indo-Muslim culture and history on the basis of which claims to nationhood had been so eloquently made' prior to Independence (2005, 320).

The novel's pan-Indian ideal can be traced back, as Nandy suggests, 'more than a millennium' to that 'other India', known as 'Hindustanis' or 'Hindis', 'only a partly territorial entity that has been a point of convergence of a number of civilizations and cultural areas' (2005, 543). This 'other India', navigated from Bombay, offers a position from which the failures of the modern postcolonial nation-state can be interrogated in the novel, while opening itself to a critique of its nostalgic, mythopoetic sensibility. In her reading of the national idea in Rushdie's work, Sara Upstone argues that it 'would better be termed a state' as a rejection of a colonially inflected nationalism (2009, 48), yet clearly, the idea of the state in South Asia has been similarly tarnished by the notion of 'an imperial state internalized during the colonial times' (Nandy, 543). *Midnight's Children* critiques not the state, Upstone claims, but 'statism', yet she falls short of acknowledging an active, positive engagement with the 'political state'. Rushdie 'does not reject India as a state' (47) is as far as the argument can proceed. A far more enabling perspective is offered through Rushdie's sense of the city as a democratic, if utopian, space of disputation, a form of which is envisaged in the magical space-time of the midnight children's conference, convened from Bombay. While it mimics a Westminster-style democracy, it has non-Western precedents, evoked in Rushdie's most recent novel, *The Enchantress of Florence*, as we shall see in Chapter 7. Rushdie judges the failures of the Indian national imagination against the ideal 'other India' of which the Mughal emperor Akbar also dreams in *The Enchantress* and which he names 'Hindustan' (EF, 34). There, as in *Midnight's Children*, its subversive potentialities are coded urban. Bombay in *Midnight's Children* and Fatehpur Sikri in *The Enchantress* offer a positive paradigm of multiplicity, co-mingling and openness while challenging the structuralities of the state/empire and the primordial, originary, feminized body of the nation/homeland.

Midnight's Children's project of reclaiming India from the canon of Anglo-Indian literature employs an ambiguous tectonic metaphor that is also Bombay-specific and has a very real presence in the city's post-Independence history as a legacy of its colonial origins – the late 1660s' land reclamation projects of the East India Company, which joined the original seven islands into a single peninsula (MC, 93). Rushdie comments on Bombay as a 'British invention' within this scheme: the 'whole city, where it now stands, is mostly built on land that was reclaimed from the sea – by the British' (CSR, 72). In the novel, the British 'myth of conquering the waves' is taken up by Dr Narlikar and Saleem's father, Ahmed Sinai, who invest in the production of 'full-sized concrete tetrapods', 'four-legged conquerors triumphing over the sea' (MC, 314). This act of reclamation ironically mimics the colonial conquest. The tetrapod scheme further duplicates, in miniature, the process of decolonization within what Aijaz Ahmad has described as the contexts of modernization and integration of the post-colony within a global capitalist system (1992, 30). Upon his return to Bombay, at the end of the story, Saleem is horrified by what the tetrapod scheme has achieved: 'vast monsters soured upwards to the sky, bearing strange alien names: OBEROI SHERATON' (MC, 452).

In his biography of Mumbai, Suketu Mehta also writes of the city as a product of 'a struggle against the sea' (2005, 135). He remembers himself as 'a child standing by the ocean and throwing pebbles into the water', an exercise he interprets as a manifestation of 'an atavistic urge to construct land, to conquer water' (135). Although he notes the irony of the term 're-claimed land' – it is 'as if we had a legitimate claim on it in the first place' (134) – he acknowledges the connection between this urge and the necessity of demarcating a territory in a city like Bombay. In school, the 'important thing was not to get crowded off the space you happened to possess …. The moment you left, it was up for grabs' (129). Land reclamation and demarcation are, in this sense, fundamental to the idea of the crowd – an iconic image of the nation in Indian literature (Srivastava 2008, 98), which figures in Rushdie's and Mehta's imagination as a characteristically urban trope and one which is specifically embodied by Bombay. For Mehta, the 'Battle of Bombay' is 'the battle of the self against the crowd' or of 'Man against the Metropolis' (589) echoing the famous closing scene of *Midnight's Children*, where Saleem disintegrates into the multitudinous Bombay crowds, a symbol of urban/national pluralism and, at once, of a perpetual fragmentation.

The urban ideals of inclusiveness and pluralism are frustrated in the proliferation of catoptric splits, partitionings and shadow selves. Partition, the novel's most prominent catoptric split, informs the incessant fragmen-tation of urban identities, histories and geographies. These bifurcations include the social, ethnic and religious polarization of the midnight's children forum in the Saleem/Shiva split and the transformation of Bombay from the city of the Midnight's Children Conference into the city of the

Midnight Confidential Club, symbolic of a new, degenerate Bombay, which mirrors Saleem's own translation from an active agent of history to its crumbling victim. Delhi also deteriorates from the city of the public announcement of Saleem's and India's birth into the city of the magicians' ghetto. India's midnight promise, its first post-Independence generation, has been symbolically exported outside the new nation's capital.

The novel employs, however, the ambiguities of the land-reclamation metaphor – both originary and hegemonic, on the one hand, and identificatory and transformative, on the other – in the imagination of history as an earth-shaping force. This force is constituted through multiple geomorphic movements that are suppressed by or coerced into the official form of history but that nevertheless continue to undermine it. Saleem's family attempt to carve out a space for themselves while riding the tides of history, and if 'riding the tides of history' seems a contrived and pretentious trope, then that is because, ironically, by virtue of his destiny to mirror the life of the nation, Saleem is also forced to repeat its clichés and hyperboles. Moreover, he recurrently describes his nationwide omniscience in global or cosmic terms as the ability to shift the tides of the world. As playthings of history, Saleem's family are thus forced to move from one city to another until they settle in Bombay, but in the process, they personalize public history in order to both make sense of it and claim it as their own:

> [t]he boatman Tai drove my grandfather from Kashmir; mercurochrome chased him out of Amritsar; the collapse of her life under the carpets led directly to my mother's departure from Agra; and many-headed monsters sent my father to Bombay, so that I could be born there. (MC, 90)

The journey to Bombay, however, is, to some extent, teleological: it refracts the imagination of the city as a national goal in the project of postcolonial modernity. It is not an urban flaw but one of national ideology that forces the Sinais to flee, after Partition, to newly formed Pakistan. The novel does not advocate stability, however, in the sense of stasis: travel is a necessary rite of reclamation. Aadam Aziz's return to Srinagar, for instance, with which the novel opens, mimics both fictional and historical re-beginnings – E.M. Forster's *A Passage to India* in the figure of Doctor Aziz, but also M.K. Gandhi's return to India in 1915 and, even further back, the migration of the first Mughal emperors South in the sixteenth century and their conquest of what was to become Mughal India. Aadam Aziz, Saleem's grandfather and, in the mock-allegorical terms of the novel, the founding patriarch of the nation, is a homecoming, home-reclaiming migrant – a detail reinforcing the idea of nations and cultures as forged through travel and inter-'leaking'.

Aziz's return to Srinagar, situated in the centre of the valley of Kashmir, however, marks yet another symbolic inception – one that is prefigured at this stage – of history as conflict. A princely state, which acceded to India in 1947, Kashmir became strategically crucial for both India's and Pakistan's national self-definition, thus triggering the tragedy of the two countries' rival land reclamations. In the novel, the ancient boatman Tai brings a summons to Aziz that would 'set history in motion', while beneath its surface, Kashmir's Lake Dal reveals 'the cold waiting veins of the future' like 'the skeleton of a ghost' (13). Kashmir is perhaps one of the few places in Rushdie's work that offers a positive affiliative engagement with the non-urban, testifying to his Kashmiri roots. It is presented as a magical repository of stories and thus a liminal, Edenic and atemporal place that would be violently brought into history as the site of contestation of political identity and nationhood, a signifier, at once, of the unitary character of the new Indian state and of Pakistan's foundations in the 'two-nation theory'. The prophecy of Lake Dal and of Srinagar's 'deceptively soft' ground (MC, 11) point even further forwards into the future, to the larger contexts of contestation in which Kashmir will figure and to which Rushdie returns in *Shalimar the Clown*.

Tectonic instability, the softness and malleability of the ground, often manifests itself, in *Midnight's Children,* in the form of urban signs and omens that come to signal or follow public, authenticated events, thus suggesting that this instability is simultaneously the cause and the effect of political divisions, which physically fracture and crack open urban ground, and that resistance against such ruptures is not to be found in the idea of urban stability, but in the process of a tectonic reconfiguration of the city, which draws its resources from the very infirmity of the ground. Whereas Saleem's narrative persistently records urban signs, he is both their victim and their manipulator as a consequence of his status as a twin of the nation. On the one hand, he is himself transformed into a sign of national history and earthography and an object of interpretation; on the other, he actively interprets signs in an attempt to impose form and meaning.

Within the earthography of official history, the cities on the Sinais' route are imagined as hotbeds of historical activity. They are often forced to coincide with official events, but this coincidence is often catoptrically distorted. Such reconfigurations reveal it in this way as exclusive, divisive and coercive. Amritsar and Delhi are each associated with an iconic public event. In Amritsar, where Aadam Aziz arrives with his new wife Naseem, he is literally plunged into history by being 'swept along by the crowds' (protesting against the Rowlatt Act) into the Jallianwala Bagh massacre (1919), an event that has become a symbol of colonial terror and, in the novel, a national wound tended by Aziz. The remoulding force of British colonialism as an exercise of imposing order on the 'chaos of India' is portrayed in the clash between the disorderly Indian crowd and the symmetrical logistic manoeuvre of General Dyer's troops: 'twenty-five to Dyer's right and twenty-five to his left' (MC, 36).

Delhi, the city of the public announcement of Saleem's conception, is the historical location of Jawaharlal Nehru's address to the nation at midnight on Independence Day from the walls of the city's Red Fort. The passage of Saleem's mother across Delhi to Red Fort for a prophecy of her son's future symbolically prefigures the nation's journey to Independence. In the spirit of Nehru's speech, she crosses the city's communal divides by rescuing Lifafa Das, a Hindu visitor in a Muslim muhalla, from the gathering mob outside her house. Yet, her journey to Red Fort is traced in cinematic parallels with the journey of her husband, Ahmed Sinai, to Old Fort to deliver a ransom to the Hindu Ravana gang so as to prevent them from burning down his property. Posing as a 'fanatical anti-Muslim movement', the Ravana gang operates, behind this façade, as a 'brilliantly conceived commercial enterprise' (MC, 72), which turns some of the key values that punctuate Nehru's speech on their head. The Ravana gang are 'ethical' in that they keep to their word to reduce 'shops fronts factories warehouses' to ashes and 'professional' in that they provide testimonial references from 'satisfied customers' who have paid up to stay in business (ibid.).

Prefiguring Partition, the national route bifurcates, before it begins, into the ambitious tropes of official history, marked by optimism and thrilling expectancy and the reality of life in the city. Agra bears most prominently the signs of this divergence. It has been infected by an 'optimism epidemic' that has been single-handedly caused by Mian Abdullah, the founder of the Free Islam Convocation, whose annual assembly is to take place on the Agra maidan in 1942 (MC, 40). The idea of an alternative to Muhammad Ali Jinnah's Muslim League, which claimed to be the sole representative of India's Muslims and which had passed the 'Pakistan resolution' two years earlier (Metcalf *et al.*, 2002, 200), is revealed in the novel as idealistic and naïve. It is symbolically annihilated in the assassination of the Convocation's leader. His secretary, Nadir Khan, is forced to hide in the basement of the Azizes' house. The subdual of this political possibility by a territorial version of Islam and its humiliating displacement underground from the public platform of the maidan, however, is presaged by the appearance of 'huge gaping fissures' in the earth of Agra, which symbolically prefigure both the ruptures of Partition and the way they are officially denied by India's celebrations of Independence. The fact that Nadir Khan fondly refers to his subterranean chamber as 'Taj Mahal' further portends the uprooting and dislocation of Indian Muslims from their cultural traditions, specifically their hybrid elite urban heritage as evinced in the fused (Persian, Islamic and Indian) architectural styles of the palace of Mughal Emperor Shah Jahan, into the fixed territoriality of the state of Pakistan. In order to imagine itself as a Muslim nation, Pakistan had to not only sever ties with Muslim material culture but to also radically abrogate the very principle of the 'united Muslim community in India' for whom it had been brought into being (Toor, 320). The escape of Nadir Khan underground would be mirrored in Delhi's Muslim muhallas, where people look inwards into the 'screened-off courtyards of their lives' and where even 'young loafers' stand in circles, facing inwards (MC, 69).

Muhammad Ali Jinnah (the leader of All-India Muslim League and founder of Pakistan) had wished to avoid what he referred to as a 'maimed, mutilated and moth-eaten' Pakistan but simultaneously desired 'parity with Hindu India' (Metcalf *et al.*, 212). In the novel, Jinnah's notorious qualifier, 'moth-eaten', acquires resonance as a motif that evokes, in its repeated use, the perpetual fragmentations of history. On the eve of Partition, for instance, Aadam Aziz inspects the already perforated sheet through which he has examined and fallen in love with his future wife, only to find that more holes have appeared in it. As he 'wave[s] her history under her nose', he yells at her: 'Look, Begum: moth-eaten! You forgot to put in any naphthalene balls!' (MC, 111). Bombay and Pakistan's cities thus stand, in the novel, for two opposed techniques for the preservation of history – the naphthalene method, aiming to preserve essence and purity, and the chutnification method, involving creativity, the mixing and transformation of traditions and celebrating the fallibility of memory as a tool for the production of something new. The novel further parodies the two-nation theory in positing Karachi against Bombay in terms of smell: the former's citizens exude the 'flat boiled odours of acquiescence', depressing to Saleem's nose, which is used to the 'highly-spiced nonconformity of Bombay' (MC, 308).

Although Bombay seems invulnerable to the communal discords of Delhi, it too is involved in rival land reclamations that are also tectonically presaged by cracks in its roads in the wake of a severe drought that afflicts the city. Such urban omens constitute an alternative, non-linear, often organic temporality that is satirized on a number of occasions but that unsettles, as we noted earlier, the linear sequence of the causes and effects of official events. Like Partition, the separation of Gujarat from Maharashtra in 1960, after which Bombay remained the capital of the latter, is not only tectonically predetermined but also over-determined. A parallel between Agra and Bombay will demonstrate the development of this geomorphic movement. As they observe with alarm the growing fissures in the earth, Agra's 'betel-chewers at the paan-shop' busy themselves in speculations over 'the numberless nameless Godknowswhats that might now issue from the fissuring earth' (MC, 39). Saleem's narrative leaves it deliberately unclear whether the cracks have been followed or triggered by the Free Islam Convocation's naïve optimism, the imminence of either Independence or Partition, or of Jawaharlal Nehru's desire for a strong central government. Similarly, the cracks in Bombay's roads simultaneously appear to be the reason for and the result of the electoral victory of Nehru's All-India Congress and its failure to attend to the demand for linguistic states (Metcalf *et al.*, 236), or of the very division of the country into states and territories (MC, 189), or of the government's indecision concerning the future of Bombay itself: 'it was to be the capital of Maharashtra; or of both Maharashtra and Gujarat; or an independent state of its own' (MC, 223). Political boundaries, Saleem intervenes to explain, are 'not formed by rivers or mountains, or any natural features of the terrain' but are rather 'walls of words', and yet, the parallel Marathi and Gujarati language marches in Bombay metamorphose into political parties, flood the city 'more completely than monsoon water' (MC, 189), collide at Kemp's corner, as a result of Saleem's direct involvement, and physically partition the state of Bombay (MC, 191–92).

Such fantastic events have been discussed under the rubric of magical realism, as employed in the recuperation of local 'codes of recognition' (Slemon 1988, 12), which subvert the linearity imposed by imperial history. More broadly, such a duplicitous temporality has been seen as an effective challenge to the systemic and monolithic construction of historical events out of the otherwise disparate individual actions that are seen as constituting them. In this sense, the idea of 'urban omens' contains the enabling duplicities of magical realism – the sense of a modern, colonially instituted temporality as interrupted by and interrupting a local and unalienable, but often metaphysical and essentialist obsession with correspondences or lust for allegory. The novel offers, in this way, a specifically urban redemptive hermeneutics, at once forecasting and pre-emptive, that is part of the everyday, in the form not of an 'Indian mysticism' but of an interpreting and interpretable cultural production of local meaning through which people participate in political life rather than being passive receptors of history. If, in many ways, India 'typifies', as Upstone reminds us, the 'fate of postcolonial nations' – including the articulation of a homogenous national narrative based on the colonially inherited model of the European nation-state (46–7) – the novel's geomorphic movements place the cities in contention with such a historical and theoretical banality.

In their treatment of Pakistani cities, both *Midnight's Children* and *Shame* modify their land reclamations. When Saleem's family emigrate to Karachi, his umbilical cord is planted in the earth where they are to build a house in a ceremonial act symbolizing their bond with their new home. Saleem observes, however, that the houses in Karachi are 'deformed' and 'grotesque', 'the stunted hunchback children of deficient lifelines', as they have grown out of 'entirely unsuitable cords' (MC, 309). For Rushdie, Karachi stands for the mutation of the urban ideal. Pakistan's cities in both novels – Rawalpindi, Karachi, Quetta and Islamabad – figure as Bombay's upside-down subcontinental twins. An irreversible historical perforation, Partition is envisioned as a 'closure of possibilities' that is imagined on both sides of the frontier, but that cannot be challenged through a reconfiguration of Pakistan's cities.

Tectonic instability intensifies in *Shame*'s Pakistan. Early on, the reader is told that the city of Q. suffers from 'periodic earthquakes' and is offered the tribals' mythical explanation of the tremors as 'caused by the emergence of angels through fissures in the rocks' (S, 23). The protagonist, Omar Khayyam Shakil, imagines as a result, a fantastical upside-down topography: 'Hell above, Paradise below' (ibid.). In foregrounding the tribals' interpretation of seismic activity, Rushdie gives a voice to a most under-represented community, the descendents of the first inhabitants of the South Asian subcontinent. This tectonic imagination of the tribals is reminiscent of Bengali activist and intellectual Mahasweta Devi's in her collection of stories, *Imaginary Maps* (1995). For her, tribes are like indigenous continents that have inhabited a parallel topography to 'the mainstream' (x–xxi), hence the imaginary maps of the title. While Rushdie shows, in this way, a peripheral interest in tribals, it is incomparable to Devi's strong local commitments. However, in the novel, theirs is one of the few voices of opposition, shared with Pakistan's women, to the political status quo: the one-party rule of Zulfikar Ali Bhutto (prime minister of Pakistan between 1973 and 1977), followed by the military dictatorship of General Muhammad Zia-ul-Haq (who deposed Bhutto in 1977 and stayed in power till 1988), only thinly disguised as, respectively, Iskander Harappa and Raza Hyder.

Shame thus continues *Midnight's Children*'s catoptric critique of Partition, as evident in the protagonist's imagination of an upside-down Q./Quetta, where otherwise 'Indian centuries lay just beneath the surface of Pakistani Standard Time' (S, 87), and develops into a full-scale indictment of post-Independence Pakistan's political and military elite. In particular, tectonic configurations work towards undermining the idea of political stability by revealing it as more phantasmal than the indigenous cosmic myths. Rushdie aims equal measure of critique at Pakistan and the West. On the one hand, the despotic regime of Hyder/Zia-ul-Haq is based on 'Stability, in the name of God' (S, 249), justifying his Islamization policies, which severely limited women's rights. On the other hand, the West (specifically, George Bush and Margaret Thatcher, as Rushdie explains in an essay) is implicated in its staunch support of Pakistan's military 'stability', rather than the country's democratic forces.

In this schema, the novel oscillates in an urban triangle, as we noted earlier. Quake-prone Q./Quetta mediates between Karachi, the 'whore-city' (S, 144), associated with the regime of Iskander Harappa ('city playboy No. 1'), with his hedonistic tendencies and his specifically 'urban gaiety', and, at the other extreme of Pakistan's political spectrum during the period, Islamabad, the 'clean' city, or Karachi 'purified with the help of the Almighty' (S, 107; 120), as reflective of Raza Hyder's puritan political ambitions.

Frequently, discussions of the novel contend that Pakistan has been magically deferred, that 'realism is impossible' and that fantasy offers a backdoor of escape (Upstone, 49–50). There are, however, significant nuances in Rushdie's urban representation that complicate such a reading. Not all cities are merely 'referred to by their initials' (ibid.). Only Quetta is ostensibly censored while also being paradoxically named 'not really Quetta at all' (S, 29). When it reaches Karachi, Rawalpindi and Islamabad, the narrative names these cities unproblematically. While Karachi does figure, within the politicized cartography of the novel, as a cipher for a city of pleasure, exclusive to the elite, it also bears witness to political brutalities as the epicentre of riots in protest against Harappa's/Bhutto's electoral corruption. Pretence is dropped completely in relation to Islamabad within what constitutes the most severe and realistically specific critique of the city – its division into the mutually exclusive 'new city' and 'old town'; the modern ambitions of its built environment, specifically through the reference to the Greek borrowings of its architectural design, at odds with the country's cultural heritage, and the historical move of the country's capital from Karachi to Islamabad. The novel's metaphor of the creation of Islamabad 'out of Rawalpindi's rib' (S, 200) is intended to reveal Hyder's attempt to justify his political and military power within a natural, authentic or organic framework.

Quetta as Q. also merits a reconsideration in its intertextual echo of Russian author N. V. Gogol's *Dead Souls* (1842). The 'remote, border town' of Q. in *Shame*'s opening sentence is reminiscent of the provincial town of N. in the first sentence of *Dead Souls*. Rather than purely a magical deferral, such typifications are a characteristic of classical nineteenth-century realism, along with the authorial interventions of an omniscient narrator. While the logic of gossip unsettles the conventions of realist historiography in *Shame*, the two discourses – magic/realism, gossip/comedy and tragedy/history – interrogate each other.

Rushdie situates Gogol in a European 'fantasized, satiric, anti-epic' tradition (which can be more broadly termed Menippean), also including Rabelais and Boccaccio (CSR, 10). In *Dead Souls*, Collegiate Councillor Pavel Chichikov sets out from the town of N. on a picaresque journey across Russia to purchase the eponymous dead souls, or non-existent serfs, and mortgage them in a money-raising scheme. The novel is, to some extent, also a critical 'national narrative' in that it offers generalizations about Russia and Russians in authorial digressions from Chichikov's travels. *Shame* shares with it a quality of the grotesque – the double murder of Iskander Harappa, for instance, echoes the brokering of dead serfs. As a starting point of the narrative and a marginal location in relation to the nation, Q. mirrors the backward (feudal in *Dead Souls*) provincialism of N., but it is also a broader comment on all of Pakistan and its cities. They appear trapped, historically, between the claustrophobic provincialism of British colonialism and the medieval form of Islam that Hyder attempts to institute.

The narrator's interventions have a tectonic effect in interrupting the events of the narrative and a catoptric effect in comparing Pakistan's cities to London. The comparisons bring the two to reflect each other in an absurdist or deforming mirror. Racism in 1980s' London, for instance, is juxtaposed with the sequestration of and violence against women under Hyder's rule. Shame, an emotion governed by ideas of honour and pride, is ironically only the mirror image of shamelessness in Pakistan's history. In the figure of Sufyia Zinobia, the novel's avatar of shame/shamelessness, tectonic and specular configurations interact most radically. Her literal bomb-like explosion is an attempt at destroying the order of things: a resistance, at once, specifically against the abuse to which she is subjected and, in general, against the social and political brutalities of her society. Specular pairs recur: Sufyia and Rani Harappa stand for opposite tendencies in the cultural reproduction of shame's violence. While the former absorbs disgrace until she bursts, the latter externalizes it by documenting the various crimes of her husband in the series of shawls she embroiders. Arjumand Harappa, or 'the virgin Ironpants' (based on Benazir Bhutto and evocative of Indira Gandhi as the Widow in *Midnight* and Margaret Thatcher as Maggie Torture in *The Satanic Verses*), contrasts with Naveed 'Good News' Hyder, whose pregnancies produce children in an arithmetic progression – twins, then triplets, quadruplets, quintuplets and so on – until she is unable to bear the 'good news' of her fertility and hangs herself.

Both *Midnight Children* and *Shame* are marked by the tectonic rift of Partition and its consequences. The former novel re-employs the idea of partitioning in order to interrogate the absolute principle of the centre of history, the story, the city and the nation through a series of symbolic centre partings. Methwold's and the Widow's central hair partings, for instance, form part of the text's catoptric critique of colonialism and authoritarian state politics. The latter novel offers a similar catoptric re-envisioning in the mirroring of shame and shamelessness. Borders in both texts are not only created but also sustained through a massive cartographic and political hypnosis. After Partition, Karachiites in *Midnight's Children* have the 'slipperiest of grasps on reality' and rely on their leaders to decide for them what is or is not real (MC, 308). In *Shame*, the border moves to that between Pakistan and Afghanistan, near which Quetta is situated. There, broken pieces of mirrors are tied to the frontier posts, and this is the inspiration for Omar's hypnosis of Farah Zoroaster (52). Rushdie's point, however, is that the massive hypnosis of the Partition frontier has been undergone, however unwillingly, by both India and Pakistan and will continue to be visited upon their futures.

Chapter 3

Bombay, London, Jahilia: Di/versifications and Di/versions in *The Satanic Verses*

Reading *The Satanic Verses* is an increasingly complex matter. If it has been impossible to read it outside the events of the Rushdie Affair, it has since continued to reverberate and, often, to be forced to reverberate with contemporary events and their interpretations and with political rifts and realignments. The effects of the novel itself can be described in tectonic terms, not only for the massive and frequently violent urban response across the world that it triggered: the public protests, riots and attacks in London, Leicester, Bradford, Islamabad, Karachi, Bombay and Ankara, among other cities. Writing on the occasion of the book's twentieth anniversary, Malise Ruthven referred to the Affair as a 'watershed in the globalization of Islam' and a 'catalyst in the process of creating a British Muslim identity' by bridging diverse Muslim traditions and even generation gaps and by shaping, in this way, a 'common platform' for a domesticated British Islam (2008, 138). Ruvani Ranasinha, however, reminds us that it has also led to a post-fatwa tendency to homogenize Muslims despite the differences in their responses to the book and the Affair, as well as triggering a liberal support in defence of the freedom of speech against religious intolerance that dangerously posited an enlightened Western secularism against an Islamic dogmatism (2007, 47–9).

That the book has served as a catalyst for mobilizing and articulating British Muslim interests is, nonetheless, undeniable. English-language British Muslim publications emerged after the book's release, such as the *Muslim News* (first published in February 1989) whose foundational objective was to provide a platform for British Muslim voices at a time when the mainstream media largely excluded them (Gilliat-Ray 2010, 237). Gilliat-Ray notes that the novel paved the way for a recognition of the 'power that could be derived from unity' and led to the formation of organizations, in the wake of the Affair, such as the Muslim Council of Britain or 'Women against Fundamentalism'. The latter one rejected, as some of Rushdie's female characters do in the novel, both Islamist ideology and the British state's Orientalist assumptions (ibid., 219; 257).

The novel, however, has also been vulnerable to hijackings by various groups, interests and theorizations (most controversially by statements in line with Samuel Huntington's thesis (1993) of intercivilizational clashes of cultures and religions) in a political climate increasingly exacerbated by such cataclysmic events as the 9/11 attacks on New York or the London bombings; the West's military interventions in Afghanistan and Iraq and the 'war on terror'. In this climate, the publication of the Islamophobic 'Mohammed cartoons', portraying the Prophet as a terrorist, by the Danish newspaper *Jyllands-Posten* in 2005, consciously played with religious and cultural sensitivities and forced an analogy with the novel's satirical representations of suicide bombers and extremist religious leaders. The 9/11 attacks in particular had given an unexpected resonance, in the West, to the images of Rushdie's fictional suicide bomber Tavleen (responsible for the destruction of a plane bound for London and the death of most passengers) and the imagined Imam, exiled in his London flat, where he plans an Islamic revolution in his native *Desh* ('country'). Seen out of context, these representations have served a stereotypical demonization of Islam. Even seemingly 'benign' gestures have had the same effect. In the wake of the London bombings, the media consciously attempted to reject publicly the identification of Islam and terrorism by reconfiguring the 'enemy' into terrorist misreadings of Islam. Nevertheless, leaders of the British Muslim communities were invariably asked in front of television cameras if they condemned the terrorist attacks on London and New York. This media strategy evoked the verbal denouncement of the devil in witchcraft trials and, ironically, mirrored the metamorphosis undergone by Saladin Chamcha in *The Satanic Verses* – there, he is the literal product of hegemonic stereotyping.

Commenting on the attacks on New York, Rushdie himself argued, in November 2001, that the disclaimer, '[t]his isn't about Islam', was 'not true':

> For a vast number of 'believing' Muslim men, 'Islam' stands, in a jumbled, half-examined way, not only for the fear of God . . . but also for a cluster of customs, opinions and prejudices that include their dietary practices, the sequestration . . . of 'their' women, . . . a loathing of modern society in general, riddled as it is with music, godlessness, and sex, and a more particularized loathing (and fear) of the prospect that their own imme-diate surroundings could be taken over – 'Westoxicated' – by the liberal Western-style way of life. (SATL, 395)

The explicit us-them division in this passage echoed earlier ones constructed through the West's defence of the author after the announcement of the *fatwa* in 1989 and revived constructions of Islam as the West's other. Rushdie argued further that the blows on New York, imagined as 'the bright capital of the visible', were the responsibility of the 'forces of invisibility' and urged that 'we . . . must now ensure that . . . the world of what is seen triumphs over what is cloaked, what is perceptible only through the effects of its awful deeds' (SATL, 391). In this way, the author seemed to claim that the terrorist attacks were the only indicator of the subversive existence of a phenomenon that he defined as being 'about Islam' and that he assigned to the urban underground of the Western metropolis. *The Satanic Verses*, however, employs the same metaphor of the invisible city, suppressed underground by 'Proper London', in order to undermine the powerful discourse of the migrant as an other, to reclaim it and to use it against racist or Orientalist stereotypes and their homogenizing effects. Although, as Sabina Sawhney and Simona Sawhney (2001) note, in his non-fiction published after 11 September 2001, Rushdie seemed to defend the most dominant stereotypes of Islam, in his novel, *The Satanic Verses*, he exposes the power of description. Moreover, as Feroza Jussawalla (1996) proposes, the novel can be understood as Rushdie's 'love letter to Islam', or be defined, as Sara Suleri suggests, as a 'deeply Islamic' book (1994, 222). Although in his post-9/11 political writings, Rushdie seemed to align himself with the project of exclusive Western visibility, his fiction, with its novelistic dialogicity and its multiple catoptric splits, unsettles the monologic nature of this voice and demonstrates that Islam can be an idea that is capable of compromises, even when it is strong.

The Satanic Verses is a multilayered narrative that juxtaposes the migrant experiences of two Bombay-born actors, Saladin Chamcha and Gibreel Farishta, in 1980s' London. The omniscient narrator, whose self-description evokes a caricatured image of Rushdie himself, interrupts the narrative, in a mock-authoritative/divine fashion, on a number of occasions: 'I know the truth, obviously. I watched the whole thing. As to omni-presence and -potence, I'm making no claims' (SV, 10). The novel opens with the two protagonists falling towards England, after the plane on which they have been travelling from Bombay to London is blown up by a group of Sikh terrorists led by the enigmatic Tavleen. Each goes his own way, reconnecting with past relationships and finding himself drawn 'under' into a series of invisible-city existences, centred around spaces such as the Shaandaar Café, the Club Hot Wax and the London Underground system. With the protagonists' literal explosion into Britain, however, their histories, their

Bombay selves and, in the case of Saladin, his memories of past East-West journeys, also erupt onto the surface of the London narrative. Gibreel Farishta (the Angel Gibreel), born Ismail Najmuddin, has been a well-known face, the biggest star in the history of the Bombay theologicals (a pointed pun on the popular Bollywood genre of the *mythological*). In these theologicals, Gibreel has been impersonating the deities of the various religions of India and has developed, as a result, a pathological belief in the divinity of his own persona. This belief has replaced his faith in God, which Gibreel has lost in the process of recovering from a mysterious illness, shortly before he leaves for London. The novel's London narrative is punctuated by the eruption of the intermittent, schizophrenic/cinematic visions of the increasingly delusional Gibreel, who can no longer distinguish between his waking hours and his dreams, or between his own life and his film roles. This nocturnal punishment of dreams forces Gibreel to witness, direct, film or participate in three serial narratives.

The first one is the story of the businessman-turned-Prophet Mahound, Rushdie's fictional Mohammed figure, and the emergence of Islam. The adoption of the name 'Mahound', an early Christian name for the devil and an Orientalist stereotype, is part of the novel's main subversive strategy, the attempt to 'turn insults into strengths': 'whigs, tories, Blacks all chose to wear with pride the names they were given in scorn' (SV, 93). The story is set in the desert city of Jahilia, Rushdie's seventh-century Mecca, and relates the incident of the satanic verses whose historicity has been greatly disputed by Muslim historians. The account of this episode comes not from the *Qur'an*, as F.E. Peters notes, but 'rather from Quranic commentary', most notably that of al-Tabari, a historian and 'one of the premier exegetes of medieval Islam' (2003, 61). The novel tells the story in the following way: the Grandee of Jahilia makes an offer to Mahound to accept three of the goddesses of the city, Al-Lat, Al-Manat and Uzza, as Allah's intermediaries. Mahound initially accedes, having received as revelation the following verses – '"Have you thought upon Lat and Uzza, and Manat, the third, the other?" . . . "They are the exalted birds, and their intercession is desired indeed"' (SV, 114) – but later repudiates them, having realized that he has been tricked by the Devil who had come to him in the guise of the archangel. The satanic verses are said to have been added to, and later removed from, Sura 53 of the *Qur'an*. According to Muslim commentators, the whole incident may have been fabricated by non-believers in the time of early Islam and/or by Orientalist scholars of Islam in an attempt to question the authenticity of the *Qur'an* (Aravamudan 1994, 187; Kuortti 2007, 134; Teverson 2007, 154). It was the novel's dramatization of the satanic verses incident and, in general, the Jahilian sections of the book that were found blasphemous by Muslim communities. As Srinivas Aravamudan suggests, the disputed historicity of the satanic verses incident explains 'the threat of a metonymic de-legitimation of the religious veracity of the rest of the sacred text' (197). While it can be argued that the novel places an accent on inauthenticity, thus questioning the methods of historical verifiability and blurring the boundary between story and history, the defence of satirical readings of Islam can, if decontextualized, contribute to the ideology of Western cultural imperialism (Aravamudan, 187). Sara Suleri offers a reading of blasphemy as a mode of historical introspection, but observes that the writings in defence of Rushdie contain an implicit understanding of the author as 'one of us' and cautions that 'the desacralizing of religion can simultaneously constitute a resacralizing of history' (222). Gayatri Spivak argues that, in the context of the fatwa, Rushdie can be seen merely as the writer-as-performer, while the Ayatollah fulfils the author-function by representing himself as an 'unmediated testifier for the immutable essence of Islam' (1993, 217–41).

The city of Jahilia bears the name of the period of 'ignorance' (IH, 398) or the 'age of barbarism', *al-jahiliyya*, before Islam (Peters, 33). In his defence of the novel, Rushdie wrote that this was done not to insult Mecca Sharif, but because the dreamer, Gibreel, had been plunged into the condition the word describes (IH, 398–99). Before the Prophet, however, Jahilia is a city of annual poetry competitions, during which poets, such as Baal, feel free to compose verses that lampoon those in power, if only as part of the carnivalesque performance of their recitations. The arrival of Mahound replaces these satirical poems with the Qur'anic verses. The dominant urban order is thus continually eroded through poetic dec-lamations. In an ongoing battle of the verses on the site of the city, Mahound's message is, in turn, eroded, though only momentarily, by the Devil's versifying work.

Gibreel's second dream narrative describes the London exile of 'the Imam' in his Kensington flat, where he is literally closed off (by curtains and guards) from the visible city and where he has created an atemporal sub-city: the hotbed of the planned Islamic revolution. Although he is iconophobic, the Imam has kept a few postcards on his mantelpiece: conventional images of his homeland. It is one of these images, the city beneath the postcard mountain, to which the Imam dreams of returning. Ensconced in the middle of London, he is nevertheless not of it. The Imam is based on the Ayatollah Khomeini, the leader of the Iranian, subsequently known as the Islamic, Revolution of 1979, which overthrew the Pahlavi monarchy and instituted an Islamic republic. The Imam's exile in London in the novel parallels Khomeini's exile in Paris, before his triumphant return to Tehran, the unnamed city beneath the postcard mountain. In Rushdie's analysis after the announcement of the fatwa, Khomeini's revolution was more 'intensely nationalistic' (IH, 383) than religious. He had managed to harness the people's grievances against the oppressive regime of the Shah, instituted, as a guardian of U.S. interests, in the 'CIA-sponsored' Iranian coup of 1953, which overthrew the democratically elected Mosadeqque government (Ghamari-Tabrizi *et al.*, 2009, 2). Rushdie explains that a key phrase describing the Iranian Revolution, coined by one of the revolution's main ideologues, Ali Shariati, is 'a revolt against history' and the novel satirizes this perception of history as 'a colossal error' that the revolution set out to undo by turning back the clock (IH, 383). The Imam thus announces that after the revolution there will be no clocks (SV, 214). In light of Rushdie's comments, the figure of the Imam can be seen as a response to the Orientalist construction of Islam not only as a 'medieval, barbarous, repressive' idea that is 'hostile to Western civilization', but also as a 'unified, homogenous, and therefore dangerous' one (IH, 382). Such monolithic constructions obscure Khomeini's claim of the 'support of the Almighty' to justify his position of worldly power, a claim with many precedents in Western European history.

Gibreel's third dream story traces the pilgrimage of the Titlipur villagers, led by a prophetess named 'Ayesha' (as is the Imam's enemy), through the Arabian Sea, which they have been promised will part so they can walk on to the city of Mecca. The Ayesha episodes fictionalize a historical incident, related by Sara Suleri, the 1983 'Hawkes Bay case' in Pakistan, where 38 Shiite Muslims, inspired by a young woman, 'who claimed to be in direct visionary contact with the twelfth Imam', walked into the Arabian Sea, expecting that the waters would part so they can walk on to the holy site of the Karbala (in Iraq). Most of the pilgrims drowned before the Karachi police reached Hawkes Bay and 'proceeded to arrest the survivors, on the grounds that they had attempted to leave Pakistan illegally, without visas' (1994, 232).

London in *The Satanic Verses* is initially constituted almost entirely through its unseen diasporic suburb of Brickhall (a combination of Brick Lane and Southall, both London areas known for their Asian communities) with its even deeper, darker spaces of the Shaandaar Café and the Club Hot Wax; the city of Bombay with its catoptrically inverted temporality, since 'if you turn your watch upside down in Bombay, you see the time in London' (SV, 41); the city beneath the postcard mountain that the Imam has brought into his London of exile; the dreamed-of sand-city of Jahilia and its water-counterpart of Medina and the desired holy city of Mecca, which the Titlipur pilgrims never reach. Common to all these seemingly unreal, subterranean cities, and what eventually translates them into visibility, is the activity of *versifying* – the production of erosive verses, magic spells, commandments, prophecies and satirical poems that have the power to undermine, or even explode on, the visible surface of the metropolis. Those who pronounce these performative utterances engage, simultaneously, in *di-versification*, the process of bringing newness into the world, of rejecting, challenging or reclaiming dominant ideological verses and tropes. The Latin *versificare* derives from *versus* and the linguistic and conceptual newness of Gibreel's, Jumpy Joshi's, Pinkwala's, Mahound's and Baal's verses partakes of this quality of being against established discourses, of producing satanic interpretations of the dominant order of things or of reading *against* the grain.

These versifying strategies are the focus of the first part of the present chapter, where I explore the broad spectrum of diasporic tensions in Rushdie's postcolonial metropolis and the numerous Londons they bring into being, as well as the interactions between the multiply defined city and its underground, dream-counterparts through the process of di-versification. The popular conceptualization of terrorism, and particularly the teaching of terrorism, as a form of explosive versifying that needs to be extinguished, suggests the inexhaustible power of metaphor, its ambivalent potential to constrain and demonize, while reclaiming and di-versifying. The discussion examines such forms of satanic versifying that can be seen, metaphorically, as tectonic functions of the East, which are being forced up against Western hegemonic discursive formations, comparable in their simultaneous rigidity and fragility, to what geoscience terms *tectonic plates*. Such versifying, initiated at the margins of these plates, is irregular and varying in force and effect. It leads to the eruption of the narratives of the other onto the site of the metropolis or gnaws it into new shapes.

Equally, in the novel, di-versification instigates spatial and temporal di-versions, dreams, routes and intertexts that interact with and transform the metropolis, while leading away from it. The geographically identifiable London is thus not only di-versified, but also displaced through the process of satanic versifying. The second part of this chapter engages in a reading of urban spatialities and temporalities as reconfigured through fictional, physical and intertextual routes. It examines the catoptric processes that impact on the urban condition, such as revelation, translation or dreaming, and assesses the novel's urban politics through the specifics of its urban marginalia and inter-urban spaces.

This chapter concludes with an examination of the novel's overt commitment to women's experience of the postcolonial metropolis and its strategies of exposing their exclusion from a number of urban discourses and
practices. It explores the relationship between women's characteristically
unstable identities and the text's strategy of doubling female figures' names
across the catoptric frontier of dreams and travelling.

Explosive Versifications

The novel's emphasis on the subterranean quality of cities articulates a
London that shares its characteristically Dantean imagery with such
modernist representations of the city as T. S. Eliot's infernal/unreal vision
of London in *The Waste Land*. Although Rushdie can be seen as writing in
response to the modernist construction of the city as a site of exile (Saladin's
alienation in his satanic metamorphosis is a case in point), the configurations
of the city in Rushdie's novels move beyond the idea of an urban Dantean
Vestibule of Hell. Tectonic urban configurations engage in the process of
di-versifying such discourses that operate towards the construction of
hegemonic verticalities – urban centres and peripheries, developed and
developing/First and Third World cities – or in practices of exclusion, the
geological suppression of the stories of the other beneath official, visible/
audible urban narratives. The metropolis's subterranean or subconscious
narratives are shown to operate tectonically, moving beneath or up against
what only appears to be its untroubled, rigid surface and, as a result, transforming this surface. Di-versification is best illustrated in the recuperative
transformation that the term *satanic* undergoes in the text: from a racist
stereotype, with its derogative connotations in Western Christianity (which
often equates *satanic* and *Muslim*) to an empowering, counter-hegemonic
category. As Rushdie explains, 'Trotsky' was the name of Trotsky's jailer and
that by taking it for his own, he 'symbolically conquered his captor and set
himself free' (IH, 402).

In his study on postcolonial London, John McLeod notes that both
Salman Rushdie and his book have come to occupy a privileged space in
postcolonial representations of the city. McLeod's reading reveals elements
that contradict Rushdie's 'seemingly celebratory narrative of London's
mongrel self': for instance, Gibreel's and Saladin's 'cosmopolitan and
media chic', or Gibreel's tropicalization of London as a project analogous
to the Imam's challenge to London's unreliable wetness (2004, 147), his
attempt to simulate the climate of his native Desh by turning up the heating

to the maximum in his London flat. In addition, however, it can be argued that in delineating a multiplicity of migrant sentiments towards the host metropolis, the text also engages with the contradictions in these sentiments or the undercurrents that trouble them. One of the ways in which London celebrates its mongrel self in the text is by not turning a blind eye on those migrant strategies of translation that seek to possess the metropolis in its entirety – what can be termed the migrant's totalizing impulse. Gibreel's project of tropicalization and the Imam's re-creation of the climate of Desh in his flat both reveal a desire to conquer London, though in different ways – respectively, by translating London into 'home' and by transporting 'home' into London. At the same time, both translation strategies expose the translator's profound rejection of hybridity. Both positions are effectively outside the metropolis: Gibreel has to fly high above London to tropicalize it and the Imam has symbolically built himself out of the city, though within his flat: the curtains are kept drawn all day, because otherwise 'foreign-ness, Abroad, the alien nation' might sneak into the apartment (SV, 206).

Gibreel's and Saladin's 'cosmopolitan and media chic' is limited, respectively, to the Indian subcontinent and to the South Asian diasporic community in London. An important distinction between the two characters' careers elucidates the dynamic relationship Bombay–London, as well as the distribution of visibility on the novel's postcolonial urban map. Both protagonists are actors: one is a famous Bollywood face, while the other an invisible, disembodied voice, inhabiting the simulacrum of London's 'ethnic universe'. Neither mask – face nor voice – stands for unproblematic mimicry. Though he has occupied a prominent position in his home city, Gibreel begins to bleed on the inside. Just as his skin masks a mysterious illness, visible Bombay conceals, in Gibreel's imagination, its imperceptible underworld: in his mind, people and objects continue down below the surface of the city, most of their reality concealed from his eyes (SV, 21).

Tensions between the apparent and the hidden, and the multiple and the singular, characterizes both Gibreel and his home city. He deliberately mixes the Muslim and Hindu lunch compartments in the tiffin tins he carries as a boy, thus scandalizing the community by causing the two main cultural and religious monoliths of Bombay, the understandings of what it means to be Hindu or Muslim, to explode on the surface of everyday life. Yet, in his movie career, he crosses religious boundaries without giving offence and lives in a double-vista apartment (SV, 13). Gibreel's multiple/ omnipresent God-like persona, developed through his filmic impersonation of deities from various religions, mirrors the 'many-headed, many-brushed Overartist' of *Hamza-nama* cloths, a multiply co-authored artistic form, which encapsulates the idea of Mughal synthesis (SV, 70). By referring to this form, Rushdie draws attention to the mixed cultural heritage of India.

Gibreel's illness, however, problematizes this possibility of multiplicity, of impersonating Bombay in its entirety and, at the same time, erodes his position above the city: 'the highest home in the highest building on the highest ground in the city' (SV, 13). His illness suggests that he is internally torn between his various religious impersonations and that such a unifying or omniscient role is not only politically but also existentially difficult to sustain. This hesitation between pluralism and individuality foreshadows his personality split and the geographical division of cities or urban dimensions in his mind into visible and invisible, overground and underground.

Saladin's childhood Bombay foregrounds, instead, the clash between an invisible magic-lamp promise, the realization of which is retained till the end of the novel, and the desire for his dream-city, *Ellowen Deeowen London.* His father's 'magic' lamp would only pass into his possession if he remains in Bombay. Yet, in Saladin's mind, the Bombay of dust and vulgarity, of confusion and superabundance, longs for Proper London, with its 'crisp promises of pounds sterling', its poise and moderation and its 'Saintpauls, Puddinglane, Threadneedlestreet' (SV, 37–9). This idealistic image of grand London, an imperial fiction supported by the popular tourist imagination of the city – a landmark cartography of capital letters and seductive names – is the only one accessible to Saladin. Its essence becomes an alphabetical conundrum to which the city's name provides 'the key'. *Ellowen deeowen* (L-O-N-D-O-N) defamiliarizes *London.* The process of renaming, or the erosive versification of the city, in which both protagonists are involved throughout the novel, problematizes the metropolitan cultural identity of London.

The text's protagonists, Saladin Chamcha and Gibreel Farishta, can be seen as catoptric doubles, or as each other's negative twins. This is not only because during their fall towards England, one is metamorphosed into a devil and the other into an angel, but also because of their clashing views on London. Saladin worships while Gibreel loathes the city. Together they produce an ambivalent image of London, a city that accommodates alternative, and mutually opposed, translated migrant identities. This catoptricity delineates the idea of the migrant as an actor and the city as the stage on which his/her identities are constantly being played off against one another and which precludes closure. This celebratory narrative of the unproblematic performativity of identity, however, is eroded first by the fear of the loss or dilution of originary individuality, conceptualized in an essentialist way, and, secondly, by the danger of its being fixed into an item of exchange within popular culture. Both possibilities, as we shall see, come into play in Saladin's conquest of the metropolis. In the case of Gibreel, the possibility of a multiple identity, one that crosses religious and cultural frontiers and transforms him into a 'United Nations of gods' (SV, 200), also reveals the existence of a schizophrenic multiplicity of parallel migrant Londons, which he brings into the city and which thus collide with the narratives of the readily recognizable London. These subversive migrant stories simultaneously foreground the irreducible hybridity of the novel metropolis and drive Gibreel towards suicide.

London and Bombay can also be seen as each other's catoptric doubles or negative twins, as demonstrated in Saladin's upside-down watch metaphor. Catoptrically speaking, the two cities are divided by an invisible, 'looking-glass' frontier. Travelling across it, the characters are translated or transformed, as we shall see in the next section of this chapter. In a tectonic sense, Bombay, a city that has been perceived as a distant outpost, or indeed an edge, of the British Empire in colonial discourses, as situated somehow geologically *beneath* or historically *behind* the metropolis, is symbolically 'unearthed' to challenge London's privileged geopolitical location.

The inverted twin-ness of the two cities is also apparent in the understanding of migration as a body–soul split. Long before the protagonists' meta-morphoses, when Saladin has just decided to settle down in London and work as an actor, his father, Changez, writes to him: 'I have your soul kept safe, my son, here in this walnut-tree. The Devil has only your body' (SV, 48). This London/Bombay antithesis can be seen as a variation on the Dantean concept of metamorphosis, understood as leading to a reduction of identity to the point of obliteration, as Marina Warner suggests (2002, 37). In Changez's understanding, actor/migrant identity is the result of a dissociation of body from soul, where London and Bombay are the two dimensions of Saladin's translated urban self, the corrupt and the pure, the unreal and the 'natural', the feigned and the 'original'. Though essentialist, this conception of identity reveals the erosive undercurrents beneath Saladin's seemingly coherent London self, as well as ironically opening up possibilities of transgression. Having carefully constructed himself as the Man of a Thousand Voices and a Voice, Saladin has, in effect, transformed himself into a ghost (SV, 61), thus becoming marooned, or ghettoized, within invisible London. His disembodied voice-overs in the television programme called *The Aliens Show* are the literal realization of his father's accusations, of Changez's fears that his son has become 'an imitator of non-existing men' (SV, 71). *The Aliens Show* features phantasmal extraterrestrials, from animals through vegetables to minerals, which mirror the strange 'aliens' at the Detention Centre hospital, the literal monstrous products of the discursive postcolonial clash between cultures. At the same time, the success of the programme is predicated on the marketability of race, which has been commercially fixed into an item of exchange. The creator of *The Aliens Show*, Hal Valance, refers to the category of race as 'the ethnic universe' in the same way as he speaks, in marketing jargon, of 'the chocolate universe', the 'slimming universe' and the 'dental universe' as examples of the 'total potential market of a given product or service' (SV, 264). Patronizingly, he makes the point explicit to Saladin: 'The product, you bastard, being you' (SV, 266).

Saladin's later metamorphosis into a devil also appears to prove Changez's ideas that the Devil has only his body. For Saladin, however, this satanic transformation, although in effect the result of the process of hegemonic description – what Homi Bhabha terms 'difference into demonism' (1994, 226) – is the realization of his own Fanonian subconscious fears that the bad or black Indian he has suppressed might erupt and overwhelm his public self-made image of the 'goodandproper Englishman' (SV, 43). Yet, whereas Changez describes the play involved in trying on different identities as 'Shaitan's best work' (SV, 48), Saladin's transformation into a devil ironically takes up this possibility of transgressive mimicry, of impersonating hollowness (or 'non-existing men'), the invisible gaps in the describers' discourse.

Muhammad Sufyan, the Bangladeshi owner of the Shaandaar Café in Brickhall High Street, where Saladin hides in his satanic form, also attempts to make sense of this devilish transformation. He proposes two theories of metamorphosis, as based on his classical reading: the first one, based on Ovid's *Metamorphoses* (8 CE), conceptualizes identity as an immutable essence – we are 'still the same forever, but [we] adopt in [our] migrations ever-varying forms' – and the second one, based on Lucretuis' *De Rerum Natura/About Nature* (c. 70 BCE), sees identity as characterized by constant mutability: the old self has to die for the new one to be born (SV, 276–7). By the end of the narrative, it seems that Saladin has embraced the latter by becoming so other as to be another, in line with the post-structuralist emphasis on the decentred, plural, constantly changing self as opposed to the essentialist notion of identity as an inherent, ever-present sameness. This Ovidian/Lucretian duplicity of metamorphosis, however, consistently haunts the narrative and forms a dominant element of the catoptric make-up of urban configurations in the text, as we shall see in the next section of this chapter.

In the London/Bombay split, as envisioned by Changez, the soul is an Ovidian immutable essence, tied up with traditional family values and the concept of roots, as indicative in the metaphor of the walnut tree. For Saladin, however, migration involves the regurgitation of the past and opens up ever newer, and thus Lucretian, possibilities of identification. He explains to his Bombay lover, Zeeny Vakil, that in Kashmir a 'birth-tree' is treated as a financial investment. When a child grows up, his walnut tree is treated as an insurance policy (it can be sold to pay for his wedding). In this way, the adult's childhood is the price he pays for his later life by unsentimentally cutting it down (65).

The most crucial aspect of Saladin's metamorphosis, however, is that it serves to reveal to him the unseen city of Brickhall London and to enable the translation of the metropolis itself from Proper London into Jahannum, Gehenna or Muspelheim (SV, 254) – a city, which he derogatively describes as hell, but which just as ironically mimics the gaps in hegemonic description and achieves a tectonic potential. In diasporic London, Muslim (Jahannum), Judeo–Christian (Gehenna), and pagan (Muspelheim, borrowed from Norse mythology) cultures and texts are brought up against each other in the image of a hell-fire city. The ambivalence of the figure of the devil in the novel thus backfires at the producers of descriptions: 'Shall there be evil in the city and the Lord hath not done it?' (SV, 323). It is the seismic power of dreams that helps reclaim this figure – Saladin appears in his satanic form in the dreams of the Brickhall community: 'rising up in the Street like Apocalypse', singing verses in a 'diabolically ghastly' voice and burning the town (SV, 286).

The text delineates a broad spectrum of migrant urban narratives that crystallize around the 'satanic' diasporic spaces of Brickhall High Street, the Shaandaar Café and the Club Hot Wax – spaces that supplement and effectively haunt the image of 'Proper London' in the novel. The previous name of the Club Hot Wax, the 'Blak-an-Tan', refers simultaneously to the brutal military force used to subdue the Irish, and to the dog breed, Black-and-Tan Coonhound, known for its specific markings (allegedly the source for the nickname of the black-and-tan soldiers, who wore dark-and-khaki uniforms). Thus, the Club Hot Wax points both to Britain's colonial past, palimpsestically overwritten by history on the site of the metropolis, and to Brickhall London's hybrid ethnic make-up. Most visibly, Hanif Johnson – a light-skinned Asian man, a savvy lawyer and 'local boy made good' (SV, 185) – and the prancing Pinkwalla – a seven-foot albino with Indian features, who has never seen India, a 'white black' man (SV, 292) – immediately disrupt any pattern of categorization. Brickhall High Street is a mythological battleground onto which the Indian epic of the *Mahabharata*, imported by the Indian migrant communities, erupts to produce the hybrid *Mahavilayet* (SV, 283), an epic of modern, migrant urban myths. It consists of the minority stories and histories of a number of street characters, such as the nostalgic accountant, who pretends each evening to be the conductor of a single-decker bus bound for Bangladesh, who interrupt the narrative of a self-contained London.

The Shaandaar Bed and Breakfast, where Saladin hides in his demonic form, is classed as 'temporary accommodation', a phrase that evokes the Thatcherite register of administrative discourse, the categories of 1980s' London's metropolitan council authorities. In an essay on such forms of allegedly 'temporary' housing, Rushdie draws attention to the conditions in which black and Asian families were forced to live for years (IH, 139–42). In the novel, Proper London both suppresses and is haunted by the existence of numerous such places of temporary accommodation and by their inhabitants, Kafkaesque 'temporary human beings'. Their very existence, however, somehow both within and outside the city, disrupts the idea of linear metropolitan temporality.

The name of the Club Hot Wax alludes to the duplicitous, flexible and manipulable, but also indefinable and unpredictable, Lucretian nature of migrant individuality, which is always in the making. At the Club Hot Wax, which Saladin visits with his 'own people' (253), wax effigies of racist politicians, including those of Enoch Powell and of Margaret Thatcher, are ritually burnt to the music beat. The metaphor of the melting pot, associated with a specifically American assimilative and homogenizing policy on immigration, is turned on its head at the Club Hot Wax. There, versifica-tion takes the form of dub poetry – '*Now-me-feel-indignation-when-dem-talk-immigration-we-no-part-a-de-nation* . . .' (SV, 292, original emphasis) – that seeks to symbolically melt down the conception of pure national identity and exorcize the Madam-Tussaud's-like monumentality of Maggie Torture's (Margaret Thatcher's) 'Chamber of Horrors' Britain.

One of these horrors immortalized in British national mythology and, respectively, at Madam Tussaud's – the murders of Jack the Ripper – re-enacts the terror of late 1880s' London on the site of the contemporary metropolis. A serial killer is rampant in London and since his victims are invariably elderly women, he is popularly labelled 'the Granny Ripper'. The mythology surrounding the figure of Jack the Ripper reveals, as Alex Murray notes, a paradoxical failure of the Enlightenment tradition, specifically, of its rejection of the superstitions and irrationality of pre-modern thought: he 'represents the great unknown: that which the rationalizing discourse of modernity has failed to uncover. . . . At the heart of [the quest to uncover the identity of Jack the Ripper] is a faith in rationality that is inherently irrational' (2004, 58).

In one such rationalizing gesture, the authorities frame a black man for the Granny Ripper murders. The scapegoat is Sylvester Roberts, who has renamed himself 'Dr Uhuru Simba', thus choosing to occupy the 'old and honourable' role of the 'uppity nigger' (SV, 414). The plain 'Sylvester Roberts', a name redolent of British colonialism, has become not simply 'Uhuru Simba' (a cod-African name meaning 'lion of truth'), but 'Dr Uhuru Simba', where the title, 'Dr', undermines the African roots by adding to them a sense of European intellectual authority. In this name, there is a clashing not only of cultures and worlds, but of the *ideas* of cultures and worlds, from the perspective of the displaced and deracinated. The appropriation of a European educational accolade in conjunction with the African name seems to undermine the former's superiority, institutional, intellectual and imperial. But it can also be seen as Rushdie's attempt to caricature self-identified icons of cultural resistance. Such gestures are made undoubtedly ironic today in the wake of Rushdie's acceptance of a knighthood, which produced 'Sir Salman Rushdie'. That Rushdie was uneasy, at the time at least, in describing such leaders of resistance, can further be seen in the association of the figure of Dr Uhuru Simba with a history of sexual aggression. Unsurprisingly, it is Saladin who points this out. Others, however, insist that the man's record of violence should be set aside, that what 'we have here is trouble with the Man' (SV, 415). In light of Saladin's dislike for the use of 'such American terms' as 'the Man' or of the pan-African liberation anthem, *Nkosi Sikelel' iAfrika* in 'the very different British situation' (SV, 415), McLeod reads this episode as indicative of 'Rushdie's squeamishness towards the rhetoric of black power' and his refusal to grant its cultural resources the translative potential he otherwise reserves for his Indian Muslim heritage (154–55). Rushdie's scepticism, however, could be explained by Saladin's overall 'squeamishness' towards 'improper London', including 'his own people', and even its 'improper' manifestations in himself, which, in effect, render him a Fanonian 'new man' when members of the Brickhall community begin to wear horns, T-shirts, badges, posters and banners with the image of the 'Goatman' into which he has thus been doubly metamorphosed. Crucially, movements of cultural/political significance in the novel seem to leave open the invisible-city door for ambiguous 'man' figures who become targets for the 'Man'. It is in the 'undeground' urban space where such identities are forged, but in the 'over-ground' city where they are vulnerable, where their dubious pasts can be exploded.

The charging of Dr Uhuru Simba with the Granny Ripper murders exports culpability outside the 'common sense' of the metropolis into the dark space of the irrational other. The extensive evidence of the existence of witches' covens throughout the Metropolitan Police, an irrationality at the heart of Proper London, is suppressed in the same way. Official London is, as a result, revealed as 'a Crusoe-city, marooned on the island of its past, and trying, with the help of a Man-Friday underclass, to keep up appearances' (SV, 439). The mysterious death of Uhuru Simba while awaiting trial and the existence of witches' covens in the Metropolitan Police are tests for Saladin's hospitable London of assiduity, restraint, moderation, self-reliance and family life (SV, 257).

The text caricatures these decidedly Podsnappian values in the simulacrum of Dickensian London, recreated at the Shepperton film studios to serve as the setting for a party, where Gibreel and Saladin meet again. The giant stage of Dickensian London echoes the setting of Podsnappery in Dickens's novel *Our Mutual Friend* (1865) – the party in honour of the eighteenth birthday of Miss Georgiana Podsnap, which gathers the 'grand chain' of Victorian society (141). Instead of the Frenchman, whom. Mr Podsnap addresses in Dickens's novel, the Podsnap chorus in *The Satanic Verses* teaches an 'invisible' foreigner about the unique qualities of Englishmen (modesty, independence and responsibility) that can be found in the streets of London (424).

In Dickensian satire, the notorious quality of Podsnappery combines Victorian chauvinism and middle-class social consciousness that dismiss foreigners and the poor with the same flourish. In *The Satanic Verses*, the Podsnappian society at the film studios – fashion models, film stars and politicians – also evokes the assembly of auctioneers at the Grand Saleroom in Rushdie's short story 'At the Auction of the Ruby Slippers' (1992) who bid for Dorothy's cherished footwear in *The Wizard of Oz*. In the contemporary world, the ruby slippers have been commodified and transformed, in this way, into an empty simulacrum that can be filled in with any one from a variety of fictions, including that of 'home'.

In the novel, counterfeit London, with the fake grandeur of its English Podsnappery (satirized in Dickens' novel as putting 'the rest of Europe and the whole of Asia, Africa and America nowhere', 137), also includes a dark Thames, from which a man is recovered unconscious by an actor impersonating Gaffer Hexam. The man is Jumpy Joshi, a leftist poet and anti-war activist as well as the new lover of Pamela Lovelace, the meta-morphosed Saladin's estranged English wife. In his verses, Jumpy Joshi urges that Enoch Powell's notorious metaphor of the rivers of blood should be reclaimed, made 'a thing we can use'. A street, Jumpy proposes, is a river and we are the flow, or, the rivers of blood flow in our bodies (SV, 186). Ironically, Jumpy nearly drowns in the trope he attempts to reclaim, the Dickensian Thames, a symbolic river of blood. Yet, this episode foreshadows Jumpy's death: he will be killed, along with Pamela Lovelace, as they attempt to prove the existence of witches' covens in the Metropolitan Police. The novel places an emphasis, however, on the role of the Dickensian Gaffer Hexam, who keeps watch over a stretch of the Thames for floating corpses to steal their valuables before handing them over to the police. The dust-heaps of London are, potentially, both a source of wealth and a dark repository in Dickens' text. In *The Satanic Verses*, the urban 'refuse', which the English, in their imperial Podsnappery, have discarded as junk, comes back, having been washed up on the river bank, to haunt them. It is the same metaphor of recycling, reclaiming or re-versifying that transforms the mounds of dust into a treasure in *Our Mutual Friend* and turns 'insults into strengths' in *The Satanic Verses*.

At the party, Saladin recognizes, in Gibreel's derision of this complacent London, an 'inverted Podsnap' (SV, 426). Whereas Saladin attempts to conquer London by taking over its 'cherished identity', by becoming *it* as in a game of grandmother's footsteps (SV, 398), or by translating himself into the medium of the metropolis, Gibreel is determined to redeem the city, to make it his own by versifying or translating it. He embarks on this project of a counter-conquest through re-description in several different ways. First, he approaches Geographers' London, attempting to correct its 'capricious, tormented' nature and restore its sense of itself (SV, 320). As he traverses London, bent on retribution, Gibreel does so with the help of the city's popular simulacrum of the *A to Z*. This itinerary formats the metropolis into a standardized map and subverts the project of colonial cartography, specifically, its attempts to validate and fix empire's inscription of the space of the colonized. Here, we see Gibreel attempting to re-appropriate the city, a project itself doomed to failure since the city refuses to surrender to the cartographers and persistently changes shape. Instead, he arrives at what Graham Huggan (1989) refers to as a 'decolonization' of the map: his recognition of the failure of cartographic representation to empower him, because the metropolis is irreducible. The uncharted wastelands, the anonymous parks and the holes in the roads, burnt by acid dripping from the sky (SV, 327), frustrate the legitimacy of the *A to Z*.

Earlier in the text, in his flight from Rekha Merchant (a woman whose death he has caused indirectly and whose ghost repeatedly haunts him after he leaves Bombay), when Gibreel descends to the London Underground, he finds it constantly changes shape, 'protean and chameleon' (SV, 200), to mirror the logic of his own 'insanity'. Like the *London A to Z*, the map of the London Underground offers no solution, for frenzied Gibreel, to the 'labyrinth' of the subterranean city. David Pike discusses Harry Beck's map of the London Underground as a modernist technological conquest of 'irrational space' (2002, 104–07). In the novel, Gibreel is unable to read this text of the city's perpetual underground motion. Instead, under the controlled geometry of its multiple lines, he uncovers the suppressed space of the other – a psychogeographical 'hellish maze' (SV, 200) that mirrors the landscape of his own mind.

His second translation of London – this time, literally, by way of its underground dimension – has comic overtones. Having discarded the street atlas, he arrives at the Angel Underground, a place that, as its name suggests, would presumably facilitate his divine intervention. The incident with the Underground worker, the suggestively named Orphia Philips, reveals a love-triangle story and produces the tragic–comic subterranean landscape of material and emotional space, whose occupants' lives revolve around the incessant, repetitive and meaningless, descent and ascent in the station's two new elevators. As Gibreel descends into the city's underground, like an Orpheus himself, he finds an analogue of his own story, the love triangle Gibreel-Alleluia-Saladin. Undeground London becomes a subconscious projection of Gibreel's jealous determination to protect his lover, Alleluia, from other men's lust and an anticipation of his failure to predict Saladin's betrayal of his trust. Later on, driven by envy, Saladin will take revenge on Gibreel, which takes the form of 'telephone verses'. Using his talent to imitate voices, Saladin will make a series of telephone calls to Gibreel and Alleluia, reciting insinuating verses, which will set the lovers against each other. This underground episode confirms the psychogeographical significance of the city's subconscious/subterranean realm: its quality of a projection of Gibreel's mind that is simultaneously subversive of the rationality of the metropolis. Gibreel's subconscious fears of rejection and of the possibility that his endeavour to translate the city might fail or turn out to be meaningless haunt his rational self and, respectively, the overt existence of London, its overground level.

Gibreel's most comprehensive attempt at reconfiguring the city – by tropicalizing it – involves an epistemologically different position, a bird's-eye view, which Michel de Certeau refers to, theoretically, as that of the 'urban cartographer' – the 'voyeur-god' who observes the panoramic 'texturology' of the city spread out before his eyes (1988, 92–3). Gibreel is no longer attempting to read the metropolis, but magically hovers above it, trying to impose on it a new urban order. This translation strategy subverts, in Bhabha's analysis, the colonial discursive construction of the European other – 'the heat and dust of India; the dark emptiness of Africa; the tropical chaos that was deemed despotic and ungovernable and therefore worthy of the civilizing mission' (1994, 169). At the same time, the 'proposed' metamorphosis of London, mimicking, with its 'benefits' and 'disadvantages', the scientific claims and methodology of the colonial enterprise, is construed as a totalizing project that foregrounds urban authenticity, rather than a recognition of the metropolis's hybridity: since truth is 'extreme' and 'heated' (SV, 354, original emphasis). Like the Imam's experience of the city, Gibreel's narrative of London emphasizes displacement and nostalgia for the clarity of home as opposed to the 'slippery' and 'devilish' quality of London that he finds in its 'endless drizzle of greys' (SV, 353). Hence, his persistent conscious attempts at versifying the city.

Intermingled with these conscious reconfigurations of London and increasingly indistinguishable from them are Gibreel's serial dreams of the Imam, of Mahound and of Ayesha. If in *Midnight's Children*, Saleem succeeds in uniting the generation of India's midnight promise through his magic power, Gibreel's divine omniscience gives him access to London's telepathic, subconscious and subterranean migrant narratives, which are thus both his and not his articulations. In an interview, Rushdie says of the story of Islam: 'I felt that I had inherited the culture without the belief, and that the stories belonged to me as well' (1996, 62). The plurality of these serial stories throws urban temporality into a state of schizophrenic multiplicity, while the dreamer – an interpreter, a cameraman, a spectator or a god – grows unable to observe the boundaries between them and experiences the city as a babble of narratives, a *Babylondon*. It would seem that Gibreel lives out a characteristically post-structuralist perspective on meaning, yet the simultaneity of London and its sub-narratives is destabilized by the continuous quality of his dreams, by the nostalgia for the certainty of linear chronology, of picking up the story where we left it. The chronological narrative mode of Gibreel's visions clashes with the emphatically nonlinear, frequently proleptic or analeptic main narrative. The stories of Mahound and Ayesha are always 'picked up' from the exact point at which they have been paused before. They seduce the reader and Gibreel, who is otherwise torn between dreams and reality, with their deceptive clarity and coherence.

London's sub-stories of the Imam's city of exile and of Mahound's Jahilia, on which we will now focus, foreground the novel's secular historicized point of view on Islam. The image of the Imam, modelled after Ayatollah Khomeini, the Shiite mullah who returned to Iran from his Paris exile to overthrow the Shah and construct a new Islamic Republic, evokes the modernist trope of exile understood as a necessary displacement. The Euro-American modernist conception of exile, as Caren Kaplan suggests, 'works to remove itself from any political or historically specific instances in order to generate aesthetic categories and ahistorical values'; it is construed as an 'ideology of artistic production' (1996, 28). While the Imam does not aestheticize homelessness (he was exiled for opposing the oppressive regime of the Shah), he shares the essentialist idea associated with modernist exile: the notion that it is 'natural' to be at 'home' and that a separation from that location can never be assuaged by anything but return. He is also involved in the production of ahistorical values, in versifying that attempts to annihilate History. Rushdie ironically remarks that 'despite all the restoration of ancient laws, time in Iran persists in running forward' (IH, 384).

The Imam's exile in London is referred to as his 'Elba, not St. Helena' (SV, 205), that is, the first exile of the French Emperor Napoleon Bonaparte, during which he planned his return to Paris and the throne, rather than his second exile, after his defeat at Waterloo, when it was only left to him to write his memoirs on the island of St. Helena. This comparison of the Imam and the French emperor is a tongue-in-cheek allusion to Ayatollah Khomeini's 'French' exile as well as to the nature of his ambitions. The idea of the island is also a significant reference. The island is a potent image in the iconographies of British nationalism and colonialism: what Marina Warner describes, in her essay 'Home: Our Famous Island Race', as the notion of an ancient national insularity (1994, 82). It is this image that the Imam embraces and imposes upon the city, while distancing himself from everything British. His London is the site of an 'existential dislocation' (ibid., 85). The Imam's curtained Kensington flat produces an image of London as the 'overheated' laboratory of the Islamic Revolution, an urban pocket of messianic time, which is an implacable rejection of the realities of this other city in which the Imam is living, yet which mimics the colonial behaviour of the British. This can be seen, for example, in the colonial re-creation of an isolated 'little England' in cities such as Bombay and Delhi in *Midnight's Children*, where the custom of the cocktail-hour is diligently adhered to on Methwold's Estate in Bombay and, in Delhi, where a new city of pink-stone palaces built by 'pink conquerors' has succeeded in isolating itself from the old city's realities (MC, 69). The energy of the Imam's rejection of London increases the tension within the enclosed simulacrum, Desh, to explosion point: it forces together two opposing cultures, which can be compared to what the text refers to as the city's uranium and plutonium, its ability to juxtapose incompatible realities because when they meet, they explode by making each other decompose (SV, 314).

At the same time, the Imam's confinement within a simulation of the climate of his native Desh is self-imposed – a mini-tropicalization of London, since, it is important to emphasize, the Imam is the dream creation of Gibreel. This narrative voices a nostalgia for hot certainties and plays out a diasporic identity that is an absolute rejection of translation, apart from its subversive use of Western technology – the heating system that conjures up Desh; the American filtration machine that sustains ideological purity and the radio that makes revolutionary messages possible. The Imam's London becomes, in turn, a subtext of the dreamed of city beneath the postcard mountain: 'what is first uttered in the impotence of an overheated apartment becomes the fate of nations' (SV, 209). This absolutist versifying contrasts with the multiplicity of the metropolis and erodes its visibility. Unlike the subtexts of Jahilia and the pilgrimage from Titlipur to Mecca, which take a serial form, the dream narrative of the Imam is confined within a singular account, its monologic nature contrasting with the multiplicity of London, which, at the same time, paradoxically contains it. The Imam muses: 'Such a welcoming city, such a refuge, they take all types. Keep the curtains drawn' (SV, 208).

The dream city of Jahilia is based on the same potentially explosive urban formula: the inclusive *many* that accommodates the exclusivist *one*. There, the dominant narrative of sand – with all its concomitant elements: polytheism, multiplicity, inconstancy, elusiveness, shapelessness and the memory of nomadic culture – is still one with the minor narrative of water – a ghostly, subversive underground presence, since where it drops, it erodes the city; holes appear in the earth and houses start tilting and swaying. The Muslim name 'Jahilia', denoting, as we noted earlier, the period of ignorance before Islam, excludes the religion, while paradoxically being its own, if retrospective, articulation. Jahilia 'before' the Prophet exists in a suspended temporality within the discursive timeline of Islam. Within the secular, multiply historicized urban temporalities of the novel, the narrative of Islam is presented as a tectonic insurgence. The businessman Mahound, excluded from the mercantile elite, heads a 'revolution of water-carriers, immigrants and slaves' (SV, 101; 102). Initiating a war of the elements, Mahound offers a message of dangerously monolithic singularity, thus eroding the multiplicity and inconstancy of sand by mobilizing the unity and purity of water.

This urban ambivalence between the one and the many, between Ovid and Lucretius, is a process of their mutual subversion and versification, an articulation of 'verses and converses, universes and reverses' (SV, 123). If Mahound's message of monolithic singularity censures the multiplicity of the city from which it rises, the satanic verses lampoon the certainty of the recitation of which they are a part. The separation of the divine from the satanic, as the text stresses, is a recent fabrication. By contrast, the repudiation of the 'satanic' verses articulates multiple discursive splits – sacred/blasphemous; prophecy/satire; water/sand; oasis/desert; Yathrib/Jahilia; truth/mirage; knowledge/ignorance; fixity/rootlessness and purity/profanity – that partition the city and ultimately deprive it of its 'provisional quality of a mirage' (SV, 360). When Mahound returns to Jahilia, the city is no longer built of sand.

The narrative of Jahilia is Rushdie's hybrid migrant translation of the story of Muhammad: he describes Jahilia as a 'radical city' that fuses India and Arabia; Mecca, New Delhi and London (1996, 55). The translation of Muhammad into the figure of Mahound mirrors Saladin's metamorphosis into a devil and participates in the novel's urban politics of recuperative versification. In contrast to the Imam, Mahound is represented as an idea that is capable of compromises. Therefore, the construal of the book's narrative of Islam as derogative by Muslim communities can be seen as the result of their adoption of a non-ambivalent view of versification, in which Islam is a passive, rather than an erosive, sub-textuality of the Western metropolis. Muslim communities condemned the book for its denigration of Islam in the eyes of the West. On the contrary, as this discussion has shown, Rushdie is even-handed in his critique: rigid constructions of Islam, on the one hand, and monolithic imaginations of a smooth, uninterrupted, pure West, on the other, ironically collide on the site of the city. Although, in doing so, they fail to destroy each other, the collision triggers a massive geomorphic shift. Verses and di-versifying in the text as well as the reclaiming 'satanic' project of the novel itself unsettle the metropolis' monopoly over visibility and push the buried ghosts of many conscious and subconscious diasporic narratives up onto its surface. In the process, versifying also lays bare migrant fears and doubts, dreams of power and retribution, and totalizing projects, whose initiators, faced with the illegibility of the city, seek what is suggested to be the impossible position of untranslatability, since Gibreel, Saladin and the Imam inevitably change as they transform the city.

The great climax of the novel, London's conflagration, leads not to the destruction of the city but to its geomorphic renewal. Having abandoned the idea of urban translation, Gibreel calls fire upon the city in his role of the avenging Angel Azraeel, but it is as if the invisible-city stories have spontaneously erupted, forming fiery 'rivers of blood' on the urban surface. Hanif Johnson describes the event as a 'socio-political phenomenon' (SV, 469), which signals a monumental change in the history of Britain. As the riots cool down, new cultural formations and identities are created and, although Saladin and Gibreel fail to confront each other in this burning Babylondon, Gibreel's 'hot certainties' dissolve as he rescues his adversary, while Saladin travels to a new, reconfigured Bombay.

Routes and Diversions Through the Looking-Glass

The novel's project of urban di-versification, disruptive of the Western metropolis's exclusivist claim to visibility, produces a dynamic postcolonial topography that expands and contracts with the migrant's/migrating narratives. Within this shifting topography, urban spatialities and temporalities undergo a number of multi-directional catoptric processes – diversions that continually re-chart and redefine them. The novel articulates a chain of catoptric associations that can be arranged, according to the semantic schema of the novel, in the following way. First, these associations stand for activities denoting a transition or a passage of a catoptric quality that inform interurban travel, such as migration, translation, metamorphosis, reincarnation, rebirth and pilgrimage. Secondly, the novel provides catoptric patterns of linking urban spatialities and temporalities that problematize epistemological hierarchies, such as dreaming, revelation/ prophecy, cinema and intertextuality. Finally, catoptric associations include motifs of splitting, doubling and multiplication, such as the parting of the sea, Partition, schizophrenia and the division of cities into those *in* which one dreams and those *of* which one dreams, a division that produces further catoptric echoes or correspondences: Gibreel/Mahound or London/ Jahilia. In London, for example, Saladin hears an ominous voice warning him against returning to Bombay: 'When you have stepped through the looking-glass you step back at your peril. The mirror may cut you to shreds' (SV, 58).

The idea of postcolonial migration and return as journeys analogous to Alice's mirror adventure in Lewis Carroll's *Through the Looking-Glass* (1896) takes us not only to the understanding of Bombay and London as each other's negative twins in the metaphor of inverted urban temporality, developed in the previous section, but also to the novel's motif of glass skin, the discursive catoptric cage, which imprisons the other. I will argue that the mirror boundaries that separate cities, partition cartographies and imprison the self are made to reflect, through their inconsistencies, duplicities and shadow selves, their own translucence, illusiveness and absurdity. The bipartite model of original and reflected image, of Same and other, that informs colonial discourse, is replaced in the novel by the paradigms of the inverted mirror and of the mirror reflected in another mirror, which compromise the concepts of origin, teleological directionality and cultural purity.

This section focuses on the catoptric aspect of postcolonial travel as reflective of the production and metamorphosis of urban spatial and temporal configurations and urban identities in what appears to be the novel's forked-path world. The travellers themselves, the main characters Saladin and Gibreel, are each other's negative twins, who negotiate, in the imagination of the passage from Bombay to London as a process of translation, two alternative, catoptrically opposed versions of postcolonial identity. Lawrence Venuti's notion of translation as a violent social practice can be brought to bear on the angelic/devilish reincarnation of the protagonists that begins in inter-urban space. In Venuti's view, translation inevitably involves a degree of violence by which the foreign text is being reconstituted into certain hierarchies of dominance and marginality that determine the production, circulation and reception of texts.

> The aim of translation is to bring back a cultural other as the same, the recognizable, even the familiar; and this aim always risks a wholesale domestication of the foreign text, often in highly self-conscious projects, where translation serves an imperialist appropriation of foreign cultures for domestic agendas, cultural, economic and political. (1996, 196)

Venuti follows Friedrich Schleiermacher in distinguishing between two translation strategies: a *domesticating* method – an ethnocentric reduction of the foreign text that 'brings the author back home' – and a *foreignizing* method that exercizes an ethnodeviant pressure on these values, registering the linguistic and cultural difference of the foreign text, to produce a translation that 'sends the reader abroad'. Historically, Venuti notes, foreignizing translation has always been marginalized in Anglo-American culture (ibid., 197–98).

Although Venuti's theory seems to be based on an understanding of cultures as distinctly separate entities and, therefore, conflicts with the novel's accent on culture's impurity, it is useful in explaining the violence involved in the catoptric split of Saladin's translation into a target medium, on the one hand, and the actual product of this translation, his demoniasis, on the other. Even if we assume, however, that Saladin is a self-translated man, his re-fashioning, outlined retrospectively in the opening chapter of the novel, is marked by his target – English, middle-class and urban – culture's canons and practices. His metamorphosis into a devil, which we discussed as the product of hegemonic versifying in the previous section, becomes synonymous with the processes of translation and migration as the sites of multiple determinations. Saladin's metamorphosis can only be reversed if he embraces and re-appropriates his demonic form – an act in which the translated migrant not only undoes the descriptors' ethnocentric project but also foreignizes the metropolis, the target medium itself.

The text opens in the *medias res* of the interurban space of translation that is experienced by the travellers as a void or a transit lounge: 'most insecure and transitory of zones, illusory, discontinuous, metamorphic' (SV, 5). In the work of James Clifford (1991; 1997), the transit lounge becomes a trope for the contemporary condition, along with the hotel lobby, the station, the hospital and the airport terminal, all of which are seen as places of transit, where encounters are fleeting and arbitrary, gesturing towards culture's borderland location, constituted through diasporic travel. A site of multiple reflective inscriptions, yet ultimately unmarked by epistemological hierarchies or teleological directionality, this notion of interurban space carries the theoretical potential of Homi Bhabha's concept of the Third Space of enunciation, where culture's hybridity is articulated and where meaning cannot be controlled. However, this model is problematized, as we shall see, by the destruction of the plane bound for London in the city's airspace. Outside the context of the novel, the international, in-between space of migration/translation has continued to mean, for many migrants in search of a better life in the West, the limbo of detention centres, where they may remain stuck for years en route to their destination, the target medium or land of promise into which they will, in this way, forever seek to transfer themselves, rather like the 'temporary human beings' described in the novel.

The airspace of the Bombay–London interval reverses colonial discursive structures of domination through the figure of an inverted mirror mediating between the two cities on the characters' journey west. For instance, 'unnatural selections' (SV, 133) occur during their fall that frustrate the logic of Eurocentric time as conceptualized in the scientific paradigms of progress and evolution and that contradict the 'natural' direction of travel they articulate. The protagonists' fall, compared to meteor lightning or divine vengeance, functions as a postcolonial *Deus-ex-machina* interruption of the space-time of the metropolis. Yet, as we mentioned earlier, the plane bound for London explodes above the city. It is as if London eliminates, in its airspace, what it finds to be alien, dangerous or illegal. For instance, many children upon whose legitimacy the British Government has cast its 'ever-reasonable doubts' mingle with the remnants of the plane (SV, 4). The liminal, intercultural zone that surrounds the metropolis is therefore also its 'protective' buffer, manufactured through British immigration laws.

The protagonists' fall into 'Englishness' simultaneously reflects the journey of Lewis Carroll's Alice down the whole to Wonderland (SV, 6): an intertextual passage that caricatures the course and tropes of colonial travel, while delineating the Western metropolis as a constantly fluctuating, upside-down world that parodies the absolutes of colonial epistemology. Once she has fallen into Wonderland, Alice attempts to determine her identity by establishing what she knows for fact. She resorts to mathematics and geography, two of the foundational sciences of Victorian certainty, yet their laws are not only invalid but meaningless in the curious parallel universe of Wonderland. Her efforts to pinpoint her constantly metamorphosing location by relating it to the idea of herself as a stable point of orientation are of no avail – her shifts in size are unpredictable and even the promising symmetry of the height-changing mushroom cannot regulate them consistently. In Rushdie's novel, Saladin also questions his identity, after his metamorphosis into a devil, and initially arrives at the conclusion that he has fallen into an inverted, 'not-England', an 'improper-London' world that produces an absurdity of place, which he perceives as a grotesque 'wrongness' (SV, 132). Like Alice's size, Saladin's shape, whether a product of hegemonic description or a necessary transformation that enables him to see the invisible city, simultaneously produces and is produced by the surrounding space. Alice's growth and involuntary invasion of the Rabbit's house are mirrored in the symbolic process of Saladin's growth out of the Shaandaar attic room.

Alice's journey parodies the genre of colonial adventure by, ironically, leading her into the 'exotic' space of imperial absurdity – a world that is, on the one hand, decidedly the negation of its overground counterpart, since, there, shoes are done with *whiting*, you have to *dig* for apples, and the sentence *precedes* the verdict (42, 99, 117), and, on the other, one that is remarkably similar in its hierarchy, since Wonderland also has a queen, albeit a queen of hearts. Alice and the reader are thus left unable to separate the familiar from the dissimilar and the same from its mirror image. It should be noted that the precursor of *Alice in Wonderland* is entitled *Alice's Adventures under Ground*. In *The Satanic Verses*, the protagonists' entry into London/Englishness is similarly conceptualized as a descent that reconfigures the discursive notion of the antipodes in colonial discourse. This notion is also meaningfully satirized in Alice's comically mispronounced version, the 'antipathies' (17), revealing the underlying sentiment in the catoptric ideology of the colonized other as the inverted and perverted image of the Self.

As Susan Sherer notes, there is no backward motion in Wonderland, because of the impossibility of returning to an established place (1996, 5). In comparison, in Saladin's mind, the idea of return to the home city fluctuates between his utter refusal to look back and his rehabilitation of Bombay as *a*, rather than *the*, home city, at the end of the narrative, through its association with his father. The migrant's 'home-coming', as we mentioned earlier, is seen as analogous to Alice's passage through the looking-glass, yet one that foregrounds the impossibility of such a route or the dangers it poses. In what seems to be a similar journey in Lewis Carroll's *Through the Looking-Glass*, Alice attempts to leave the looking-glass house, only to find herself back at its doorstep. In this *contrariwise* world, it is necessary to move away from an object in order to get closer to it. In Rushdie's novel, the protagonist's postcolonial route produces a catoptric anomaly as bewildering as Alice's walk towards/away from the house. Like Alice, Saladin returns to a topographically and psychologically altered past.

The character's fears of the 'homebound' route reveal his necessarily complicated conceptions of the city and of migrant identity. When he finds his speech undergoing an unexpected transformation into his Bombay lilt on one of his journeys from London to Bombay, Saladin decides that it had been a mistake to go home, that it feels like a 'regression' or an 'unnatural journey' (SV, 34). Saladin literally travels within the colonial understanding of the journey East as a regression or a return to the past from the advanced or superior condition of the Western metropolis.

On his return to Bombay, at the end of the novel, however, 'back home' no longer rings false to him. The text ends with Saladin's turning away from the view of his childhood home's window and its old and sentimental echoes, thereby refracting the notion of return through the idea of a constantly metamorphosing, Lucretian identity, that is always open to new

translations. Andrew Teverson argues that the novel does not fully assert
either the Lucretian or the Ovidian model but both: 'some aspects of identity are translated, and some remain untranslatable' (2007, 151). I would
argue, more precisely, that the novel's paradigm of identity *is* the Lucretian
one, which is not to suggest that it excludes the Ovidian paradigm. Lucretius negotiates Ovid in the text in the manner in which the city of Jahilia is
governed by the idea of the inclusive many (Lucretuis) that accommodates
the exclusivist one (Ovid).

The juxtaposition of the seemingly opposite routes, Bombay–London
and London–Bombay, foregrounds their catoptric relationship, as eluci-
dated through the text's allusions to Lewis Carroll's *Alice* books. As we established above, the journey to London mirrors Alice's fall into Wonderland
and the journey to Bombay, Alice's passage through the looking-glass. This
bifurcation presupposes no stable point of orientation or origin and frustrates the Manichean opposition same/other or same/mirror image. If
Alice in Wonderland destabilizes the colonial notion of the antipodes as based
on the asymmetrical geographical binary up/down, *The Satanic Verses*
exposes the arbitrariness of the division East/West as analogous to that of
left/right and the unequal values assigned to each side of the mirror in
hegemonic description.

The Alice intertexts also highlight the duplicitous quality of the migrant
traveller – the catoptric twins Saladin and Gibreel – and the splits of Gibreel's
own persona, as well as the multiple dreamed-of cities he brings into being,
to which the discussion now turns. In Wonderland, Alice remembers how
she has tried to 'box her own ears for having cheated herself in a game of
croquet she was playing against herself' (21). As Jan B. Gordon points out,
Alice's fall is a disintegration of the self into complementary components.
The child realizes that the defensive posture she assumes is itself a mode of
self-multiplication and that her journey is a metaquest (1987, 23). The clash
between Saladin's and Gibreel's Londons can be defined as the migrant's
duplicitous, angelic/devilish or foreignizing/domesticating translation of
the metropolis. If Alice's self-reflexive duplicity mirrors and is mirrored by
the self-proliferating citizenry of Wonderland, the doppelgängers in
Rushdie's novel foreground the ambiguity of postcolonial London. This
ambiguity is characterized, in the case of Saladin, by a schism between
official, visible London and its underground Brickhall version. In the case
of Gibreel, the ambiguity is exemplified by a schizophrenic multiplicity of
worlds, linked through the processes of cinema, dreaming and revelation,
which function as catoptric strategies of juxtaposing ontologically different,
yet interdependent, cities.

On his fall from Flight AI-420 into London, Gibreel sings the opening song from the Bollywood movie *Shree 420* (Kapoor, 1955). Srinivas Aravamudan discusses the significance of the number '420' to the Indian imagination. It is associated first, with a section of the Code of Criminal Procedure, itself a legacy of the juridical apparatus installed by the British colonizers, which declares imprisonment as punishment for cheating; secondly, especially in the popular imagination, with the broadly perceived 'villainy of politicians and businessmen'; thirdly, with the State of Emergency, which 'relied on a panoply of ambiguous statutes, including perhaps Section 420'; and, finally, with the combination of Sanjay Gandhi's four-point programme, including sterilization, and Indira Gandhi's 20-point programme for national growth, that, added together in an Orwellian fashion, produce the sum '420' (191–92).

In the film, the number '420' corresponds to the distance, in miles, between a crossroads in the country and Bombay, travelled by the Chaplin-like protagonist, Raj, an orphan, who heads for the city in search for work. *Shree 420* was produced during the 1950s' Nehruvian era of Hindi cinema, when the city became synonymous with exploitation, crime and danger, so that the film's heroes were the peasants and the urban working-class (Ganti 2004, 24–29). Throughout the film, Bombay is associated with greed, deception and the dehumanization of the individual. A beggar on the street tells Raj: 'this is Bombay, it's a big city, if you look for work, you'll never find it. If you live by lying and cheating, there are four-hundred and twenty ways'. Symbolically, Raj sells his honesty medal before he is dragged into the corrupt high society of the city, where he is involved in a number of fraudulent deals with the rich Seth Dharamanand, whose car's plate number is 840, presumably pointing to his *double* dishonesty, as the same Orwellian arithmetic suggests.

The distance between Bombay and London in the novel is approximately the same catoptric/cinematic 'length'. The flight number, AI-420, alludes, in Aravamudan's view, to the plane bound for London as an allegorical 'ship of state', detonated by Sikh extremists, just as Indira Gandhi was assassinated by her Sikh bodyguards in 1984 (192). Yet, a more literal source for the opening scene of the novel is the 1985 bombing of an Air India jet by Sikh extremists. In this catoptric replacement of Bombay with London as the destination city, associated with prejudice and double-standards, and village India with Bombay as the impoverished colonial periphery, the site of felled family trees, the protagonists, Saladin and Gibreel, disillusioned with state politics, embark on a postcolonial journey that, ironically, leads them to the very source of four-hundred-and-twenty-ness. Raj's 'song of the

road' (Mishra 2002, 108), 'My Shoes Are Japanese', a version of which
Gibreel sings during his fall unto London, formulates an idea of Indianness,
which approximates the Ovidian notion of identity and contrasts with
Saladin's choice. Inhabiting a plurality of cities or worlds, Gibreel, who
wishes to remain an untranslated man, ultimately self-destructs in a failure
to reconcile his schizophrenic multiplicity of selves with the Ovidian
immutable essence. Yet, the blurring of his cinema roles and his off-screen
persona parody the lives of actors – politicians such as N.T. Rama Rao, who
headed the government of Andhra Pradesh while devoting his career to
star roles in Hindi mythologicals (Fischer *et al.*, 1990, 122). The same
erasure of the boundary between cinema and politics marks Indian election
campaigns, where, as Tejaswini Ganti notes, 'political parties . . . produce
and circulate audio-cassettes of their political slogans set to the melodies of
popular-film songs' (2004, 79). Gibreel's multiple self then satirizes film
stars' semi-divine status in India – 'If Gibreel died, could India be far
behind?'(SV, 29) – and the manipulation of popular culture and its
celebrities for the purposes of endorsing political agendas.

Bollywood cinematic paradigms permeate the narrative of Bombay in the
text. Ganti points out that much of the discussion within the industry is
about how the newness of a story derives from its presentation and treatment,
since most stories are considered not to be unique (ibid., 75). Similarly,
Bombay is 'a culture of remakes' in the novel, its architecture mimicking
skyscrapers and its cinema continuously reinventing *The Magnificent Seven*
and *Love Story* (SV, 64). Lalitha Gopalan (2002) discusses Indian cinema as
one structured around and celebrating spatial and temporal discontinuities
and, in the text, Gibreel's story is also characterized by such cinematic
ruptures. The boundary between dreams and waking hours becomes
increasingly indistinct for him until it disappears altogether. The cities *of*
which he dreams leak into the cities *in* which he dreams and vice versa, so
that the relation between the dream urban narratives, of Jahilia, of the
Imam's London, and of the pilgrimage to Mecca, and the waking-hour
ones, of Bombay and London, becomes that of the catoptric model of a
mirror reflected in another mirror.

This catoptric quality of cinema as a paradigm of a world within a world
is most prominent in the narrative of Jahilia. The story of Jahilia is, to some
extent, an intertextual revision of a film narrative, the popular movie *The
Message* (1976), produced and directed by a Muslim film-maker, Moustapha
Akkad, who, like Rushdie, lives in the West. In the film, the figure of the
Prophet is literally invisible, in line with the Islamic tradition according to
which the impersonation of the Prophet is considered offensive 'against the

spirituality of his Message'.[1] As a result, when they talk to Muhammad, the other characters in the film seem to be addressing an imaginary or metaphysical figure, which, like Brickhall London, is there, but is unseen. The director of photography explains that a special technique was designed in order to avoid showing the person of Mohammed. It involves using the 'camera as the Prophet' so that all actors who are speaking to the Prophet look, while doing so, directly at the camera and also, in this way, the viewer of the film. Significantly, it is other characters that render Muhammad's words, thus mediating between him and the viewer, so that his utterances are always channelled and never autonomous. When they address him, looking at the lens of the camera, we see what he sees. In this way, the makers of the film succeed in representing unrepresentability through a hybrid strategy that involves the technological/artistic adaptation of Mohammed. Curiously, however, the technique also has the effect of placing the figure of the Prophet within the ontological level of the viewer or the cameraman. It is precisely this technique that Rushdie borrows and develops in the novel and whose effects throw light on the catoptricity of the processes of revelation and prophecy. Gibreel's point of view is sometimes that of a camera or of an observer, at other times of a movie fan with Jahilia as his silver screen (SV, 108); or, he is inside the Prophet himself, and it is impossible to determine who has dreamt whom (SV, 108–10). Gibreel serves, like the Prophet in *The Message*, as a sort of a catoptric camera device. What could otherwise be seen as the novel's characteristically postmodernist technique of linking parallel ontological levels is revealed as an attempt to reclaim existing, already hybrid, sacred *and* secular, modes of representing and disseminating the story of Islam. (A similarly hybrid contemporary strategy is recorded in Monica Ali's novel, *Brick Lane* (2003), where Muslim Londoner Karim has set up prayer alerts on his mobile phone.)

For Gibreel, the movie star, the cities of London, Bombay and Jahilia are linked, as would be expected, cinematically. His dream narratives of these cities share a focus on Muslim religious leaders – the Imam, Mahound, Ayesha and, significantly, their journeys of return – the Imam's journey, on Gibreel's shoulders, back to the dreamed-of city below the postcard mountain; Mahound's triumphant journey back to Jahilia from the oasis of Yathrib; and Ayesha's journey to Mecca, through the Arabian Sea, a symbolic return to the roots of Islam. The city of return, a metaphorical Jerusalem in the context of Mohammed's spiritual Night Journey, is never achieved by the dreamer himself. If the Imam's and Mahound's returns frustrate the idea of a stable point of origin, since they radically transform the cities to which they travel back, Ayesha's and the pilgrims' journey to Mecca is realized in the ambiguous event of their passage across the bed of the Arabian sea. Migration, return and pilgrimage are juxtaposed, in this way, through Gibreel's multiple catoptric itineraries.

Underlying the Titlipur narrative in the text is the opposition between the tree (or the village) and the route (or the journey towards a city). Titlipur has grown in the shade of an enormous banyan-tree, 'a single monarch' that has ruled the village with its 'multiple roots' for so long that it is impossible to differentiate between the tree and the village (222). If Saladin's birth tree in Bombay is felled to help pay for his life in London, the Titlipur banyan tree just as meaningfully burns down upon Mirza Saeed's return to the village from the pilgrimage that both has and has not ended. The pilgrimage is thus at once an outward journey, a migration that necessarily denies the notion of roots, associated with the idea of the village in the text, and a metaphorical journey of return, understood as an incessant process, a perpetual search for a city that is both accomplished and unaccomplished in the undecided event of the parting of the Arabian sea.

In the catoptric correspondence between the parting of the sea and Partition, the pilgrimage can be read as the national search for integration, which ironically bifurcates, or partitions, into the *hajj* (Muslim) and the *padyatra* (Hindu). As a result, Partition, like the miracle of the parting waters, is an invisible and unbelievable event, since it produces a split along discursive lines, and yet also, an event that has and will continue to produce division.

The parting of the novel's urban topography into dreamed-in and dreamed-of cities also parallels that of Mikhail Bulgakov's *The Master and Margarita* (1966), a novel Rushdie identifies as a major influence. *The Master and Margarita* shuttles between Stalinist Moscow, which satirizes the city's literary society, and Jerusalem, specifically, the story of the interrogation, trial and execution of Yeshua Ha-Nostri (Jesus). The Jerusalem narrative consists of several intermittent sections, each of which is articulated by a figure in the Moscow narrative. The latter focuses on the Soviet literary elite articulating an image of the city as a collection of institutions, such as the Variety Theatre or the literary establishment, MASSOLIT, whose name evokes the idea of literature that is produced uniformly and *en masse*, and echoes many communist neologisms.[2] It also conjures the image of an imposing, *massive* and yet seductive 'Proper' city, comparable to Saladin's *Ellowen Deeowen*. The 'underground' spaces of Brickhall's Club Hot Wax and the Shaandaar Café mirror the modest basement of the Master's flat buried beneath the expensive and exclusive restaurant of MASSOLIT, various theatre offices and the flats of literary critics. The two urban narratives of Moscow and Jerusalem reflect each other in their common motifs, allusions, events and themes, which further assert a parallelism of Roman power and Stalin's regime, particularly through the figures of the angelic/devilsh Yeshua and Woland. As outsiders to the cities they enter, both these characters disrupt the established urban order as Saladin and Gibreel would do in *The Satanic Verses*.

Bulgakov, as Andrew Barratt suggests, lived an extraordinary double life as a writer, divided between official and secret, subversive, writing activities – a condition, which Aleksandr Solzhenitsin has described as 'literary schizophrenia' (Barratt 1987, 39). In his novel, a number of characters suffer from the same 'catoptric' condition, reflective of the fundamental discrepancy in state communist rhetoric between words and deeds, which effectively renders existence into a collective pretence. In the Moscow narrative, Bezdomny is diagnosed as a schizophrenic. He splits into two Ivans – the Old and the New – or between disbelieving and believing in the existence of Jesus and the devil, or between writing his conformist poetry and continuing the Master's novel. In the Jerusalem narrative, Pilate suffers from a notably *asymmetrical* illness: hemicrania, a form of chronic headache marked by continuous pain on one side of the face, which is reflective of his hesitation between his duty as a governor of a Roman province and his desire to condone Yeshua.

This duplicitous logic saturating the world of Stalinist Moscow is radically interrupted by the unexpected appearance of the Devil, or Woland, and his suite, who turn the city on its head by engaging in what I referred to earlier as 'satanic versifying'. They transform the chairman of the Variety Theatre into a suit that is constantly writing something and pompously pretends to be busy with important matters or they have the workers at the branch office of the Theatrical Commission sing, in a collective involuntary reflex and beyond exhaustion, 'The Song of the Volga Boatmen', thus, in effect, over-fulfilling the wish of the branch director to organize a choral society (Bulgakov, 217–22).

Another important similarity between Bulgakov's and Rushdie's works is the projection, on the one hand, of Moscow and of London/Bombay as decentred, chronologically disrupted contemporary urban narratives that contain supernatural elements, and on the other, of Jerusalem and of Jahilia as contrastingly linear, realist and historicized urban narratives. This carnivalesque inversion frustrates the expectations of a miraculous account of the birth of Christianity or Islam, while inserting figures from Christian or Muslim cosmology into Moscow and London. In Bulgakov's novel, Woland and his retinue speak and act like party activists, but with an ever-greater conviction, which takes these words and deeds, only too familiar to Muscovites, to the point of absurdity, thereby causing communist rhetoric to fold in on itself. It is this strategy that Rushdie re-fashions in order to turn insults into strengths. Both novels revisit and reclaim religion as a narrative in the stories of, respectively, Jesus and Mohammed, in an interrogation of the political order.

Cartographic Re-Inscriptions of Gender and Sexuality

The Satanic Verses engages with a critique of women's status in Islam, undertaking, for instance, as part of its subversive project, a satanic (di-)versification of such practices as the sequestration of women. Although the book attempts, to some extent, to 'liberate' Muslim women from seclusion and veiling, and thus echoes, since it is written in the West, the Orientalist practices, defined by Gayatri Spivak, as 'white men saving brown women from brown men' (1988, 297), it successfully articulates a necessarily ambiguous specular paradigm that counters women's 'double colonization' through its construction of urban space. However, as I will argue, this project is limited, almost without exceptions, to the narrative of Jahilia. In the greater part of the novel, the defence of women's causes seems to fail, as indicative, for instance, in the number of female characters who die from various causes: Rekha Merchant, Tavleen, Rosa Diamond, Alleluia and Elena Cone, Pamela Lovelace, Mishal Akhtar, the Madam of The Curtain and the Prophetess Ayesha. The novel's characterization of women, as related to its urban configurations, often splits along specular lines. Female figures are either unstable, lacking confidence and searching, like Alleluia Cone, for an intangible, otherworldly city of ice, or they stand, like the Prophetess Aeysha, for the idea of an absolute, pure urban goal. Playing the roles of fanatic religious leaders, or symbolically standing for the body of empire or for the notion of urban 'roots', the female characters embody ideas that dangerously seduce or even hold the protagonists captive.

The catoptric duplicity of the novel's doppelgängers, as reflected in the parallel split of London into visible and invisible and the division of the novel's urban cartography into dreamed-in and dreamed-of cities is informed, to a considerable degree, by women's specularized images. For example, residual traces of Saladin's alternative translations of self and of Gibreel's personality splits can be discerned in the doubling of women's names, such as 'Hind', across the catoptric frontier of dreams and travelling, or in their multiplication, such as the one that the name 'Ayesha' undergoes.

Hind and Ayesha reflect certain versions of the protagonists' urban selves and stand for ideas that are simultaneously tempting and dangerous.

The seductions of the alternative route, of the self's other, which inform the twin-ness of the novel's protagonists, also become apparent in Rushdie's comment on the character of Saladin as his own, fictional, inverted image:

> I love going back to India. . . . But the decision I have made for the moment about my life is that I don't want to go and live there. However, then it's very interesting to have a fictional character who makes the opposite decision. . . . You send him off to do it and you don't have to do it yourself. I think that certainly had a lot of interest for me, in the Chamcha character (CSR, 121).

Notably, Rushdie refers to his character by the Anglicized version of his name, thus once again, consciously or subconsciously, distancing himself from Saladin's choice of return, while the phrase 'you don't have to do it' reveals a degree of obligation with which Rushdie regards such a homecoming. While the novel places a post-structuralist emphasis on the decentred and plural subject, as highlighted, for instance, in Saladin's choice of Lucretian identification, the protagonists' journeys and dreams reveal a degree of anxiety that accompanies this choice, in the case of Saladin, or that aims to reconcile the plurality of selves, in the case of Gibreel. These anxieties find outlets mostly in the *margins* of urban representation. It is through women and the female body that the protagonists, consciously or subconsciously, seek what Jacques Lacan refers to as 'orthopaedic totality'– the self-fiction that the subject assumes during the Mirror Stage in order to ward off its otherwise inevitable fragmentation into self and other/mirror image ([1949] 2004, 5).

As Catherine Cundy argues, the satanic verses incident participates in the novel's central concern with the importance and power of women (1997, 67). The text undertakes to expose their inferior status both in *al jahiliyya*, in pre-Islamic times, and in Mahound's, or Islamic, Jahilia. This is made evident in, respectively, the comment of Mahound's first wife – 'It isn't easy to be a brilliant, successful woman in a city where the gods are female but the females are merely goods' (SV, 118) – and in Mahound's repudiation of the Jahilian Grandee's offer to accept the three goddesses as Allah's archangels. Ghada Karmi proposes that Islam can be seen as an agent of change in an Arabian society that was already moving in the direction of patriarchy (1996, 79). In his offer, for instance, Abu Simbel is clearly motivated not by a desire to empower Jahilian women, but by a fear of losing the city's patron deities as a magnet for pilgrims.

The novel celebrates the idea of doubt – both religious and identificatory – as the opposite of absolute faith or a monologic articulation of identity. Strength is located in the critical ability to doubt certainties of all kinds and, even more radically, in the ability to compromise. Mahound's hesitation during the 'satanic verses' incident, specifically, his flirtation with the notion of polytheism as embodied in the three most worshipped goddesses of the city, therefore, constitutes, in the secular terms of the novel, a moment of strength.

It would seem that the novel juxtaposes monotheism and male sexuality on the one hand, and polytheism and female sexuality on the other, but such a facile antithesis is unsettled by the specular illusion of a second 'harem' in Jahilia, which appears after the city's submission to the new faith. As in *Midnight's Children*, brothels appear, in Rushdie's analysis, as the result of the sequestration of women. The brothel in *The Satanic Verses*, The Curtain, mirrors Mahound's harem at the oasis of Yathrib: as the twelve prostitutes enter their roles, the alliances in the brothel come to mirror the political cliques at the Yathrib mosque. The concept of the *hijab* becomes, in this way, a specular boundary between the harem and the brothel, or the sacred and the profane cities in the novel. The *hijab* has been associated, at once, with the sequestration *and* emancipation of Muslim women. It has participated both in Orientalist and in feminist discourses, while in the latter, it has been critiqued as a discursive trope of patriarchal control and re-articulated as a counter-discursive figure, symbolic of the resistance against the Western gaze. Both the veil and the harem have been read as phenomena that introduce sexual segregation and seclusion. For instance, Fatima Mernissi argues that Muslim sexuality is territorial, its regulatory mechanisms consisting primarily in a strict allocation of space to each sex, yet, ironically, sexual segregation intensifies what it is supposed to eliminate: the sexualization of human relations (2003, 489–91). Similarly, Sarah Graham-Brown suggests that the segregation of space and control over the visibility of women have been forms of patriarchal control that emphasize the need to channel and contain women's sexual power (2003, 503). However, as Meyda Yeğenoğlu notes, the practice of veiling and the veiled woman have figured in the Orientalist imagination, specifically, in speculations about what might be hidden behind the veil. Therefore, veiling has been embraced by many Muslim women as a practice of resistance: 'the veiled woman can see without being seen' (2003, 546). In colonial discourse, the harem has been articulated either as the space of untrammelled sexual pleasures or as the space of promiscuity, in which women are forced to live in conditions akin to those of a brothel (Graham-Brown, 503). Seen out of context, the Jahilian brothel appears both unnecessarily provocative, in its scandalous equation of the Prophet's wives with prostitutes, and Orientalist, in its confluence of harem and brothel. What the text seeks to scandalize, however, are the antitheses in the imagination of Muslim women – the Orientalist split imagination of the harem as erotic or imprisoning and the patriarchal codes of Jahilian society where women become associated either with purity or with profanity. To this end, the novel revisits the hijab as a specular frontier that separates Muslim women and Muslim men, Muslim women and European men, or East and West. The erotics of oneness, of monotheism and of the Ovidian articulation of identity is subverted through the specular split in the idea of the city, which in this way, invites resistance both *against* and *through* the hijab. Within a year of the brothel's existence, the twelve prostitutes have become so skilful at their impersonations of Mahound's wives that their previous identities begin to fade away, their 'edges' blur and their images appear 'doubled, like shadows superimposed on shadows' (SV, 382). This is, literally, the visual effect of patriarchal and Orientalist 'descriptions', and it mirrors the metamorphosis of immigrants into 'aliens' at the Detention Centre.

When Mahound's soldiers close the brothel, they attempt to symbolically unveil its innermost secret, the identity of the Madam of The Curtain. Instead, they find a dead, three-feet-tall woman who looks like a 'big doll' (SV, 388). Mahound, it seems, has destroyed his profane other, his critical mirror, but the unveiling has ironically only revealed another veil. The Curtain remains an urban space of resistance, reflective of the emancipating status of the hijab: Yeğenoğlu takes her cue from Lacan in arguing that the very act of representing the veil is only ever represented as a reflection on a veil (Yeğenoğlu, 549).

Rushdie's novel, then, undoubtedly espouses women's causes and successfully critiques patriarchal and Orientalist constructions of femininity. It remains, however, at the same time, inscribed within others. It morphs, for instance, its urban cartography and the female body. The prominent Menippean motif of ideas' travels, tests and transformations is often articulated by the omniscient narrator in the form of the question: 'what kind of idea are you?' The women of whom this question is asked – Tavleen, Hind Simbel and the Prophetess Ayesha– all appear as the embodiments of absolute, uncompromising notions, which are further explicitly eroticized and act as temptations for the male characters. Tavleen, for instance, is associated with the margins of urban representation, interurban travel or specifically, the journey West and the fears that the protagonists associate with it. She is also, however, seductive. She is the suicide bomber responsible for the destruction of the plane and the death of most passengers, but her destructive power is symbolized by 'the 'arsenal' of her body, the 'grenades like extra breasts nestling in her cleavage, the gelignite taped around her thighs' (SV, 81).

Another woman of unyielding convictions, Hind Simbel, opposes most categorically Mahound's 'translation' of Jahilia into a city of a single god. Her obdurate resistance to urban transformation is also inscribed onto her body: while Jahilia decays, Hind's body remains unwrinkled and firm. Jahilians come to think of her, rather than her husband, as the city's 'living avatar' (SV, 361). At 60, Hind is still sexually voracious and has slept with every writer in the city. Her refusal to surrender Jahilia to Mahound, as contrasting with her husband's immediate admission of defeat, anticipates the analogous representation of urban fall in *The Moor's Last Sigh*, as we shall see in the next chapter. There, the last sultan of Granada, Boabdil, is reproached by his mother for yielding control of the city to the Catholic monarchs of Spain. In both novels, men are weaker than women in the defence of the cause of the many against the cause of the one. In the figure of Hind, however, the mobilization of female power, though subversive of such demonizing images of woman as the witch or the necromancer in the text (Hind is believed to be both), appears to be deployed in the service of a re-mythologizing gesture, instrumental to urban representation. Hind is portrayed as simultaneously an advocate and a symbol of urban pluralism.

In Hind, whose name evokes the Indian nation, the text seeks to demystify the concept of 'Mother India'. Hind is a duplicitous, decentred figure, split between Jahilia and London. If the Jahilian Hind is associated with predatory sexuality, the London Hind stands for the opposite extreme: she objects to her husband performing his 'obscene acts' upon her body (SV, 248). 'Mother India' further symbolically partitions into the idea of an 'imaginary homeland' in the Jahilian Hind and the concept of a diasporic 'gastronomic pluralism' (SV, 246) in the London Hind. Such demystifications, however, often lead to a caricaturing of women – a criticism often aimed at Rushdie's writing. Having accepted her homelessness in the 'demon city' of London, Hind Sufyan transforms her own body into a home by devouring the Indian dishes that she cooks. Gradually, she comes to resemble the 'wide rolling land mass' of the 'subcontinent without frontiers' (246).

Even as it strives towards, or is encouraged to positively symbolize, unlimited gastronomic migration, hybridity and pluralism, the 'Mother India' idea ends up a mere parody of a nostalgic return to 'home' cuisine.

Hind's cooking draws people from all over London, but she remains trapped within her own body.

Whereas Hind's boundless body serves to symbolize the tragic effects of inscribing the Indian subcontinent, cartographically or corporeally, into diasporic London, official London acquires the shape of a woman's breast. In the re-creation of Dickensian London at the Shepperton film studios, Saladin finds himself transfixed by a woman who exposes one of her breasts and offers it to him, pointing out that she has drawn on it the map of London. The metropolis 'summons' him but he manages to pull away. Saladin is thus held, momentarily, in the erotic spell of Empire, embodied in the figure of the anonymous woman, who is both eroticized and associated with mothering. The milk of the feminized Metropolis's imperial breast that 'nurses' her colonial subjects is poisonous, since the woman is compared to a cobra and Saladin needs to pull himself away from her fatal allure. In this way, urban space withdraws, in a *mise-en-abyme* fashion, first into the simulacrum of Dickensian London, and then, through the Podsnappian woman, who inhabits this simulacrum, into the map drawn on her breast. On his first flight to London, Saladin imagines that the aircraft is 'a metal phallus' and the passengers 'spermatozoa waiting to be spilt' (SV, 41). This postcolonial journey, though an inversion of colonial exploration, is still complicit with the long tradition of male travel, which Anne McClintock terms an 'erotics of ravishment' (1995, 22).

Saladin's catoptric double, Gibreel, is held captive by another woman's narrative sorcery. Like Tavleen, 88-year-old English woman, Rosa Diamond, into whose house Saladin and Gibreel are literally washed up after the explosion of the plane, inhabits the margins of urban representation. The protagonists' joint fall towards England from flight AI-420 and down a 'long, vertical tunnel' (SV, 6), a metaphorical birth canal, has them reborn through Rosa Diamond. Inscribed into the novel's map of inter-urban itineraries, the old insomniac woman stands for a temporary deviation from the characters' urban destination, the British metropolis. The web of her stories of Argentina, from which Gibreel cannot escape until her death, is characteristically self-contradictory. In Rosa's hallucinating mind, alternative visions of her life in Argentina clash with the recurring sameness of the imagination of the battle of Hastings and the ghost of William the Conqueror to produce a complex parody of the myth of English national origins as 'dating back' to the Norman conquest, but torn by alternative histories. Similarly, in his extensive commentary on the figure of Rosa Diamond, Homi Bhabha proposes that she represents the English *Heimat* or homeland, constituted through 'cracks and absences', which she tries to patch with the cultural memory of William the Conqueror and the battle of Hastings (1994, 167–68).

Whereas Gibreel is caught in a parody of imperial romance, Saladin flirts with the idea of the nation as embodied in the figure of the Queen. In the Detention Centre Hospital, he finds himself dreaming of making love to the Queen, the 'body of Britain, the avatar of the State' (SV, 169). Notably, these enticements both occur within the metropolitan margins. The male protagonists' journeys to London are necessarily conditioned by imperial seductions or tainted by the colonial legacy. It is in the breadth of non-urban space that nation/empire, in its feminine attire, is at its most dangerous and at its most brazenly beguiling. Rosa Diamond and the abstract figure of the Queen inform the text's specularly split, masculine subversive strategy of 'writing back'. On the one hand, Gibreel is entrapped by empire's last revelation, by empire as an aged idea, that is desperately holding on to old memories of a 'grandstand view' and of exotic adventure, praying for the Norman fleet to pass, once again, 'through her front door' (SV, 129–130). On the other, Saladin finds himself seduced by the body of empire as the essentialist idea of Englishness. His dream of sleeping with the Queen can be seen both as an expression of his desire to become one with this idea, to translate himself into a 'goodandproper Englishman', and of the need he feels to assert his masculinity against the land, as feminized in the image of the Queen. The dream betrays, at once, male megalomania and an acute fear of a loss of identity.

The doubling of female figures, in Rosa and the Queen, and in the London and Jahilian Hinds, mirrors the male protagonists' duplicity, as apparent in their conflicting realizations of postcolonial identity: Ovidian versus Lucretian. The instrumental role of female characters is also prominent in the multiplication of the name 'Ayesha'. In one of Gibreel's dream narratives, the Empress Ayesha is the Imam's enemy, who stands for History – an idea that the Imam's revolution aims to abolish. Srinivas Aravamudan notes that since 'Shi'ite Muslims are followers of Ali, the Prophet's son-in-law, whose caliphate was greatly undermined by civil war with Muhammad's favourite wife, Ayesha, it is entirely credible for the Khomeini figure to choose Ayesha as his devil' (Aravamudan 198).

In the Jahilian narrative, as we saw above, the Ayesha figure splits into two, wife and prostitute. We discussed the bifurcation of this figure as a specular strategy of subverting the erotics of oneness, yet, it is difficult to reconcile Ayesha as the Imam's enemy and the Jahilian split Ayesha with the prophetess in Gibreel's revelation of Titlipur. Gayatri Spivak argues that in Rushdie's attempt to write women into the narrative of history, we need to record an 'honourable failure'. She points out that Ayesha, the female counterpart of Mahound, lacks the existential depth of the businessman prophet and that to her the archangel sings in popular Hindi film songs: '[h]er traffic with him is reported speech' or 'mere play'. In comparison, Gibreel's speech through Mahound is, according to Spivak, 'high on the register of validity, if not verifiability' (1993, 223–24).

Sara Suleri suggests that Ayesha's extraordinary desirability is matched only by her chastity, her language is both imbecilic and prophetic, so that 'its very uncertainty enhances the power of seduction' (233). 'Everything will be required of us,' says Ayesha, 'and everything will be given' (SV, 233). This pronouncement convinces, for instance, Mishal Akhtar that once she has completed her journey to Mecca, her cancer will have disappeared. The pilgrimage to Mecca develops the idea of the city as an absolute, pure, transcendental goal. Ayesha symbolically stands for the concept of this spiritual journey. In his vision of the Prophetess, Gibreel flirts with the concept of oneness, while also finding himself seduced by the linear discourse of her route and her story.

Whereas women such as Ayesha, Hind, Tavleen and Rosa Diamond threaten masculine urban identity, female characters such as Alleluia Cone and Zeeny Vakil serve, by contrast, to comfort and assure it. The lovers of the protagonists, these two women mirror, respectively, Gibreel's London and Saladin's Bombay selves. Urban representation is most palpably polarized in the specular duplicity of Saladin's women. Pamela Lovelace, his English wife, is the inverted image of Zeeny Vakil, his Indian lover, just as London is the inverted image of Bombay in the metaphor of the upside-down watch. Pamela campaigns against the victimization of Dr Uhuru Simba, but refuses to see the similar circumstances of her husband's demonization. Like Alleluia, she is characteristically insecure: 'graceful like gazelles', but 'frail like porcelain' (SV, 59). She strives to escape her family background, rebelling against the traditional 'English' values that her father espouses and his legacy: her own voice, composed of tweeds, summer pudding, headscarves, hockey sticks, thatched houses, large dogs and philistinism (SV, 180). Having married Saladin in an act of defiance, she ironically finds herself in the role that she has so desperately tried to avoid, but which is so irresistibly attractive to him: the role of Britannia. Pamela is killed while attempting to expose the existence of witches' covens in the Metropolitan Police. She dies a death that is necessary for Saladin, symbolic of his rejection of the image of the "good and proper Englishman" and of his choice of a route to a re-configured Bombay. He remarks, 'I put down roots in the women I love' (SV, 59).

Saladin travels away from the British metropolis and towards the idea of the city as associated with Zeeny Vakil, a mother figure. This journey narrates the desire for return to the Imaginary order. Thus, early in the novel, when Saladin first touches Zeeny's breasts, she weeps 'hot astounding tears the colour and consistency of buffalo milk' (SV, 53). To his translated, anglicized self, her breasts are 'forbidden' (SV, 61). As Catherine Cundy and Sabah A. Salih note, Zeeny is a person of several impressive accomplishments: a medical doctor, a part-time art critic, who mirrors Rushdie's own views on artistic eclecticism, and a committed political activist, working with the Bombay homeless and the victims of the 1986 Union Carbide chemical disaster in Bhopal (Cundy 79). She appears to be 'over-qualified' for her role in the novel. Her achievements are, however, subordinated to her role as the 'saviour of Saladin's Indian self' (Cundy, 79), his return to 'Salahuddin'.

The Satanic Verses, however, exposes a number of mirror associations, fixed in colonial discourse, while employing the same, catoptric *modus operandi*, to subvert them, rather than to merely break the Eurocentric mirror that produces an inverted image of the Same. The glass skin of the phantasmal migrant creature at the Detention Centre Hospital, Glass Bertha, vividly illustrates this duplicitous postcolonial predicament. Simply smashing up her encaging skin, as the immigration officers do, would not release her from her mirror imprisonment. As the novel demonstrates instead, the glassy metaphors of the descriptors reflect their own negation and bring into being new cities and identities.

Chapter 4

War of the Worlds: Bombay Diptychs and Triptychs in *The Moor's Last Sigh*

Traditionally associated with European, and particularly Christian, culture, the diptych and triptych forms are commonly employed to stand for the interconnectedness of and dynamics between, respectively, two or three images or ideas. Both are often and readily translated into literary criticism as metaphors for interrelated paradigms or texts. The concept of the diptych relies on a correspondence between the media of text and painting, between the linguistic and the visual arts. In Ancient Greece and Rome, *diptych* stood for a book or a notebook, consisting of two writing tablets hinged together as well as to a hinged pair of painted or carved panels. As artistic formats, diptychs involve the construction of meaning through the pairing of images such as double portraits, tapestry panels, altarpiece wings, images in manuscripts, printed books or sculptural groupings. A major element of the diptych format is the principle of duality, which invites the comparison of juxtaposed images as each other's reflections, inversions or variations. Both diptychs and triptychs can be interpreted as visual books that may include an outside image, painted on the reverse of the two side wings. The specificity of the triptych as a format is its inclusion of an inside central panel, which is structurally most significant and thus presupposes a position to which all other images direct the viewer's eye.

As this chapter demonstrates, there is an inherent catoptricity in the diptych and the triptych forms through which urban configurations in *The Moor's Last Sigh* challenge the ideas of spatial/temporal linearity and unity of vision. On the one hand, the idea of the city in the text is informed by a reciprocity between verbal and visual media. The historical and geographical configurations of the city dynamically reflect the artistic periodizations and thematic divisions of the paintings of Aurora Zogoiby, the mother of the protagonist and narrator, Moraes Zogoiby. In her art, Aurora recurrently employs the diptych format in order to envisage the city. Yet, the narrator is also a 'narrated figure' (MLS, 301) in these paintings, and the painter is also a character in Moraes Zogoiby's tale. On the other hand, while in Christian iconography, both diptychs and triptychs foreground unity as a structural and thematic principle, the di/triptych nature of Rushdie's text enables, as we shall see, the existence of mutually contradictory narratives, the unsettling of boundaries and the suspension of linear temporality. The urban cartographies of the novel open up the order of the map, which is no longer a horizontal surface, but a dynamic, folding and unfolding, synchronic and diachronic configuration. Whereas both text and painting attempt to frame the narrative, the itinerant characters 'slip' from one panel into another and the city expands and contracts across panel frames.

Published six years into the *fatwa*, provoked by his satire on exclusivist fictions of Islam in *The Satanic Verses*, *The Moor* remains one of Rushdie's darkest novels, marked prominently by the theme of captivity. This theme would also inform his subsequent novel, *Fury*, where, as Chapter 6 demonstrates, it develops into a broader exploration of the afterlife of Rushdie's fictions. Nevertheless, *The Moor* displays the author's extraordinary intellectual vivacity, attempting a sweeping revisionist historical fresco of Christian, Jewish, Islamic and Hindu relations in twentieth-century Bombay. As we saw in the Introduction, the city was radically transformed in the early 1990s, as a result of the rise of the Hindu right, and renamed *Mumbai* in an attempt at a reclamation of a pre-colonial, vernacular urban identity, yet one that, for Rushdie and many other commentators, has effectively sought to reformulate the city within linguistically chauvinist, regionally primordial and ethnically pure terms (Appadurai 2000, 629). For Rushdie, this forceful metamorphosis of the city has destroyed its classical 1950s–1960s' image of free-spirited, cosmopolitan openness (SATL, 196), explored in his earlier Bombay novel, *Midnight*. The two novels have often been juxtaposed in critical discussions, which envision the texts' interconnectedness as a continuum (Baker 2000, 51), an enduring conversation or a parallel history (Moss 1998, 122). The two novels' Bombays can also be seen as forming an intertextual diptych, which parodies the form of the sequel and evokes, instead, the tumultuous journey of Dorothy Gale in director Victor Fleming's *The Wizard of Oz* (1939). In his monograph on the film, Rushdie notes the 'rhyming' in its plot: the paralleling of characters in Kansas with those in Oz, the echoes of themes bouncing back and forth between the monochrome and the Technicolor worlds (WO, 40). In a similar way, characters are translated across the boundary/frame between the two Bombays – most notably, A(a)dam Braganza undergoes a negative transformation from being the heir of India's midnight promise, its hopeful future, in *Midnight*, to a representative of the new generation of corporate Bombay in *The Moor*. Adam symbolically steals Moor's role as Abraham Zogoiby's 'legitimate' successor and becomes one of those responsible for the destruction of the city. The continuity of urban ancestry thus relies on 'fraudulent' ties and whereas *Midnight* celebrates Saleem's mongrel self, *The Moor* foregrounds the adulteration of the ideal of hybridity. Adam and the urban generation he represents are impostors: they need to self-destruct, so that the city can be born again. In a mirror image of Dorothy's passage, the colourful Oz has been replaced by a sharply divided, black-and-white, Kansas-like landscape.

The Moor's Bombay is situated, spatially and temporally, *between* the Indian port of Cochin and the Spanish village of Benengeli – landscapes that not only invite historical, mythological and aesthetic comparisons with the central urban panel, but also ones that reconfigure it by mirroring and reiterating its themes. Like the side panels of a pictorial triptych, Cochin and Benengeli flank Bombay. The text's di/triptych urban configurations – thematic and narrative, artistic and geomorphic, and geographical and historical – intersect, interact and transform each other.

In Rushdie's panoramic/textual triptych, modern Bombay encounters a simulacrum of medieval Moorish Spain. This utopian/heterotopian 'Mooristan/Palimpstine' is an idealized place of intercultural tolerance and 'home' for the Moors, which the narrator, Moraes Zogoiby, also known as 'Moor', and his mother, the artist Aurora Zogoiby, repeatedly attempt to re-articulate in text and painting. Moor begins his story at a fortress in the Andalusian village of Benengeli, where he is imprisoned by the artist Vasco Miranda in the early 1990s. Like Scheherazade, Moor has to sustain his captor's interest in order to stay alive. From this position at a Mooristan denied (as we shall see, the ideal of Mooristan/Palimpstine is frustrated in the village of Benengeli), he looks back at the story of his family and the history of India and his home city, Bombay, from the beginning of the twentieth century to his captivity and subsequent escape.

The title of the novel points to the legend of the Christian re-conquest of Granada in 1492. Allegedly, the Moorish ruler Boabdil sighed in despair as he cast a last glance at the city he had just lost to the Catholic monarchs of Spain, Fernando and Isabella. In this way, the title of Rushdie's text encapsulates the moment of Granada's fall that becomes the prism through which the narrator articulates the violent history of post-Independence Bombay. Stilled at the scene of the Moor's last sigh for his city, the title provides an image that serves as the exterior panel of Rushdie's fictional cartographic triptych and guides the reader's understanding of the central urban panel inside.

Rushdie's Moorish Granada is a sentimentalized urban landscape, a place of tolerance and enlightenment that is seen to have been disrupted by the Christian re-conquest. Yet, as Richard Fletcher notes, although the inter-action between Islamic and Christian civilizations in the medieval West was extremely fruitful, Moorish Spain was more often a land of turmoil than it was a land of tranquillity as evinced, for instance, by the feuding Berber tribesmen, the *taifa* statelets of the eleventh century and the Moroccan fundamentalists who succeeded them. The tolerance of the 'magnificent Emirate of Cordoba' is also revealed as a myth in the massacre of the Jews of Granada in 1126, while the learning with which it has often been associated was almost exclusively concentrated within the 'tiny circles of the princely courts' (1994, 172–74). Rushdie himself acknowledges that Moorish Granada existed on the basis of an Islamic imperialism (CSR, 156).

The novel borrows a further legend from medieval Spanish history, which bears upon the tale of the protagonist: the story of El Cid Campeador, the mercenary soldier, hero of Spanish national mythology. Whereas El Cid has been extolled as a crusading warrior who waged wars of re-conquest against the Moors, in his time, there was hardly any sense of nationhood, crusade or re-conquest in the Christian kingdom of Spain. El Cid (Rodrigo Díaz) was a successful professional soldier, who was as ready to fight alongside Muslims against Christians and vice versa (Fletcher 1989, 4). Rushdie's novel juxtaposes an idealized Moorish Granada and an internally torn version of the Cid's Spain to look upon Bombay and its grand-scale Hindu–Muslim antagonisms that lead to an urban Armageddon.

The protagonist and first-person narrator, Moraes Zogoiby, embodies the elements from both myths. Disowned by his mother, he is banished from his Edenic Bombay into the world of Bombay Central, where he is caught between the city's warring Hindu and Muslim gangs, serving both before he is forced to flee the city. He is also a Moor figure, nostalgically recreating his city in narrative. The text appropriates conflicting myths of the medieval Spanish past alongside components of their official, historically verified versions, thus problematizing both the authenticity of historical accounts and the sentimental wish for return to the golden-past city. Ironically, what breathes life into the story within is a sigh, an expression of grief and desperation. The novel parodies the nostalgic myth of a Golden Age of peaceful Christian–Muslim coexistence. It situates the story at a moment *outside* the longed-for city of Granada but, at the same time, fixes the gaze upon it.

The novel's tectonic and catoptric urban configurations interact in and through the form of the triptych. Catoptrically speaking, the central urban panel representing Bombay is dynamically refracted through the narratives of Cochin and Benengeli, while all three spatio-temporal scenes of the novel point to and reconfigure what we have referred to, metaphorically, as the outside panel: the moment of the Moor's last sigh for his city. The text's triptych form is also tectonically subversive in reconfiguring an Orientalist three-fold understanding of Indian history. Barbara and Thomas Metcalf note that Indian history was forged in a framework created by the British as they themselves devised a national history for their own emerging nation:

> Central to their image of themselves, as well as to their image of what they came to see as a backward but incipient nation, was what the historian David Arnold has called the Orientalist 'triptych' of Indian history. In this vision, ancient 'Hindus' had once created a great civilization. With the advent of Islamic rulers in the early thirteenth century, Indian culture rigidified, political life gave way to despotism, and the gap between foreign 'Muslim' rulers and a native 'Hindu' populace of necessity made for a fragile structure. Moral arguments, particularly a focus on what became a caricature of Aurangzeb's 'intolerance', were central in explaining 'decline'. Stage three brought modern British colonial rule with its enlightened leadership, scientific progress, and – for some adherents to this vision more than others – tutelage to independence. This tripartite schema was explicit in much British writing, and it often underlay even anti-colonial Indian nationalist historiography. Even today it has been tenaciously persistent as unrecognized 'common sense' in historical writing; and [has been] treated as fact in Hindu nationalist ideologies. (2002, 2–3)

It is between the historiographical 'layers' or 'frames' of this colonial discursive triptych that Rushdie's characters find themselves trapped. In the novel, the Hindu nationalist movement, led by Raman Fielding, taps into Bombay's geological accretions of antagonism, articulating a fiction of an ethnically pure city. Abraham Zogoiby, the upholder of a rival claim to Bombay, engages in similar excavations, but in order to unearth the city's profitable secrets and to play upon Hindu–Muslim animosity. In eventually colliding with each other, Bombay's warring urban fictions explode the very Orientalist triptych of history out of which they have risen. The tripartite cartography of the novel – Cochin, Bombay and Benengeli – offers a horizontal re-envisioning of the vertical/geological/historiographical triptych articulated in Orientalist discourses. Bombay negotiates its present on the borderline, a seismic fault line, between past and future hegemonic narratives, respectively, colonial (in Cochin) and global capitalist (in Benengeli).

Moor's story begins in the port of Cochin, historically, a strategic point on the Europeans' routes of discovery and trade as the first European settlement in India, founded by Vasco da Gama in 1502. Here, in the many conflicts of the day, the narrator historicizes the collision between Abraham Zogoiby's and Raman Fielding's fictions of Bombay, developed in the central panel. Cochin's political and religion-fuelled divisions are mirrored on the scale of the family and the self: nationalism versus anglophilia, religion versus secularism, Christian versus Jewish, pro-British versus Communist and discourse versus praxis. The divisions of Cochin's Christian community stand out in the celebration of Christmas – a unifying tradition that paradoxically causes segmentation. A mock-Bethlehem, Cochin is more akin to the Biblical Babylon, with its warring Christmas denominations: English Protestant, Catholic, Syrian Orthodox and Nestorian (MLS, 62–3). The British community of Cochin is represented by the clergyman, Reverend Oliver D'Aeth, whose photophobia and Anglican Christianity are at odds with the Indian 'Christianity of Uncertainty': 'the gentle reasonableness of the Church of England [is met] with great clouds of fervent incense and blasts of religious heat' (MLS, 96). The idea of the Indian heat dogging Oliver D'Aeth reflects the image of the enveloping 'foreignness', surrounding the English enclaves of Fort Cochin and the Indian Ocean, encroaching on the illusion of England, created by the British on an Indian shore (MLS, 95).

Looking back at the period around Independence, the narrator thematizes in the Cochin panel the origin of the grand-scale conflicts that would lead to the destruction of Bombay. Paul Brass notes several tensions, particularly relevant to *The Moor*, in Indian political culture, shortly after Independence. First, while the leadership of the country respected British political traditions, some (especially India's first Prime Minister, Jawaharlal Nehru) were also influenced by the Soviet model. Secondly, while the leaders self-consciously maintained many features of the colonial legacy, they realized that those had to be adapted to the social structure of Indian society. Thirdly, many politicians, who proclaimed their adherence to secularism, actually harboured Hindu communal sentiments. Finally, although soon after Independence, the leading opposition parties were the Communists and the Socialists, these ideologies bore little relation to the social structure of Indian society (2001, 2–17). In the novel, the nationalist/pro-British conflict between Francisco and Epifania, Moor's great grandparents, also divides their sons, Camoens and Aires. Rushdie shows the blind spots of both positions: Francisco announces that the British must go, while standing 'beneath the oil-paintings of his suited-and-booted ancestors' (MLS, 18). Epifania continues to believe in 'the omnipotent beneficence of the British' even after the Russian Revolution, World War I and the Amritsar massacre (MLS, 22). In Francisco, Gandhi's 'insistence on the oneness of all India's widely differing millions' (MLS, 22) and Nehru's internationalist modernist building project combine to produce an idealistic, Quixotic quest that is doomed to failure.

At first a follower of his father, Camoens later embraces communism, only to find out that it is 'not the Indian style' (MLS, 31). Through the figure of Camoens, Rushdie critiques the emerging Indian nation's imitation of foreign models, which results in a discrepancy between rhetoric and practice. Camoens, a veritable personification of Indian political life around Independence, tries on various roles. He is a 'millionaire flirting with Marxism' and 'a nationalist whose favourite poems [are] all English'; he is also equally convinced that 'the British *imperium* must end and the rule of princes along with it' (MLS, 32–3). Finally, Camoens turns to Nehruvian ideals, business and technology, progress, modernity and the city, but wears Gandhi-style clothes.

Cochin, Bombay and Benengeli are linked through Nehru's ideas in the figure of Moor himself. Nine months to the day before he was born, Moor's mother had spent a night with Jawaharlal Nehru (MLS, 177). Respectively, Moor's life follows the history of his country and his home city, Bombay, by virtue of a tentative, illegitimate genealogical link. Moor carries the misbegotten line of Nehru's political ideas – a narrative that parallels, as we shall see, the transformation of the Edenic Malabar-Masala Bombay into Bombay Central and the adulteration of the ideal of Moorish Granada into the hellish ghost town of Benengeli. Rushdie looks for the roots of Bombay Hindu–Muslim hostility in the secular ideology existing at Independence. Historically, secular nationalists emphasized the need to remove religion and the sense of community from the centre of Indian politics and to establish the independent Indian state as a neutral force standing above these antagonistic forces (Brass, 229). Brass argues that the secular ideology itself, together with the persistent centralizing drives of India's state leaders, has also been responsible for the failures to resolve the political problems of non-Hindu minorities, which has contributed to the rise of the militant Hindu nationalist movement (192–93). In the novel, the politics of state centralization and the failure to recognize religious pluralism lead to the persistence of Hindu Muslim antagonistic sentiments in Bombay.

The resultant urban instability, however, is construed by the characters as symptomatic of an urban malaise, rather than as the very condition that makes the idea of the inclusive city possible. Such diagnoses, premised on essentialist notions of place, at which Rushdie levels his critique, lead to attempts at 'healing' or 'beautifying' the city. Communal divisions, the product of the cumulative understanding of the city as a rigid, uni-temporal structure, literally 'grow out' of the land, causing tectonic disturbances and, eventually, urban fall. The mutually antagonistic fictions, which aim to beautify the city, rely on the idea of what A. K. Ramanujan terms the *orthogenetic* city. As opposed to the *heterogenetic* city, anticipating the Foucauldian notion of the *heterotopia*, the orthogenetic city is organized around the idea of moral order, placing an emphasis on cultural homogeneity and allowing no possibility of subversion and heresy. Cities of orthogenetic character, argues Ramanujan, were established by purposeful acts of founders (1999, 63–4). In the novel, the search for urban foundations, origins or purity is most characteristic of the Hindu fundamentalist fiction of the city, espoused by Raman Fielding and exhuming elements from the discursive Orientalist triptych of Indian history. In modelling Bombay in his image, Abraham Zogoiby also probes into its history, but ironically, to excavate its weaknesses and to manipulate them in order to achieve control of the city. Whereas Fielding's Bombay is unequivocally informed by the orthogenetic idea of the city, the negation of its heterogenetic character, Zogoiby's exploits the *understanding* of the orthogenetic city, without believing in it. The novel caricatures both the projects.

Bombay is partitioned in this way into two mutually hostile fictions, the articulations of exclusivist urban discourses that claim the city. This Bombay diptych is thus nestled within the narrative's overall triptych structure. Though the city is central within the national triptych, its centrality is problematized by the urban split: the criminal entrepreneurial da Gama-Zogoiby Axis manifestly dominates the urbanscape – Abraham Zogoiby's skyscraper towers over Bombay – while the Hindu nationalist Mumbai's Axis (MA) inhabits the city's underground, eroding the visibility of its rival. These competing urban fictions, the product of a continuous accretion of antagonism on the site of Bombay, are seen as plaguing its body. The idea of the ailing city is connected with the notion of the body politic, which informs Moor's narrative of Bombay. His unnaturally rapid growth parallels that of the city – he 'mushroom[s] into a huge urbane sprawl of a fellow', expanding without time for 'proper planning' (MLS, 161–62) like 'a skyscraper freed of all legal restraints, a one-man population explosion, a megalopolis'(MLS, 188). Moor's life mirrors that of his city: like Bombay, he ages prematurely.

The text's analogies between the concept of the body, particularly Moor's body, and the envisaged corporeality of Bombay lead to a mind/body split in the urbanscape:

In Bombay, my old hovel'n'highrise home town, we think we're on top of the modern age . . . , but that's only true in the high-rises of our minds. Down in the slums of our bodies, we're still vulnerable to the most disorderly disorders . . . . There may be pet pussies prowling around our squeaky-clean, sky-high penthouses, but they don't cancel out the rat-infested corruption in the sewers of the blood. (MLS, 145)

The metaphor of the mind's unawareness of the existence of the plagued body participates in the larger context of the urban narratives of Rushdie's texts – the visible/invisible or overground/underground urban split. The city's projected modernity conceals its rotten flesh and it is this urban duplicity that imprisons the protagonist. He finds himself caught 'between coats of paint' (MLS, 318); between the visible skyscrapers, built by Abraham Zogoiby, and Zogoiby's invisible dealings; between his Edenic life in Malabar-Masala Bombay and his imprisonment, first, in Bombay Central lock-up, and later, in his service to Raman Fielding. The competing fictions of the city lead to Bombay's Armageddon: as the art critic, Zeeny Vakil, remarks, 'The followers of one fiction knock down another popular piece of make-believe, and bingo! It's war' (351). The image of the dissected Bombay, informed by the notion of body politics, is laden with assumptions about what constitutes a better, or healthier, body (O'Conner 2002, 406). Respectively, the resulting 'war of the worlds' (MLS, 318) is between the two main 'Beautifiers of the City' (MLS, 350), Abraham Zogoiby and Raman Fielding: 'the long-awaited duel, the heavyweight unification bout to establish, once and for all, which gang (criminal entrepreneurial or political-criminal) would run the town' (MLS, 351–52).

The novel's Bombay diptych carries Rushdie's critique of the corruption in Indian politics and the ideology of religious fundamentalism. In terms of Michel de Certeau's dualistic model of the economy of urban space, Moor can be seen as an ordinary walker, who is trapped between the cartographies of the competing Concept Cities, produced respectively by Abraham's 'criminal entrepreneurial' aspirations for a Bombay of gold and Fielding's 'political criminal' ideology of a pure Hindu Bombay (MLS, 352). Through his invisible, underground dealings – bribery, blackmail, drug-trafficking, money laundering, flesh trade and smuggling of nuclear bombs – Abraham systematically amasses a fortune and earns control of the city. He begins by studying Bombay's history, disinterring the secrets of 'the great houses' networks of connections' (MLS, 181), purporting that the motivation for his excavations is merely humanitarian. The fiction of the ailing city, in which Abraham envelopes his underhand business deals, renders him a benevolent saviour of Bombay. This fiction is based on the assumption that the amputation the city allegedly needs is natural and scientifically justified. Geological accretions of antagonism are delineated in organic or physiological terms. The body of the city is seen as being traversed, manipulated and mutilated not only by the course of history, but also by the accumulation of discursive constructions of history. Abraham Zogoiby engages in mining the urban body/text.

The name of Moor's father ironically echoes the Old Testament Abraham, who is associated, most notably, both with the notion of fatherhood and with the readiness to sacrifice his own son. He is the anti-image of the 'National Father' (MLS, 168), fashioned after Mogambo, the villain of the Bombay *masala* movie *Mr India*, and, as such, the combination of 'a potpourri of elements' that is designed to appeal to the broadest range of audiences. Whereas the biblical Abraham is considered to be the patriarch of Judaism, Islam and Christianity, Abraham Zogoiby carefully chooses the nickname *Mogambo*, so as to avoid offending any of the country's communities and to succeed in manipulating all. Despite being a Cochin Jew, he craftily unites the Muslim gangs controlling the city's organized crime. Another ironic effect of the analogy between Zogoiby and the biblical forefather is the attempt of the former to secure a god-like position – his Cashondeliveri Tower reaches for the sky, while his initials (A. Z.) point to his despotic omniscience. Abraham's architectural giant, however, depends on its underground counterpart – an invisible city, built by the 'spectral' migrants from the countryside who have settled in Bombay after the latest census and whose very existence, therefore, is officially denied by the municipal authorities (MLS, 212).

The breach between Abraham's overground and underground dealings parallels the discordance between rhetoric and reality in post-Independence Indian political culture: characterized by an all-pervasive instrumentalism, which washes away party manifestos and effective implementation of policies in an unending competition for power, status and profit (Brass, 19). Rushdie's critique of the model of the state that exists for its own sake is succinctly contained in Vasco Miranda's Indian variation upon the theme of Einstein's General Theory: '*D equals mc squared, where D is for Dynasty, m is for mass of relatives, and c of course is for corruption, which is the only constant in the universe*' (MLS, 272, original emphasis). This equation appears to mobilize the forces of 'nature' to produce the explosive formula of Mumbai's shadow economy.

Abraham's fiction of Bombay, a tower of rhetoric built on the bodies of the ghostly inhabitants of the city, entraps Moor between its layers. His fall from Malabar-Masala Bombay into Bombay Central is presented as a descent from the sentence of his own story into an 'other, outlandish, incomprehensible text' that has been lying beneath it (MLS, 285). In this way, he is assimilated into the text of his father's fiction of the city: 'the stomach, the intestine of the city' (287). Having slipped, in what seems to be a carnivalesque inversion, off the upper and into the lower half of the city, Moor becomes part of another urban fiction: Raman Fielding's Mumbai. In an essay, Rushdie names Bal Thackeray, the head of the Shiv Sena, as the prototype for his fictional character, Raman Fielding (SATL, 196). In the novel, the leader of the militant Hindu movement, Mumbai's Axis, is a caricaturist, rather than an artist, similar to the head of the Shiv Sena, Bal Thackeray, who is a newspaper cartoonist-turned-politician. In a parody of Aurora Zogoiby's pictures, Fielding signs his caricatures with a little frog that is usually shown making some snide comment in the edges of the frame, which earns him the nickname *Mainduck*. The name *Fielding* is also meaningful in its echoes of the eighteenth-century English author, Henry Fielding (Bal Thackeray's name echoes that of William Makepeace Thackeray). Yet, Rushdie ironically relates the etymology of his fictional Fielding's name to the game of cricket. While according to legend, Raman Fielding's cricket-mad father used to wander round the Bombay Gymkhana, pleading to be given a chance to play – 'just one fielding?' (MLS, 230) – Raman rewrote his father's tale by telling journalists that his educated, 'internationalist' father had taken the name of 'Fielding' as a genuflection to the author of *Tom Jones* (MLS, 232). The two explanations of the name's origin symbolically reflect the divergence of Raman Fielding's cultural aspirations and political practice, while, in fact, both etymologies lead to the same country of origin: England. The fictional Fielding's belief in cricket as an essentially Hindu game mirrors the exclusivist politics of the Shiv Sena leader, who is known to have banned Pakistani cricketers from Indian territory (Ghosh 1998, n. pag.).

In the novel, cricket is at the roots of Fielding's political philosophy and his movement, Mumbai's Axis; his 'dedicated cadres' are grouped into 'elevens' and headed by a 'team captain' to whom absolute allegiance is sworn (MLS, 231). The structure of Fielding's hit-teams mirrors that of Shiv Sena membership, which is formed into small local groups called *shakas*, each led by a *dada* (Trousdale 2004, 100). Rushdie caricatures Hindu nationalism by portraying it as empty politics of game-playing, as a team involved in a meaningless war game that needs to undermine the value of sportsmanship in order to win. Hindu communal politics mirrors the us–them division of sports culture in which Fielding's crack teams are involved in nothing more than fan hooliganism. When choosing a name for his political movement, Fielding hesitates between a Hindu cricketer – 'Ranji's Army, Mankad's Martiners' – and a Hindu goddess – 'Mumba-Ai, Mumbadevi, Mumbabai', finally succeeding in 'uniting regional and religious nationalism' through the choice of the latter (231). The absurdity of the MA origins is in the combination of Hindu pride and the affiliation to a game introduced by the colonizer, especially since Fielding swears by a 'beautiful goddess-named Mumbai' as opposed to 'this dirty Anglo-style Bombay' (293). In comparing the structure of the Hindu nationalist movement to totalitarian hierarchies and militant alliances, Rushdie joins political commentators who have noted that the Shiv Sena's policies in Bombay display many of the symptoms of a murderous pre-fascist stage, which has produced a number of localized *Kristallnachts* in many urban sites (Brass, 354). Fielding's divisive politics construct an exclusivist image of Bombay that relies on essentialist representational practices: the fiction of ethnic purity and the belief in a golden age.

As the city is partitioned into Mainduck's and Mogambo's, the protagonist loses his name, his 'Moor'-ings, and is reduced to the metonymic nickname 'Hammer', when he becomes part of an MA crack team. The split in the Moor figure mirrors the split in the urban fabric. Through this urban diptych, Rushdie critiques the model of the city of international capital and corruption, on the one hand, and the city of religious fundamentalism, on the other: the model of the 'god-and-mammon' city (MLS, 351). The two shadow selves of the protagonist, Adam Braganza and Hammer, are the reciprocal embodiments of Abraham's and Mainduck's versions of the city. Adam Braganza, rising from the ranks of Abraham's 'Siodicorp' – 'the first financial institution from the Third World to rival the great Western banks in terms of assets and transactions' (MLS, 334) – replaces Moor as Abraham's successor. Thus, Abraham realizes the biblical motif of his name's etymology, ironically, by sacrificing his son to the new 'mammon' Bombay.

While in a formal sense, the narrative of Bombay occupies a central position in the text, its centrality proves to be an impossible goal. Centrality is what both Abraham's fiction of a corporate Bombay and Fielding's fiction of a pure Marathi Mumbai aim to achieve, thus producing, ironically, a bifocal city. After having continuously ground, scraped and abraded each other in this way, Bombay's economic and political monoliths spectacularly explode: Fielding's MA building and Abraham's Cashondeliveri Tower are both bombed and numerous buildings in the centre of the city are destroyed, leaving the streets covered in bodies. Bombay 'bl[ows] apart' and Moor wonders if the city is 'simply murdering itself' (371).

Bombay's Armageddon signals the destruction of the ideal of urban tolerance that is the catoptric analogy of the precedent of Arab Granada's fall to Catholicism: 'Just as the fanatical "Catholic Kings" had besieged Granada and awaited the Alhambra's fall, so now barbarism was standing at our gates' (MLS, 372). Though Rushdie has his narrator speak of collective guilt – 'the barbarians were . . . within our skins' (MLS, 372) – his attack, consistent with the politics of urban representation in his previous novels, is aimed at fundamentalist practices. Rachel Trousdale notes that as a secular Western-educated Muslim, Rushdie is both vehemently opposed to and unwelcome among the Hindu nationalists (97). It can also be argued that Rushdie is at pains to demonstrate even-handedness in his critique of Christian and Hindu fundamentalisms in this novel as well as of Muslim exclusivist fictions of the city in *The Satanic Verses*. The greatest villain and betrayer of the city, however, 'the biggest dada of them all' (MLS, 331), and thus the main object of critique in *The Moor's Last Sigh*, is Abraham Zogoiby: a Jew of Moorish origin, who stands at the head of a mostly Muslim axis of capitalist self-interest.

Bombay is successively shrunk to a series of incarcerating spaces that echo the author's condition under the fatwa – the prematurely aging body; the home, where Moor receives private tuition, and the prison, in which Moor is locked up after falling from grace with his parents. At the same time, the city invisibly and paradoxically expands with Abraham's secrets and the nightly assaults perpetrated by Mainduck's crack teams. Although urban space is flexible and self-rejuvenating and has the power to heal itself by diluting the spirit of 'adversarial intensity', it is also manipulable and defenceless against the rest of the country (MLS, 351). Bombay, the novel's triptych structure suggests, is imprisoned within modern India, just like Moor is imprisoned in his body and in his Scheherazade-like captivity within his own tale.

Moor embarks on a Quixotic quest to find the true Mooristan/Palimpstine, thus escaping Bombay's imprisonment, only to stumble upon an 'anti-Jerusalem' (MLS, 388) in the phantasmal Spanish village of Benengeli. Named after Cide Hamete Benengeli, the fictional author of Miguel de Cervantes' *Don Quixote*, the right-wing panel of the novel's triptych evokes the tradition of self-reflexive writing. More specifically, *The Moor's Last Sigh* intertextually re-envisions the idea of inhabiting fictions, of reading of oneself, which is the self-imposed fate of Cervantes' protagonist. The name of the only taxi driver willing to take Moor to Benengeli is 'Vivar', an echo of the hero of Spanish national mythology, celebrated in the popular ballad tradition for hundreds of years: Rodrigo Diaz, or El Cid Campeador, or the Cid of Vivar. In the novel, Vivar ('Vivar' is the birthplace of the Cid) is reduced from the legendary status of the Cid to the Hollywood stereotype of an incomprehensible 'Third-World' New York taxi driver: the 'broken argot of dreadful American films' (385) that he speaks is the only language in which Moor and he can communicate.

The text, particularly Moor's route to Benengeli, foregrounds the idea of urban inauthenticity, but not, for instance, as the concept of culture's or origin's mongrel nature (celebrated in all of Rushdie's work), but as usurpation, imposture and plagiarism. A series of stand-ins frustrate expectations and the image of Benengeli as an impostor replaces the ideal of Mooristan. Vasco Miranda's commercial art, an empty imitation of Aurora's paintings, is divested of their political significance. Benengeli's neighbouring town of thieves, Avellaneda, shares its name with that of Cervantes' slanderous contemporary, the author of the illegitimate sequel of the *Quixote*, the second book of Don Quixote's adventures published before Cervantes' own Part II.

Travelling to the city from which the Moors had been cast out in the fifteenth century, Moor finds himself in a kind of anti-Oz, a place where his only connection with Bombay is the plagiarist of his mother's art, Vasco Miranda, whose name is further suggestive of the project of discovery and colonial exploitation, through the allusion to the Portuguese explorer Vasco da Gama. Benengeli is a fraud, a geographical and historical elapse. On his passage from Bombay to Benengeli, the protagonist metaphorically 'falls' off the edge of the urban panel. The failure of Rushdie's protagonist to reach/achieve the urban goal asserts the novels' dissociation from epic fate and historic teleology, but it also points to Rushdie's critique of the destruction of the urban ideal through the negation of Mooristan/Palimpstine in Benengeli, a canvas/fiction that strips the notion of cultural inauthenticity of its inspiring potential.

In Benengeli, the idea of the cosmopolitan city of cultural hybridity is reduced to the trope of the discourse of globalization – the global village – and seen against the effects on place of contemporary multinational capitalism. In this way, Rushdie's extended critique of international commercial self-interest, as embodied by the unifying figure of Abraham Zogoiby, bridges Bombay and Benengeli to transform the latter into a grotesque vision of empty, anonymous multiculturalism. Such is the vision of Benengeli's Street of Parasites: it is full of non-Spaniards, who have no interest in the local customs and who behave more like city dwellers rather than village people. It is flanked by a lot of expensive boutiques, bearing international brand names, and eating places that offer all the national cuisines of the Western world. The Benengeli section of the text experiments with and deliberately exaggerates a variety of narrative conventions, such as those of the genre of detective fiction, to parody this culture of empty pastiche. Many of these conventions are interwoven in the episode of Moor's captivity in Vasco Miranda's fortress and are, thus, indicative of Moor's imprisonment in the same degraded culture.

Life Painting and the Woman Behind the Canvas

In its attempt to reclaim the past, early modern Indian art was informed by a marked paradox. This past, as Daniel Herwitz points out, was at once the product of colonialism's 'museumizing' imagination that petrified Indian cultural moments for the Western gaze and, yet, a past 'living on each and every street corner' (2004, 216). During its history, modern Indian art has offered various ways of 'working through' (ibid. 223) this contradiction, including a 'quest for indigenism', (Kapur 1978, 43), a Westernization, whether strategically selective, revisionist or wholesale, and a modifying eclecticism (Kumar 1999, 14–21). In the novel, these complexities in the experience of the postcolonial artist are opened out and lived as manifest urban contradictions through the figuring of 'living art'– art in the process of being lived and life in the process of artistic representation as dynamically mirroring and transforming each other. Bombay, in particular, and the urban trope, more generally, undergo a series of artistic transformations as articulated through the mediating commentary of the narrator on the paintings of his mother, the Bombay artist, Aurora Zogoiby. Her pre-Independence works, the charcoal sketches of British-ruled Bombay, foreground the colonial museumizing gaze by representing the city as paralyzed by the naval mutiny of 1946 when 'that super-epic motion picture of a city [i]s transformed overnight into a motionless tableau' (129). After veering between imaginary, mythological themes and a patriotic 'mimesis' (173) in the decades after Independence, Aurora finds a solution in making Moor the central figure of her work. Her treatment of the urban trope can be traced in her vision of the juxtaposition and/or collage of post-Independence Bombay and medieval Moorish Granada as connected through and foregrounding the Moor figure, itself inspired by history, biography and legend, by the last of the Nasrid Sultans, Boabdil, and her only son.

The city is thus doubly represented through the media of visual and verbal narratives. Urban representation is further complicated through the double status of Moor, a narrator and a narrated figure, and of Aurora, an artist and a character in Moor's narrative. On the one hand, it is Moor's perspective on the multiply refracted city to which the reader has access and which is, therefore, privileged. On the other hand, Moor's perspective is that of the viewer/model, who is also 'the talisman and centrepiece' (174) of the work of art and can only offer a 'wrong-side-of-the-canvas version of the finished work' (219). The novel's figurations of living art thus dramatize the postcolonial contradiction between a museumized and a lived/living past, allow a metadiscursive commentary on this contradiction in the forms of art criticism (Moor's commentary on Aurora's paintings) and life-writing (Moor's story of his life), and intervene, in this way, into the specific codes of visibility and visual subjectivity that have produced it. Living art portrays not only self/representation at work – in the mode of Diego Velazquez's *Las Meninas* (1656), cited in the novel as an influence, in its 'sight-lines', on one of Aurora's 'Moor' paintings (246) – but also art's stepping out of the canvas, acquiring a full-fledged existence, at once as and among its prototypes, and entering postcolonial historicity.

The novel responds to the construction of the fall of Granada as a visual event as well as a historical narrative that functions, stilled at the scene of the Moor's last sigh for his city, as the exterior panel of the story's cartographic triptych, as I argued earlier. The scene of Granada's surrender and the moment of the Moor's last sigh have been the object of many artistic works and reproductions, including most notably Spanish painter (and Francisco Goya's brother-in-law) Francisco Bayeu's ceiling fresco *Surrender of Granada* (1763) in the then new Royal Palace of Madrid (Bray 1996, 479) and, over a century later, the Orientalist paintings *Surrender of Granada* (1882) and *Sigh of the Moor* (1892) of the Spanish painter and museum official, Francisco Pradilla, commissioned for the Conference Room of Madrid's Palace of the Senate (Castro 2010, 244). These works have been on display as surrounded by, or part of, images of Christian and Spanish national iconography and stand as milestones in the careers of the artists, who were eventually to be promoted, respectively, to the status of court painter and to the position of director of Madrid's Museo del Prado (Tomlinson 2001, n.pag.). In Bayue's fresco, winged angels float above and oversee Boabdil's bowing capitulation outside the walls of Granada. Pradilla's paintings are the result of his historical research, including an 1879 trip to Granada, where he copied in watercolour a wooden relief entitled 'The Delivery of the Keys of the City of Granada by King Boabdil to the Catholic Monarchs' (Castro, 249). In his *Surrender of Granada*, a small downtrodden Muslim group headed by Boabdil on a black horse stand to the left facing an overwhelming Christian force, headed by the victorious monarchs (Isabella on a white and Ferdinand on a brown horse), that stretches all the way back to the walled city of Granada in the distance, while also appearing to overflow on the right. The two groups are emphatically distinct, further separated by a rutted track. Even Bobadil's horse seems to be bowing, while in the process of moving towards the absolutely still Christian side. It is also interesting to note that the main conflict seems to be between Boabdil and Isabella, as the contrasting colours of their horses seem to suggest, with a clear Manichean indication of white/Christian moral superiority, while the figure of Ferdinand is made less significant, placed behind that of Isabella and serving to symbolically reinforce her power. As María Castro points out, Pradilla's paintings have contributed to the spatial and psychological separation of Islam and the Christian West by projecting uniformity onto the Christian side and disorder and exteriority onto the Muslim figures (ibid., 254). Pradilla's *Sigh of the Moor* carries over from the previous painting's story of surrender to the narrative of Bobadil's 'afterlife', presenting the viewer with the backs of the Moorish exiles on the hill outside Granada, now barely distinguishable in the distance, with the faceless Moor 'museumized' for future generations at the point of an eternal departure.

Within the oeuvres of the artists, these works are also situated amid imagery of Christian and classical European mythology, including, in Bayue's case, a portable oratory, in triptych form, for the Príncipe de las Asturias (1785–1786) (Bray, 480). While Rushdie's novel cannot be seen as a direct response to this particular work, his re-contextualization of Granada's fall and the legend of Boabdil's sigh parodies the contexts and formats that have contained these events, thereby mounting on them a critique of the ideas of spatial/temporal linearity and unity of vision as structural and thematic principles in Christian iconography as well as of Ferdinand and Isabella's crusading Catholicism that has contributed to the othering of Islam. The novel's pictorial triptych ironically refashions the idea of a portable oratory. A travelling alterpiece that can be folded and unfolded, this form is also etymologically related to the orator's art of public speaking, where the motifs of portability and travel point to the simultaneous rigidity and re-constitutability of the oratorical message in new contexts. These motifs complement the protagonist's role of a modern-day half-Moorish, half-Jewish Luther – he has nailed the pages of his story, we are told, 'to the landscape in [his] wake' (433), thus repeatedly 'crucifying' it (3).

Moor's oratory, then, employs and subverts what could be seen as parallel overarching Christian narratives – the triptych format, the Catholic re-conquest of Granada and Roman Catholicism – that have articulated, contained and ritually reasserted the moment of their conquest of the other. Moor's oratory/'theses' enact symbolical returns to moments of rupture: to Granada in 1492 as a world crisis in intercultural and inter-religious tolerance, and to Wittenberg in 1517 as the beginning of a religious, cultural and political revolution that shattered the authority of the Church. Essentially diagnostic and reformative in its backward glances, Moor's quest is at the same time a parody of what Charles Taylor refers to as modern 'religious mobilizations'. While modern mobilizations, such as the forms of Christian and Hindu fundamentalisms that we are witnessing today, are characterized by symbolic returns to 'purer forms', Taylor argues that it is precisely these attempts to reclaim purer pasts that become, paradoxically, 'the sites of the most startling innovation' in their reaction to modern conditions, modern perceptions of threat and modern novelties (Taylor 2006, 281–82). While Moor's Lutheran oratory seeks to critique the Christian re-conquest of 1492 from within Christianity's own discourses and precedents of self-reformation, this position is itself open to critique. Luther, as Robert Glenn Howard argues, 'liberalized divine authority by offering it to each individual' and, though 'making the unerring texts accessible to individuals', by 'claiming that there was only one truth that was comm-unicated, Luther made fundamentalism possible' (Howard 2005, 91–2). The novel inhabits the very structures and formats it critiques, and one of these is the form of a modern, secular mobilization.

The Moor offers a further mock-triptych, at once pictorial and re-historicizing, in the narrator's theoretical division of Aurora's so-called 'Moor paintings' into three distinct stages: the 'early' pictures (1957–1977); the 'high' years (1977–1981); and the undated 'dark Moors' (MLS, 218). This linear periodization, however, is problematized by the narrator's frequent parallels between her paintings and those of a number of European artists – El Greco, Velazquez, Rembrandt, Goya, Munch, Picasso, Braque, Chirico and Dali – and the diversity of artistic movements with which they are associated. The list includes a sizeable presence of Spanish painters, reinforcing Rushdie's engagement with Spanish history; the Cubist and Surrealist genealogies of modern art; and Jewish affinities, such as those of Rembrandt, in his paintings and etchings of his Jewish neighbours, which break with the medieval stereotypical portrayal of the despized Jew (Nadler

2003, 221). In this way, Aurora's art comes to stand for a vision of Bombay and Indian history that interrogates traditional European art-historical narratives and periodizations as well as provides a subversive alternative to both Abraham Zogoiby's and Raman Fielding's exclusive versions of Bombay.

Rushdie (SATL, 205) cites as Aurora's prototype the French-trained Indian-Hungarian artist, Amrita Sher-Gil (1913–1941), who claimed to have come to appreciate Indian painting and sculpture through modern European art (Kumar, 16). In Sher-Gil's blending of a 'Western idiom' with 'Indian subject matter,' we can recognize Aurora's creative fusion of the Alhambra and Bombay's Malabar Hill in 'a re-imagining of the old Boabdil story' in a 'local' setting, with her son as the Moor playing a 'Bombay remix of the last of the Nasrids' (225). Yet, Sher-Gil is best remembered with the haunting, romanticized image of the Indian villager (Kapur, 127), including a painting entitled *Mother India*, exemplary, in its treatment of 'Indian subjects, stripped of all individuality and endowed with archetypal characteristics of suffering, warmth and dignity' (Herwitz, 226–27). By contrast, Aurora is 'the city girl, as much the incarnation of the smartyboots metropolis as Mother India [is] village earth made flesh' (139). As a post-independence Bombay artist of a Portuguese/Roman Catholic background, she could be more productively compared to one of the founders of the Bombay Progressive Artists' Group (1947), F. N. (Francis Newton) Souza, born in Portuguese Goa, in a Roman Catholic family (Kapur, 3). Aurora's interest in drawing 'religious pictures' for 'people who have no god' (220) as a parodic revision of her Catholic ancestry parallels Souza's passion for caricaturing Catholic rituals and the figure of Christ in his paintings. Aurora's modernist elitism, however, is a further parodic reflection of the Progressive Group's inability to live up to its first manifesto and bridge 'the artists' community and the people' (ibid., 9). Through her work, Rushdie exposes the post-Independence split of Indian society into 'modernizing elites and non-modernising subalterns' (Herwitz, 216), mirrored in the split in Bombay's fabric into Abraham's modern panoptic Cashondeliveri tower and Raman Fielding's 'stomach of the city'.

The multiple intertextual roles of the narrator/narrated figure of the Moor inform the development of the urban trope in the text. Moor is variously cast as Boabdil, El Cid, Othello, Cervantes or Don Quixote. The city's mirror canvases provide critical commentaries on parallel historical events and reconfigure the urban trope through a number of historical, geographical and artistic journeys. The re-imagining of the history of Bombay and India through these multifarious routes has led critics, such as

Catherine Cundy, to denounce Rushdie's stance as 'limitlessly mongrelized and relativist' (1997, 113), while others, such as Stephen Baker, to defend it as a form of multiculturalism that is a 'realistic portrayal of the construction of a postcolonial culture' (2000, 51). As I have argued, Rushdie's fictional city is geared towards the critique of fundamentalist practices and the loss of the ideals of Independence. Yet, Aurora's paintings of the city, specifically, as based on the various splits in the Moor figure, also point to Rushdie's engagement with the interplay between Indian secular and religious/communal historiographies. Nehru's vision of a democratic India where 'individuals would be emancipated from their religious and affective ties and reborn as secular citizens', as Neeladri Bhattacharya points out, became one of the prerequisites for developing a secular – scientific and objective – history to counter communal narratives that posited strict boundaries between communities. In these secular revisionings, heroes were 'uncrowned' and villains 'rehabilitated', so that 'the heroes of one history [became] the villains of another' (2008, 57; 61). Rushdie parodies such inter-generic inversions in Moor's duplicitous embodiments of Boabdil as ruler and as mercenary soldier; in Granada's transition from Muslim to Christian rule; in Moor's fall from Abraham's secular Bombay to Fielding's communal Bombay; and in Moor's simultaneous roles as a Boabdil and a Luther. While Moor is easily 'hijacked' and re-programmed as a protagonist in conflicting narratives, he ironically appears to be cast in the role of a 'double agent', serving each of the polarized forces of the city in the manner of Spain's El Cid.

Aurora's paintings offer a re-periodization of Indian history through the artistic re-envisioning of the Moor figure in relation to the city. The 'early Moors' (1957–1977), produced between Moor's birth and the election that sweeps Mrs Gandhi from power, encompass, historically, the last years of Jawaharlal Nehru's premiership and Indira Gandhi's Emergency. These works are characterized by a series of fantastic substitutions, carnivalesque inversions or various corporeal transformations and experimentations with roles. The paintings parody the familio-political rule of Nehru–Indira as an Oedipal self-re-imagining of an effectively dynastic period of Indian history. I use the term 'self-re-imagining' as Aurora casts herself and her son in the roles of these political leaders and interweaves public history and her own and Moor's private lives in her paintings. Aurora and Moor pose as, respectively, 'a godless Madonna and child', as Eleanor Marx and her father Karl or as Desdemona and Othello (220–25). In his suggestively titled essay 'Dynasty' (1985), Rushdie comments on the 'continuing saga of the Nehru family' as part of a potent national mythology:

We have poured ourselves into this story, inventing its characters, then ripping them up and reinventing them. In our inexhaustible speculations lies one source of their power over us. We became addicted to these speculations, and they . . . took advantage of our addiction. Or: we dreamed them, so intensely that they came to life. (IH, 48)

While the novel traces the rise of Hindu fundamentalism 'back to those days of dictatorship and state violence' (52) through Aurora's 'early Moors', the construct of nation as family is lampooned in Moor's ironic descriptions of his family's root-searching story: 'its somewhat overwrought Bombay-talkie masala narrative, its almost desperate reaching back for a kind of authentification, for evidence' (77–8). Moor's role as Othello in Aurora's art invites comparisons between the city in *The Moor's Last Sigh* and Venice in Shakespeare's plays *The Merchant of Venice* and *Othello*. As Maurice Hunt suggests, Shakespeare's Venice in these two plays does not correspond to English Renaissance commonplaces about the city – at once, the model of republican government, the alternative to monarchy for disaffected subjects of Elizabeth I and the corrupt sister of Rome, the generic Italian locus of charlatans, lechers and courtesans. Shakespeare's Venice activates a disturbing paradigm dependant upon the city's multicultural reputation. It encapsulates the dynamic relationship between a persecutory Christian culture and what it regards as a potentially savage alien, a Turk, a Moor, or a Jew, who exists both outside and within the city (Hunt 2003, 162–63). Respectively, the duplicitous image of Venice in English Renaissance discourses corresponds to the split in the stereotype of Moors as others. In the novel, Moor can be seen as literally inhabiting a visual/discursive racial/ethnic category. The darkness of his skin makes him an outsider in Bombay, a fact also emphasized through the metaphorical significance of the selection rhyme that his siblings' and his nicknames form – 'Eeny Meeny Miney, three quarters of an unfinished line followed by a hollow beat, a silent space where a fourth word should be' (140). Moor occupies a discursive periphery, 'the end of the line', that is both linguistic and genealogical. The representation of Moor as an Indian 'Othello fellow' participates in the novel's overall critique of Christian/Hindu fundamentalist practices, which is informed by urban representation. Moor's transformation into a mercenary soldier echoes both *Othello* and the Boabdil legend.

Aurora's artistic vision of Bombay as Mooristan/Palimpstine grows darker during the 'high years', after the Emergency ends. This period of the Moor series juxtaposes the Catholic re-conquest of Granada and the devastating effect of Indira Gandhi's rule on India. The later 'Moor in exile' sequence, part of the 'dark Moors', follows Moor's fall into Bombay Central, the world of Raman Fielding and, historically, the development of Hindu funda- mentalism. In these paintings, there is no longer a position above the city, no stable, if sentimentalized, stance from which it can be observed. The Moor figure is increasingly indistinguishable from its urban setting and is composed entirely as a collage, made out of Bombay's debris.

From a central image in the early Moors, through an image occupying a distanced position of critique, outside and above it, in the high years, it becomes, in the dark Moors, an anonymous, impersonal and almost invisible figure, that is no longer 'a symbol – however approximate – of the new nation', but a 'semi-allegorical figure of decay' (303). Rushdie accedes, through his heroine, that 'the ideas of impurity, cultural admixture and melange [are] in fact capable of distortion, and [contain] a potential for darkness as well as for light' (303).

Commentators on Bombay art and cinema since Independence comment on a similar movement from a narrative of arrival to Bombay, 'featuring modern consciousness as a painful mastering of life in the metropolis' through a 'struggle to inherit the city' (while coming 'face to face with the truth of the "citizen subject" in India') to the cataclysmic events of the communal riots of 1992–1993, after the destruction of the Babri mosque in Ayodhya by pro-Hindutva fanatics (Kapur and Rajadhyaksha 2001, 18–20). In *Fiza* (2000), a film set during the riots, 'the hero performs a double patricide of the Muslim and Hindu politicians', before dying in the arms of his sister (ibid., 31). Later narratives inevitably return, like Rushdie's novel, to an Oedipal image of the city's self-annihilation. The tripartite division of Aurora's work, however, destabilizes a number of bi-partitions. The discursive diptych or bifurcation of Bombay into Malabar Masala and Bombay Central, as articulated in Moor's narrative of his own life, also informs the biographical orientation of Aurora's work.

In the triptych topography of the novel, however, another woman stands out. 'Well may you weep like a woman for what you could not defend like a man' (MLS, 80, original emphasis) were the sneering words of the 'terrifying Ayxa the Virtuous' (MLS, 80), the mother of the last sultan of Granada, Boabdil, which, according to legend, she addressed to her son on the hill outside the city as it fell to the Catholic Monarchs of Spain. The three dynamic spatial/temporal narratives of the novel, Cochin, Bombay and Benengeli, develop in relation to the outer image – weeping Boabdil and his reproachful mother looking down upon the city they have lost. The failure of the male hero to prevent the fall of his city follows the epic formula of the Trojan precedent in Virgil's *Aeneid*: a necessary tragic emplotment that enables the hero to embark upon a quest to found the city of Rome, symbolically, a new Troy. Yet, though *The Moor* incorporates some elements from this epic interurban route, the focus of the text, as the exterior image suggests, remains on the idea of urban decline. While *The Ground beneath Her Feet* places, as we shall see in the next chapter, a greater emphasis on the post-Trojan journey and, as such, concerns itself with the search for the future Troy, *The Moor* is centred around the exploration of the past and the reasons for urban fall: an altogether diagnostic and reformative quest. Hence, for example, the protagonist's Lutheran route.

Ayxa's words repeatedly haunt the male protagonist in his Boabdil role. Rushdie seems to invest his female characters with strength and power, while depriving his male characters of sufficient agency. Men tend to be feminized, while women appear superficially masculine. Having failed to defend his home city, the protagonist projects both his fears and fantasies onto women, who become compensatory mechanisms within the novel's gendered economy of urban space. A feminine agency, concealed behind this mirror of representation in the Symbolic, however, threatens to erode the totality of masculine identities and the phallic urban order, as exemplified, for instance, in Abraham Zogoiby's tower dominating Bombay's skyline. Aurora Zogoiby has concealed the image of her murderer, Abraham, beneath one of her paintings. In the realm of the Symbolic, feminine power is therefore disguized by women's mimicry of masculine agency. On the one hand, this disguise reinstates patriarchal ideologies in that feminine power is often seen as excessive, aberrant, deceitful or destructive. On the other, women's mimicry of masculine power strategically parodies or mocks masculine authority and the urban Law of the Father. Boabdil is 'forced to genuflect before an omnipotent queen' and 'obliged to suffer a further humiliation at the hands of an impotent (but formidable) dowager', who despises her son 'for yielding up what she would have fought for to the death, given the chance' (MLS, 80).

In the figure of Aurora as the 'city girl', an 'incarnation of the smartyboots metropolis' as Mother India is 'village earth made flesh' (139), Rushdie critiques the national myth of 'Mother India', of 'the land as mother, the mother as land, as the firm ground beneath our feet' (MLS, 137). The mother as land is capable, Rushdie suggests, of archaic vengeance as well as love, of destruction as well as protection. Inscribed into the text's urban fictions is, as a result, an ambivalent attitude to women, which produces the duplicitous 'city as mother/lover' paradigm. While Aurora authors/mothers the utopian vision of Mooristan/Palimpstine, Moor's lover, Uma, embodies the perversion or frustration of the idea of urban pluralism: she becomes the negative specular counterpart of Aurora. This polarization is reinforced through another parody of the feminization of the nation. Aurora and Uma are compared to the two great Cold War superpowers, respectively, 'Amrika' and 'Moskva' (3). Such woman-land analogies contribute to the antagonistic urbanscape of warring political extremes that are incompatible and irreconcilable – a polarized diptych, which mirrors the divisions of Bombay. Aurora and Uma fight their wars in art or in bed, transforming Moor, on both fronts, into their weapon and their plaything. If Aurora is Moor's Desdemona (224), Uma is Moor's 'Dis-demona' (309) – a female demon, as the name suggests, belonging to *Dis*, the subterranean city of Hell in Dante's *Divine Comedy*, or to the realm of Pluto/Hades, the lord of the dark underworld. As a result of his infatuation with Uma, Moor is banished out of the mother realm, Edenic Bombay, and into Fielding's Bombay Central, or, in psychoanalytical terms from the Imaginary to the Symbolic order of the city: 'My tumble is not Lucifer's but Adam's. I fall into my manhood' (MLS, 296, original emphasis).

A number of women in Moor's life come to be representative of the city and, like Aurora and Uma, most of them die violent deaths. Moor's sisters, Ina, Minnie and Mynah, embody three different aspects of Bombay life. Ina is the first Indian catwalk model and cover girl, a 'silent goddess of sex' (208), who dies of cancer – an ironic twist of fate, since before she falls ill, she pretends to have cancer as a ploy to win back her boyfriend. This event asserts the novel's formula of women's self-destructiveness. Minnie becomes a nun, Sister Floreas, who is one of the victims of the Bombay explosions. Mynah, the conscience of the city, qualifies as a lawyer and attempts to prove the reality of Abraham's invisible dealings. She is also the victim of an explosion. Nadia Wadia – successively, Miss Bombay, Miss India and Miss World – becomes the face of Abraham's Siodicorp and unwittingly provokes the jealousy of one of Raman Fielding's hitmen, who mutilates her face. After the destruction of Bombay, she appears on television to inspire Bombayites, bearing the scar of violence, like the city itself, but standing also for the hope of urban renewal. The face and the voice of the city, mutilated yet capable of healing her-/itself, this figure is nevertheless a metonymic reduction.

Women have instrumental/specular roles in the articulation of a distinctly masculine postcolonial identity. Despite the text's focus on urban inauthenticity, celebrated in most of Rushdie's work, male anxiety and fear of the loss of the home/mother city linger in the representation of women as informing the process of male travel. On his flight to Benengeli, Moor meets a friendly young Spanish stewardess, who tells him that the reason why she travels is the pleasure she finds in promiscuity. She leads him to the plane's toilet where they have sex: 'she reached her orgasm with a few swift movements while I was unable to do so at all, especially as she appeared to lose interest in me the instant her own needs had been satisfied' (MLS, 382). Moor interprets the incident with the mysterious stewardess, who disappears immediately afterwards, as a warning from the 'new world' (MLS, 384). If, as Anne McClintock notes, colonial discourse includes a long tradition of male travel as an erotics of ravishment (1995, 22), the terms of this erotics are inverted in Moor's sexual encounter. The flight to Benengeli, Moor's 'maiden flight' (MLS, 384), is analogous to his ritual emasculation. He becomes the passive victim consummated by his own fear/fantasy of the 'new world' that takes the form of an elusive seductress who turns out to have been just a specular illusion.

In Rushdie's short story 'Christopher Columbus and Queen Isabella of Spain Consummate Their Relationship' (EW, 1994), Columbus's search for a benefactor to fund his project of exploration figures, similarly, as a series of flirting rituals that culminate in the realization of the journey of discovery, which is also a symbolical sexual climax. Rushdie articulates the figure of the explorer as the object, rather than the subject of the latter's own discourse, whose very tropes he is made to inhabit. Columbus stands for the weak male and Isabella for the inaccessible goddess who expects to be worshipped. The novel also employs cross-dressing as a strategy of subverting gender binaries but its traffic in highly stylized figures, bearing cartographic inscriptions, ultimately collapses into the same libidinal dynamic.

The Moor's Last Sigh, then, evokes 1492 as the moment that set Moorish diasporas in motion. It employs hegemonic visual structures and forms in order to interrogate them and while it specifically seeks to avoid positing a return to a purity of origins, it offers a modern, secular mobilization. Rushdie employs a further artistic metaphor to envisage the text's indebtedness to narratives of 1492. The story of Boabdil, he says in an interview, was employed 'merely [as] background' to the novel and 'done rather like Sidney Nolan's Ned Kelly paintings' (CSR, 156). This analogy is a further reinforcement of the triptych principle of linking separate panels as well as an allusion to a fragmented, episodic structure, problematizing centrality, hierarchical order and teleology. In Australian Ned Kelly's duplicitous villain-hero status, we can recognize, once again, an ironic engagement with the epic transformations of the protagonists of secular historiographies and the processes that translate them into figures of national significance by having them step off one canvas or order and into another.

Chapter 5

Quaking Solid Ground: Trojan Falls and Roman Rises in *The Ground Beneath Her Feet*

Developing an archaeology of discourse towards an analysis of the modern social sciences, Michel Foucault employs the term *ground* as a metaphor for the history of the Same, specifically, for its groundedness in its self-produced fixities and its reliance on the systematic erasure of ruptures and discontinuities, which were seen as 'the stigma of temporal dislocation' (2001, 8). *The Order of Things* undertakes to disturb the epistemological ground of science, particularly, man's strangely duplicitous positioning as simultaneously the subject and object of scientific discourse: 'I am restoring to our silent and apparently immobile soil, its rifts, its instability, its flaws; and it is the same ground that is once more stirring under our feet' (2002, xxvi).

While the subversion of Eurocentric methods of historiography is central to postcolonial fiction, *The Ground beneath Her Feet* engages in revealing the fissures and instabilities of *urban* ground, which becomes a perspective on the global – political, cultural and economic – fault lines of the contemporary world: the idea of the U.S. as a single superpower and analogies of its role today with that of Rome; North–South divides; the nuclear arms race and challenges to nuclear oligopoly by countries such as India and Pakistan; trajectories of celebrity culture and consumerism; fraught international relations, such as those between India and Nepal, and the radical transformation of Bombay into Mumbai as the condition which sets diasporas in motion.

More broadly, urban tectonics, as I previously argued, celebrates the instability of discursive geo-historical accretions since it offers a potential for their re-configuration, for the explosive disturbance of authenticated histories and geographies. The novel presents the city of Bombay through the excavations of its layered past. In the underground memory of the city, the character V. V. Merchant, a Bombay historian, uncovers a multitude of unstable narratives, which are in the process of intersecting, colliding, or sliding under each other: relics of past worlds, ancient kingdoms, cities and proto-continents, that are at the same time part of the geographical and mythological discourses of the structure and history of the earth: Mohenjo-Daro, Gondwana, Gondwanaland, primeval fish, Hell, the Antipodes (61–2). V. V. Merchant's excavations of Bombay, reminiscent of Foucault's methodology in *The Archaeology of Knowledge*, can be seen as an activity subversive of hegemonic earthographies or such archaeological projects that are aimed at the restoration of urban origins. Instead, he unearths a number of free-floating historical propositions and labels. The urban past emerges in fragments rather than totalities, linear successions or internal coherences. The collision of landmasses, according to V. V., is still taking place; Bombay continues to experience 'impactual consequences' (GBHF, 62).

As we saw in the previous chapter, however, the 'unsolidity' of urban ground can be construed by the characters as symptomatic of an urban flaw, rather than as the very condition which makes the idea of the heterogenetic/ heterotopian city possible. This chapter examines the search for urban foundations, origins or purity, as characteristic, I will suggest, not only of the Hindu fundamentalist cause and Abraham Zogoiby's fiction of Bombay, caricatured in *The Moor's Last Sigh*, but also of the European myth of imperial urban lineage.

With respect to urban ground in the novel, travel is also informed by a prominent catoptric boundary derived from the myth of the Dioscuri. In one version of the myth, Polydeuces was the immortal son of Zeus while Castor was the mortal son of King Tyndareos. At Polydeuces' request, the twins shared the divinity between them, living half the year beneath the earth, with the dead, and the other half on Mount Olympus, with the gods. In the novel it is not the periodic change of life and death, light and dark or infernal and divine that is highlighted, but the physical boundary between them – the ground – the ability to cross that boundary, and, most of all, the choice of ground beneath one's feet as opposed to over one's head (GBHF, 54). The idea of one's position in the world is politicized in this way with respect to the ground as a normative mid-point between 'developed' and 'developing' worlds, present and past or Orphic descent and contemporary celebrity worship. The gravitational pull of the ground symbolizes entrapment, ties, and forced belonging, so that shifting ground, disorientation, and the nausea of travelling can have a positive, sobering effect on the characters.

Trojan Falls and Roman Rises: The Ground
Beneath and the Ground Ahead

While the tectonic orientation of Rushdie's cities points to their ability to stir and reshuffle the layers of the past into new configurations, the city also stands for the negotiation of one's ground within a world of political instabilities that often conspire against the characters. Reading the text as a *katabatic* narrative, Rachel Falconer argues that Rushdie repeatedly mines the same site – the ground beneath, rather than the ground ahead – for different discoveries (2001, 467). Yet, central to the idea of the city in the text is the pattern of forward movement, the 'forward pull' (GBHF, 101), complicated as it is by frequent prolepses and dreams of the future. The ground stirs not only *when*, but *because* Ormus, Vina and Rai travel. Rushdie takes the reader on a transatlantic/cross-cultural journey spanning seven decades. The novel opens in the Mexican city of Guadalajara on St Valentine's Day, 1989 (the date of the fatwa), then returns to Bombay of the 1930s–1970s, traces the characters' journeys to London of the 1960s, to New York of the 1970s–1980s and to Mexico City in 1989, circles back to the Guadalajara of the opening sentence, and moving beyond it, into Tequila, it emerges back into New York of the 1990s. Undoubtedly, it is the interplay of the motifs of the ground beneath and the ground ahead that is most prominent: mining the past is complemented by building the future, which involves, in turn, the ambition for moving on, flying away, and defying urban gravity. Moreover, in colliding and collapsing tectonic plates into each other, the text explores themes that are the concern of the geosciences and engages in geopolitical interpretations of seismic activity. Cities are built on volcanic subtexts of political, historical and mythological tensions that haunt the present and frequently erupt onto its surface.

Two significant intertexts, which belong to two considerably distinct cultural traditions, are brought to bear on the tectonic re-envisioning of cities in *The Ground*: Aztec mythology and the classical European text of the *Aeneid*. The Aztec mythological concept of time bears a close resemblance to narrative time in the novel. The series of tectonic cataclysms through which urban configurations unfold is reminiscent of the Aztec mythological idea of time as five aeonic bursts or 'suns' (Brundage 1979, 27). These aeons are arranged in an ascending tale of cataclysms, alike only in that each one is an imperfect cosmic experiment ending in collapse. The fifth and present aeon is the age of earthquakes (*ibid.*). The narrator, Rai Merchant, interprets earthquakes as 'warning signs hinting at the proximity

of the main event: which is, the end of the world. Or, the end of one world'
(503). Travel makes possible, in this way, a transition from *kenosis*, 'an
emptying' at the end of a temporal cycle, to *plerosis*, signalling the start of a
new cycle or 'the filling of time with new beginnings' (GBHF, 113). The
characters' interurban route, Bombay–London–New York, is experienced
not as a linear route, but as a series of tectonic eruptions, which both
necessitate and are necessitated by travel.

As well as borrowing themes from Aztec mythology – the end of the world,
the cult of the dead, human sacrifice and the age of earthquakes – the novel
also engages in an intertextual re-configuration of Aeneas' route: Troy–
Carthage–Rome. Mario Di Cesare takes issue with early commentators of
the *Aeneid* who note a spiritual movement from Troy to Carthage to Rome.
In his view, the individual cities contribute to the 'great metaphor' of the
city. Respectively, Carthage is merely a shadow of the city, while Rome is the
object of the ultimate urban quest. Troy is central in position, because,
although it belongs to the past, its smouldering ashes pervade Aeneas'
world (1975, 1). In *The Ground*, the fall of Bombay also impinges on all
history, on all the other cities, through which the characters travel, or in
which they settle. The tectonic upheaval of the subterranean urban realm,
or the motif of the ground beneath, thus bears upon the forward route, or
the motif of the ground ahead.

Nicholas Birns discusses the use of the Trojan myth in the idea of Western
Europe's origins. In medieval European literature and historiography, it
served as a secular paradigm for strengthening political authority by
providing the connection between the medieval present and the classical
and Biblical pasts: 'the myth was a mere adaptation of the *Aeneid*' in an
attempt 'to give a classical pedigree to non-Latin linguistic groups by
manufacturing eponymous ancestors who had come to the West, fleeing
from Troy, as had Virgil's hero' (1993, 49). *The Ground* re-appropriates this
myth of urban descent – specifically, its linking of Troy and Rome and,
subsequently, Rome and the Christian West – as developed in Virgil's epic
and employed, thereafter, by a number of imperial genealogical fictions.

Contemporary critical and political discourses, both advocating and
opposing U.S. hegemony, as Vilashini Cooppan (2005) notes, have also
made recurrent attempts to analogize the role of the United States in the
post-Cold War world and that of the ancient Roman Empire by way of
illustrating the former's power in an age of globalization. She discusses
several recent narrative returns to Rome, most notably, Michael Hardt and
Antonio Negri's *Empire* (2000) and Ridley Scott's film, *Gladiator* (2000), in
order to critique the understanding of the U.S. and Rome as 'mirror

republican empires', since such an understanding makes it impossible, she argues, 'to name, analyze, and contest the simple fact of United States' imperialism here and now' (83). Ania Loomba *et al.*, argue that as the new imperial order shapes itself in the image of earlier empires, *Pax Romana* or *Pax Britannica*, it appropriates the language of opposition: proponents of this order see themselves as the holy warriors of Anglo-American expansionism (2005, 10–12). Similarly, Cooppan suggests, *Gladiator* 'positions Americans as simultaneously Rome's slaves and its saviours, the latter-day Maximuses who will redeem Rome's vision of democratic republicanism and make the world safe for a new empire' (90). Whereas for Hardt and Negri globalization supersedes the nation, Cooppan points out that:

> *Gladiator*'s American Rome, like that invoked in current discussions of US empire, is continuous with a broader tradition in which the nation returns to Rome in order to speak its own history: the founding, for example, with its republican language; or the cold war, with its global rhetoric of good and evil empires, its domestic concerns with new social movements of liberation, and its several filmic returns to Rome. (91)

A more recent film, Wolfgang Petersen's *Troy* (2004), 'returns' even further back than Rome, to Homer's epic of Troy's fall. Yet, ironically, in terms of the chronology of Hollywood narratives, Troy superseded and relied on the glory of Rome in that *Troy* sought to parallel the success of *Gladiator*, winner of several Oscars. Rushdie's novel shares two interrelated themes with these Hollywood recreations of Troy and Rome: the alternation of old and new, the rise and the fall of cities and empires, their precedents and their descendants. Cooppan's article deliberately echoes these themes to suggest that the end of old empires and nations might be prematurely proclaimed, and also to emphasize that continuity with the past should not be sought for in the morphing of Rome and the U.S., but in the new order's use of old ideologies *as a means of* morphing Rome and the U.S. Unlike Scott's *Gladiator* and Petersen's *Troy*, Rushdie's novel allows the tensions between urban pasts and presents to bear upon his characters' inter-urban itineraries. These itineraries are informed by the tensions between the two sides of what Cooppan terms globalization's 'split personality' that also echoes the interwoven themes of decline and advance: globalization as ongoing decolonization and globalization as a new and powerful form of colonialism (84–5). The fictional map of the world offered by Rushdie's novel also problematizes the relationship between contemporary cities and long-standing narratives in its East–West tracings.

For Rushdie, as we have noted, the change of Bombay's name to *Mumbai*, as the most visible culmination of the Shiva Sena's political agenda, signals the city's irreversible decline into parochialism. *The Ground* returns to this transformation of the city in order to re-imagine it as a tectonically-triggered Trojan fall. Bombay's fall is foreshadowed in an incident at the city's Juhu Beach where the nine-year-old Rai Merchant, makes a powerful enemy in Piloo Doodhwala by offering an apple to Vina Apsara, a relative of the Doodhwalas who has newly arrived from America, rather than to any of his two daughters. Shri Piloo Doodhwala, a principal benefactor and power broker of the MA party, [3] implicated in the change of the city's name, is modelled on the Indian politician Laloo Prasad Yadav (SATL, 203). For Rushdie, the election of Yadav (who was allegedly implicated in a political double-act, claiming public subsidies for the maintenance of non-existent livestock) to the national parliament symbolizes the increasing corruption of Indian political culture. In the novel, Doodhwala is involved in a similar scheme, involving non-existent goats. Doodhwala's war for power, starting with the opening of his Exwyzee Milk Colony, can be traced back to Rai's symbolic offering, which re-enacts both the Biblical myth of the expulsion from Eden and the mythical cause of the Trojan War. Rai and Vina are expelled, in this way, from an Edenic Bombay and Persis Kalamanja, the novel's Cassandra figure, predicts that the city is 'about to fall, like Troy' (GBHF, 215). When a powerful earthquake strikes the city, the event is construed as the direct consequence of the MA party's policies and corruption:

> Bombayites had prided themselves on being quake-free. Good communal relations and good solid ground, we boasted. No fault lines under our town. But now Piloo Doodhwala's MA boys were stoking the fires of discord, and the city had begun to shake. (GBHF, 217)

Edenic Bombay is replaced in this way by Mumbai. In the novel's re-configuration of Aeneas' route, however, the nostalgic, quake-free Bombay of the past is compared to Rome: Bombay's Colaba Causeway is a Via Appia; its Malabar and Cumballa hills are, respectively, Capitol and Palatine; its Brabourne Stadium is a Colosseum, and 'the glittering Art Deco sweep' of its Marine Drive is 'something not even Rome could boast' (78). Bombay's grandiose ambition for the glory of Rome thus ends in the utter failure of Troy and the Roman 'grandeur of the metropolis' proves to be just an 'illusion of permanence' (GBHF, 78). Ironically Bombay's Roman age ends in a Trojan collapse, so that Rome is superseded by Troy. This inversion destabilizes the imperial myth of urban lineage, since Bombay's Roman age heralds its tectonic Trojan period and ultimate fall.

It is New York that comes to stand for Bombay's future. While Bombay is frequently compared to both Troy (69, 110, 215) and Rome (62, 78), New York becomes a 'new Rome' (387). Interwoven with the Mexican theme of tectonic instability is thus the myth of urban pedigree linking Troy and Rome to Bombay and New York. In the novel's cartography, London (situated between Bombay and New York) functions as a transitional city, while the Mexican cities appear to be the least seismically stable topoi, or as Falconer notes, 'the lowest hell of all' (476). In the topography of Virgil's epic, Dido's city of Carthage is on Aeneas' route from Troy to the site of future Rome, and so is the topos of the underworld, where Aeneas' father describes the glory that awaits the sons of Troy in the future city of Rome. In *The Ground*, as in the *Aeneid*, the route out of the falling city, Bombay/Troy, is by sea. It gives Rai an 'intimation' of what lies across the water: 'America, the open sesame' (59) and while V. V. Merchant chances upon an occasional relic of Rome at Juhu Beach (62), Rai is 'splash[ing] about in the future'(62). One of V. V.'s proud historical 'finds' is that Queen Catherine of Braganza, wife of Charles II, is the 'secret link' (79) between the two cities: 'Bombay came to England in her dowry; but she was also the Queen in the N.Y. borough of Queens' (GBHF, 79). Similarly, Manhattan is 'little Bombay writ large' (GBHF, 78). The dream of a new Rome or New York is thus erected on top of old Rome's/Bombay's glorious debris.

The role of London in the novel's cartography of interurban itineraries is reminiscent of the tragic city of Carthage, which is a temporary deviation on Aeneas' route to the site of future Rome, and which also burns, like Troy. Historically, the city grows into the Carthaginian Empire which is then gradually weakened and finally defeated by Rome in the three Punic Wars (264–146 BCE). Implicitly, then, New York as Rome has effectively replaced the British colonial metropolis. Rushdie's Troy–Rome re-configuration consciously by-passes and decentres London. Events in London are set in the 1960s, which allows the author to envision it as a drug-induced hallucination, 'addled by mysticism, mesmerized by the miraculous, the psychotropic' (GBHF, 287). Unreal and deceptive, London is imagined as an anachronistic space-time, a museum of the British Empire (GBHF, 330), which holds the protagonist captive.

In contrast, New York City appears, at first, to be positive and liberating. On arriving in Manhattan, Ormus 'enters a condition of worship, marveling at this new Rome, open-mouthed and slack-jawed, as did Alberti in Florence in the 1430s' (GBHF, 387). Renaissance echoes signal a newness in the idea of the city. For Vina too, New York is an embodiment of the American idea of 'a city upon a hill' for immigrants. Similarly, Rai compares the experience of New York to an acquisition, rather than a loss: 'So, this is what they feel like, I thought: roots. Not the ones we're born with, can't help having, but the ones we put down in our chosen soil' (414). These images celebrate the understanding of urban ground as a free choice, promoting the idea of a dynamic subjectivity. The journey to America is analogously imagined, as a process of healing, in Bharati Mukherjee's *Jasmine*. Her heroine, an Indian village girl, who seeks to remake herself in America, weeps at the sight of her American visa: 'I feel renewed, the recipient of an organ transplant'.[4]

In *The Ground*, the concept of 'new roots' asserts a cosmopolitan identity that is always in the process of renewal and where renewal is the product of a creative hybridity, itself feeding on the very conditions of travel, instability and difference, on the *severance* of roots. The celebratory concept of new roots has thus replaced the image of umbilical cords through which Rushdie's early novel, *Midnight's Children*, offers a critique of Partition and the mutation of the urban ideal in Karachi. The name of New York signals not only a new identity, but also the continuity between the past, Troy, Bombay, Europe and the present, Rome, New York, America. If Rome is only the prophecy of a city in the *Aeneid*, in *The Ground* new Rome/New York becomes a place of rebirth, a fresh urban start that is, at the same time, an echo of the glorious old city. New York and Bombay are 'forever yoked together' (GBHF, 354).

The myth of imperial urban continuity simultaneously relies on and precludes the possibility of difference and travelling: a 'new Troy', Rome is, at once, identical with and different from Troy. This ambiguity becomes subversive in *The Ground*. Having been permanently removed from the map and replaced by Mumbai, Bombay is transposed into New York. The city is both Troy and Troy's descendant, whereas India and Western Europe have a common fictive origin in Troy: thus, Europe contains Rome, North America contains New Rome, and India contains their common heroic yet doomed past, Troy. The mythical linkage of Troy/Bombay and Rome/New York foregrounds the unstable groundwork on which the concept of urban continuity is based, since the forward route is, paradoxically, also a return. The fantasy of imperial wholeness ironically relies on a 'Trojan split': it is both sustained and threatened by the Trojan precedent (Federico 1997, 124). By generating a series of 'new' cities (descendant from Troy – Bombay/ Troy, London/Carthage, and New York/Rome –) the text points to the questionability of the myth of urban lineage and of all cultural foundations. As we noted, in the Middle Ages, the myth gave a classical pedigree to non-Latin linguistic groups and, in contemporary narratives of globalization, it is resuscitated to envisage and justify U.S. power. In Rushdie's postcolonial translation of the myth, it points to the fragility of fictions of urban ancestry and parodies the beach-and-sandals (replacing the fringes-and-sweat signifier of Romanness discussed by Roland Barthes, 1993) filmic returns to Rome. The myth of urban ancestry rhizomatically branches out to include Bombay.

As positive and liberating as New York City appears to be, it is not immune to divisive tensions, some of them inherited from Bombay. The 'mighty pincushions' of Manhattan are set against the level of the street; its Native American past is juxtaposed with its present high-rise buildings (355). In the impressions of two of the Indian characters, Ormus Cama and Vina Apsara, who have 'made it' to New York as the lead members of a cult rock group, VTO (Vertical Take-off), New York splits into Malabar Hill ('celestial Manhattan', 387) and Bombay's bazaars ('the thronged streets of Queens', 355). Gradually, the tensions of the rest of the world, perceived as distant echoes in New York, also make their existence more palpable. As American troops withdraw at the end of the Vietnam War, the streets of the American city are filled with 'war-wounded' soldiers who remind the narrator of Bombay's beggar 'amputees' (417). In an essay, Rushdie describes New York as the 'bright capital of the visible' (SATL, 391). While all the other cities in the novel are divided into visible and invisible or overground and underground dimensions, New York's tensions are between its ground and high-rise levels, but the former stands for the invisible dimension of the rest of the world while the latter is stretched, indefinitely upwards, to include the dimension of outer space in what seems to be a reference to American space exploration. This hegemonic positioning of New York, however, is interrupted by strange incidents that take place in the city and are interpreted as a sign of people losing their humanity: rumours begin circulating of snakes sighted in urban gutters and wild pigs in city parks (391). Vina, too, has a disturbing vision, in which the Chrysler Building and the World Trade Centre change into a 'fleet of rockets' preparing to 'blast the city to smithereens and take off, leaving us to die of thirst in our ruined urban desert' (415).

The invisible dimension of the rest of the world also leaks into New York through the press coverage of a series of earthquakes: in San Francisco, Algeria, Italy, Turkey, Mexico City and San Salvador. 'Border-line' earthquakes intensify affecting, for instance, the India–Nepal border and the China–Burma line. *Time* interprets: '*Is the world coming apart at the seams?*' (451, original emphasis). The seismic instability of the world and its biggest cities, in particular, becomes a global phenomenon in making its way into New York. The tectonic upheaval is caused not only by the act of creating borders but also by the overtly unequal distribution of 'visibility' around the globe. Fault lines divide the world into regions believed to be seismically dominant and those referred to as 'seismohawks' in an allusion to the contest for influence between nuclear 'doves' and 'hawks': 'The very walls of Delhi, Islamabad and the other seismohawk capitals shout pro-quake-technology slogans. *No HARF* [Hands Across the Rifts and Faults] *measures. When we can quake land will be time to shake hand*' (GBHF, 555). The text accounts for the tremors in a number of ways: they are seen as a scientific phenomenon, a 'subterranean war', an effect caused by the collision of worlds, a result of years of covert Western activity underground, a remedy, a tool of the new hegemonic geopolitics or a Euro-American weapon against emergent economies and an act of divine punishment (471–554). The narrator, however, warns against the facile interpretation of earthquakes, or the search for their allegorical significance. In this sense, *The Ground* is reminiscent of *Midnight's Children*'s urban omens which parody what is described as the Indian obsession with correspondences, with the idea that 'forms lie hidden in reality' (MC, 300). Such correspondences are associated both with a subversive potential and with the danger of being construed as 'natural' or essentialist fictions. While it is difficult to reject the stable rock of foundations, as Eyal Amiran notes, this is the only way to reject the idea of a world of control as well as control of the world (2002, 288).

Interurban Echoes and Inversions

The interplay of the old and new, origin and mirror image, and various temporal inversions form the novel's main subversive strategy, challenging the ideas of London or New York as the descendants of Troy/Rome, of the flow of Western popular culture and of globalization as an exclusively homogenizing force. *Above* and *below* and *before* and *after* often change places in a number of cultural, political, cartographic and mythical reversals and are further unsettled through the introduction of a 'third space'. The text re-appropriates the myths of Orpheus and of Castor and Polydeuces, all of whom descend into the underworld and ascend to the surface in order to reposition its characters' journey as a descent from Bombay to London, followed by an ascent to New York. Urban configurations also reverberate across other catoptric boundaries, such as organic membranes and photographic frames.

The novel's most remarkable inversion, however, involves the mirroring of sound or music. '[W]e Bombayites', the narrator declares, 'can claim that [rock music] was in truth our music, born in Bombay like Ormus and me, not "goods from foreign" but made in India, and maybe it was the foreigners who stole it from us' (GBHF, 96). This statement, however, is complicated, in that whereas Bombay hears rock music before the West, the origin of music is other- or under-worldly. Ormus and his dead twin Gayo are a version of the Polydeuces-Castor pair. When Ormus elapses into his so-called 'cama obscuras', or 'heterotopian tendencies', the belief in the existence of an alternative world, parallel to his own, he is with his underground double: Gayo. In these visions, Ormus descends to Gayo's realm, an 'unknown but familiar' city, compared on a number of occasions to Las Vegas (253), and this is where he hears, in 1962, the 'songs of the future', including 'Eve of Destruction', 'I Got You Babe' or 'Like a Rolling Stone' (183).

The city thus appears to be proleptic, in that the songs are anticipatory; yet what they anticipate is an alternative future in which the songs of the West are but echoes of the East. Ormus's music disrupts both the concepts of cultural origins and the supremacy of Western popular culture: 'Just as England can no longer lay exclusive claim to the English language, so America is no longer the sole owner of rock'n'roll' (378). At the same time, his subsequent journey to New York, to this alternative future, is also a descent into the urban underground or the realm of the other as well as a journey across the globe. To Ormus, 'it's the West that's exotic, fabulous, unreal' (260). Through the choice of the labyrinthine subterranean Las Vegas, it is also antipodal – a simulacrum city, which is the source of words without origin or reality – which challenges a conventional view of cultural globalization as a uni-directional flow from the centre to the periphery.

Ormus's musical genius, as his name (a Latinized version of Ahura Mazda) denotes, is literally the product of the union of Parsi and classical European traditions, pointing to the cultural impurity of his home city and the similarly hybrid origins of music. Yet the name is also a pun on Orpheus, as the text acknowledges, and Ormus's travels mirror the descents and ascents of the Thracian singer. Orpheus is known as the lover who tried to win back his beloved from the dead; the minstrel whose music enchanted all nature and the shaman or psychopomp, regularly linked in Antiquity with mystery religion, special illumination, and initiation into knowledge of the secret workings of the universe. After his unsuccessful attempt to bring Eurydice back from the underworld, he is killed and dismembered by the Thracian women. Later, Ovid, in *Metamorphoses*, furnishes the myth with a further detail: after Orpheus's dismemberment, his head is washed up on the island of Lesbos and then buried in a temple, where it continues to give oracles, while his lyre is preserved in a temple of Apollo (Robbins 3–15). In *The Ground*, Ormus's route echoes various elements from the history of the Orpheus myth that inform the novel's catoptric urban configurations. For instance, the Orpheus cinema in Bombay and the Orpheum building in New York secure the connection between the two cities through the continuity of mythic imagery. From the Roman Orpheus, especially Virgil's and Ovid's, Rushdie derives Ormus's madness and migrant metamorphoses (Anderson 25–29). The novel refashions these mythical roles in the context of global diasporas and the cult of the celebrity.

If London serves as a centre of gravity in *The Ground's* urban cartography, its gravitational pull is weakening. Travelling westward, Rushdie's characters lose their East and become dis-Oriented/de-Orientalized. Ormus leaves the 'museum' of the British Empire (330) and begins his ascent to New York. This logical and effortless passage from London to New York echoes the idealized image of life in the American city as glorified in the text's echoes of the popular romantic ballad 'A New York State of Mind'(331). Ormus Cama travels in the opposite direction to popular music, from a shared, 'state of mind' myth of New York to an individual experience of the city. His journey, therefore, takes a popular echo of the city back to its 'origin' in American popular culture, where it has already been commodified. His route mirrors, however, that of his creator, first, to the privileged position of those few who can afford a New York life, as opposed to a contemplative New York state of mind and, secondly, to a position within the popular fiction of this state of mind city. Ormus Cama is romantically borne across the Atlantic Ocean 'on a pool of light' (346).

Rushdie's protagonist travels from a Bombay in which the notion of the remote metropolitan 'essence' is perceived as a shadow, to the 'pure Platonic' form that the city of New York can only reflect and worship from a distance: New York 'seems to organize itself around [VTO], as they are the principle, the pure Platonic essence, that makes sense of the rest' (382). This route inverts the direction of popular culture: now the western metropolis receives an imperfect image of the Platonic ideal and unobservable Eastern 'original', yet one relying on the semi-mythological relationship between a celebrity figure and his consumer audience. Setting out to conquer the heights of the American city, Ormus measures both his talent against his urban ideal and the city against the paragon of his unrivalled musical genius. Excluding the level of the street from his exercise of narcissistic admiration, Ormus sentences himself to isolation. Moreover, he is alone in the project of 'reversing' the flow of Western popular culture. Once he has settled into the high-rise of the city, the Rhodope building (reminiscent of his 'native' Thrace/Bombay), his music, now part of the West, echoes old routes of colonial exploration, because 'where this city leads, this Rome, all the world's cities quickly follow' (387). Ormus's conquest of the city mirrors Rushdie's route into 'celestial Manhattan' (387): both are celebrity New Yorkers whose artistic creations travel back to their 'imaginary homelands' like Plato's forms. As Stephen Morton argues, such alternatives to cultural flows do not address 'the way in which contemporary South Asian music has been packaged as World music or Asian cool' (107).

The interplay of old and new in the representation of cities in the text is also foregrounded in the travels of the narrator, whose role echoes that of Virgil's Aristaeus in the *Georgics,* the bee-keeper who *'could spontaneously generate new bees from the rotting carcase of a cow'.* As a photographer, Rai claims that he, too, can 'spontaneously generate new meaning from the putrefying carcase of what is the case' (22, original emphasis). Rai's photography is marked by the same tensions – between absences and presences or between parallel worlds – as Ormus's music. The articulation of new cities and selves is thus also premised on the imagining or generation of new images of old cities. More specifically, however, Rai's photographs seek to both preserve an image of the Bombay/Mumbai and justify his departure from it. His interest in photography stems, for Herbert, from the position into which he is forced to occupy as a marginalized voyeur rather than a participant in the city's history (2008, 147).

The role of photographic journalism in the novel has been related to paparazzi voyeurism (Morton, 114). This is particularly poignant to Rai's last most dramatic and memorable snapshot of Vina, taken at the moment of a tremor somewhere on the Pacific coast of Mexico. She becomes the face of the earthquake as the earth literally opens up and swallows her. Similar tectonic metaphors are used to describe the Vina-impersonation craze after her death: 'a tidal wave' drowns her 'under a tsunami of her selves' or a 'second seismic force . . . regurgitates her in a thousand, thousand hideous pieces' (498). Here, 'tsunami' conjures up a stereotypical idea of waves of Japanese tourists and, clearly, the metaphor is intended to parody the contemporary cult of the celebrity.

Rai sees his exit from Bombay as a necessary stepping out of the frame in order to be able to see the whole picture (203). This photographic metaphor can be seen as his attempt to author his own life rather than remain a character in the fiction of Mumbai. In New York, however, he reinvents himself as a 'Mitteleuropean' photographer, named after the psychopath prostitute-murderer Moosbrugger in Robert Musil's *The Man without Qualities* (1930). Moosbrugger's photographs of the American city reveal its dark subconscious side haunted by echoes of the old continent and threatening its newness.

Yet the narrative repeatedly returns to the idea of leaving Mumbai, offering a multitude of reasons: it is a necessary 'whirling free of the mothership'; stepping off the map as well as a rebellion against belonging as an obsession, culture as a laboratory slide, orientation as a scam and home as brainwashing (55–177). Travel is celebrated as both a political act and a crucial rite of passage against romanticized notions of localism. The novel also parodies the epic advancement from Troy to Rome within the gendered schema of the genre. Epic has traditionally been considered a masculine genre, one that takes as its subject the founding, ordering, and defending of cities (Suzuki 1989, 1).Ironically, Rai has to exit 'Wombay, the parental body' (100) and seeks to be reborn not in a depthless, over-ground New York, the paternal metaphor of Rome, but in an ordinary-life city.

As Sara Upstone points out, *The Ground* should be seen not as postmodern free play but as a postcolonial strategy of movement and nomadism which challenges the violent encounters of diaspora (2006, 35). To reach London, for instance, Ormus has to cross a 'stretchy translucent membrane across the sky, an ectoplasmic barrier, a Wall' (GBHF, 253). The membrane model, a concept of identity that emerges from cell-theory in nineteenth-century literature, science and politics, reflects scientific fears of infection and nationalistic fears of infiltration by basing identity on resistance to external forces (Otis 1999, 7). Discursive prophylactic boundaries continue to divide old centres and peripheries. Donna Haraway reminds us that expansionist Western medical discourse in colonizing contexts was obsessed with the notion of the contagion and hostile penetration of the healthy body of empire, where this 'approach to disease involved a stunning reversal: the colonized was perceived as the invader' (1991, 223).

The novel traces a multitude of journeys. Disillusioned with the chaos of Bombay, Ormus's father, Darius Xerxes Cama, longs for the white-mansion England of his dreams (GBHF, 100), a romanticized, idyllic landscape, to which he travels in his imagination. Darius' scholarly paper, '"Sent to Coventry": or, "Is There a Fourth Function?"' describes the condition of 'the leper, pariah, outcast, exile' and urges for its necessity (GBHF, 150). Yet, in stepping outside the walls of his library and outside Bombay, to travel to his fantasy of England, he ironically becomes a fourth-functional outcast himself: England leaves him 'shipwrecked, marooned' (GBHF, 163). Colonial echoes reverberate in Lady Spenta's journeys too. It is she who lives Darius Cama's dreams by marrying an Englishman and moving into his 'white Palladian mansion set upon a hill above the winding Thames' (202). Suggestively, however, Englishman's name is William Methwold, the residual trace of *Midnight's Children*'s Bombay and its colonial genealogy. Ormus, like Saleem, is fathered by a Methwold figure, but in *The Ground's* echoes of *Midnight*, it is Bombay that now claims and exoticizes England. The reality of England thus clashes with Spenta's fantasies, as it does with Darius's: she dreams of a spiritual journey of illumination.

Ormus's brothers, Virus, Cyrus, and Gayomart, through which Rushdie imagines his own as well as Ormus's shadow selves further problematize both travel and stasis. The image of 'internal exile' (138) pervades all versions of the brothers' Bombay: the narrator sees them 'as men who were all incarcerated for a time, enclosed within their own bodies by the circumstances of their lives' (138). While Virus is exiled in silence, Cyrus, who never leaves India, develops, instead, a criminal insanity that fulfils the fantasy of travelling. He is a serial killer who tempts his victims with his highly articulate and mesmerizing travellers' tales of 'glittering cities and mountain ranges like the devil's teeth' (137).

On his way to New York, Ormus is forced to stay on board a pirate radio-station ship, the *Federica*, moored off the coast of Lincolnshire. Although there he serves a sort of musical apprenticeship, the *Federica* is for him a geographical displacement from the American city. Ironically, Ormus is shipwrecked aboard a ship, an intertextual echo of Umberto Eco's *The Island of the Day Before* (1995). Eco employs the figure of Robinson Crusoe in conjunction with numerous other intertexts of the cultural era of the Baroque – a time of scientific discoveries, especially Kepler's and Galileo's – contributing to the loss of a centre in the universe (Capozzi 1996, 172). Eco's character, Roberto, is shipwrecked on a deserted Dutch ship, the *Daphne*, off the coast of an uncharted island through which the 180th meridian passes. Roberto is unable to swim and has no other way of reaching the island. He is on a mission to uncover the British attempt to find the *punto fijo*, the fixed point to measure the longitudes, which was sought by European navigators until Harrison's invention of the maritime chrono-meter. The only other passenger on board, a German Jesuit, also on a mission to find the centre of time, informs Roberto that it lies between the island and *Daphne*, dividing yesterday from today and the past from the present (Bouchard 1997, 350–1). The invisible but constricting membrane, separating Bombay and London/New York in *The Ground*, is thus a trope of cartographic discourse, as is the *punto fijo* in Eco's text. Temporally, the membrane, like the 180th meridian in Eco's novel, can only imperfectly divide the past, empire, old Troy/Bombay, from the present, new Bombay/Rome/New York. Thus London becomes an atemporal, threshold city, a permeable prime meridian that signals the transition from the past to the future.

Chapter 6

Metropolitan Desires: Glocalist Seductions in *Fury* and *Shalimar the Clown*

Rushdie's eighth novel, *Fury* (2001), was seen as marking a significant departure from his previous work's political orientation, a change often diagnosed in parallel with his transferral of urban focus from Bombay and London to New York which began with *The Ground beneath Her Feet* and the author's personal relocation to New York in 1999. In these two novels Anshuman Mondal identifies a 'profound ideological shift' in Rushdie's writing, a realignment with the North rather than the global South, with the centre rather than the margins, and with America as a global super-power rather than 'the postcolonial stage' (2007, 169). The value of Rushdie's new political position, Mondal concludes, is none at best (181). In a less categorical reading, Stephen Morton distinguishes between Rushdie's fiction and non-fiction, noting the author's tacit support of America's secular liberal values in his post-9/11 editorials as opposed to, but also to an extent prefigured in, his ambivalence towards a U.S.-led globalization in *Fury*. As a Third World postcolonial author, Morton argues, Rushdie is faced with a 'liberal dilemma': how to 'condemn political repression in the Third World while remaining resolutely non-aligned with the First World in an age of post-communist American imperialism' (120–1; 131). Rushdie's acceptance of a knighthood in 2007 prompted further, biographically-informed differentiations within his political stance. Priyamvada Gopal compared 'plain Mr. Rushdie' to 'Sir Salman' declaring *The Moor's Last Sigh* the last articulation of the former author, before he 'emerged blinking into New York sunshine shortly before the towers came tumbling down'. 'Sir Salman', she wrote, is representative of a new group of 'liberal literati who have assented to the notion that humane values, tolerance and freedom are fundamentally western ideas that have to be defended as such' (2007, n. pag.). As we shall see in the next chapter, such a pronouncement is put to a rigorous test in *The Enchantress of Florence*, a novel which was received, with a degree of cautious enthusiasm, as Rushdie's return to form. At the same time, Lindsey Moore (2010), for instance, discusses this later novel as a mere historical re-contextualization of the author's consistent political concerns.

Fury, then, has been situated, by critical opinion, in the middle of a stage in Rushdie's writing, from *The Ground* to *Shalimar the Clown*, which saw the author's involvement with the developments and effects of neoliberal globalization, the role of the global media, celebrity culture, Islamist terrorism, and America's participation and responsibility – cultural, political, military, and economic – in the shaping of these processes and their violent consequences. For some, his fiction produced during this stage re-enacted the ways in which Rushdie the person and non-fiction author was compromised in his implicit support of neoliberal values and, specifically, of the U.S. as the world's 'best current guarantor' of 'freedom' against 'tyranny, bigotry, intolerance, fanaticism' (SATL, 97–8) as well as in his own transformation into a celebrity and his acceptance of the knighthood.

Even in the pre-9/11 context of *Fury*'s publication, it is tempting to see elements of the life of the novel's protagonist, Malik Solanka, in terms of Rushdie's own choices at the time – his move to America, his separation from his third English wife, Elizabeth West, and his pursuit of a relationship with supermodel Padma Lakshmi to whom the novel is dedicated. It can even be argued that *Fury* consciously invites such an interpretation, that it anticipates and acknowledges it (or, as has been suggested that it dismisses or deflects it) in the form of Solanka's self-criticisms and, perhaps, that it attempts to exonerate its author of a perceived transgression by offering a dialogically-engaging disclaimer: 'Yes, it had seduced him, America; yes, its brilliance aroused him, and its vast potency too, and he was compromised by this seduction. What he opposed in it, he must also oppose in himself' (F, 87).

The seductions of America – more broadly, its strategies of ensuring a global capitalism and, more specifically, the effects of its policies and military interventions in South Asia – also loom large in Rushdie's subsequent novel, *Shalimar the Clown*. India/Kashmir has been seduced and then jilted by American power. *Kashmira*, *India* and *Kashmira* are the successive names of the illegitimate daughter of Boonyi Kaul (*Boonyi* means 'the earth' or 'mud', SC 46), a young and beautiful Hindu woman from Kashmir, who seduces and is seduced by Max Ophuls, the charming Jewish American ambassador to India. Since he is initially seen as a 'friend of India', and the relationship between them is 'something not unlike love', when news breaks of his scandalous seduction of Boonyi, the country feels like a 'scorned lover' (SC, 138–9). The seduction itself is compared to an international diplomatic negotiation:

> Whereupon for an hour they hammered out the treaty of their affiliation
> as if it were a back-channel negotiation or an international arms deal,
> each recognizing a need in the other that complemented their own. Max
> Ophuls was actually aroused by the young woman's naked pragmatism.
> (SC, 192)

When Boonyi and Max meet, she is married to her childhood love, a Muslim
youth from their Kashimiri village, Pachigam. Her husband, Noman Sher
Noman, is also known as Shalimar the clown, a tightrope acrobat born in the
garden of Shalimar (also the birthplace of Boonyi). Betrayed by his wife,
Shalimar renounces the art of tightrope-walking, channels his anger into
terrorism and eventually, in what is at once an act of personal and political
revenge, murders both Boonyi and Max. In the words of a reviewer of the
novel, the 'forces of Islamic fundamentalism feed on Kashmir's lost inno-
cence' (Walter, n. pag.). The American influence in the region perversely
strengthened dictatorship and fundamentalist terrorism by financing
Pakistan's military and arming Islamic fundamentalists against Soviet troops
during the Cold War. As Bruce King points out, this is 'a version of the
postcolonial empire writing back its own history' (2011, 148–9).

Fury, however, is also a post-fatwa exploration of the afterlife of Rushdie's
fictions (particularly the fate of *The Satanic Verses* and its impact on its
author), a connection explored in detail, as 'crisis authorship' in Sarah
Brouillette's (2005; 2007a) reading. A major difference, however, between
Rushdie's life and that of Solanka is that the latter does not rehabilitate
New York once his fictions' afterlife has taken its course. Criticisms of
Rushdie's (lack of) political position focused on New York as portrayed at
the beginning of the novel. For Srivastava, the novel's outlook is synonymous
with an imperial gaze and the city is the product of Rushdie's imperial
cosmopolitanism (2008, 174). Mondal acknowledges but is unconvinced by
Solanka's 'jeremiads against the debased nature of contemporary American
reality' (174–5) that New York provokes. A fundamental omission in these
readings is the global context, with its specific parameters, within which the
image of New York develops. The city, as we shall explore in depth, is both
established and undermined as the central location of the text's universe.

The turn-of-the-twentieth-century New York in which *Fury* opens is a
gravitational centre of the world, promising and embodying, but eternally
withholding the idea of America as the final destination and culmination of
limitless diasporas. On his way to his 'comfortable Upper West sublet' (29),
serviced by Punjabi construction workers, a Polish cleaner and a German
Jewish plumber, Solanka walks the streets of Manhattan, consuming its

cosmopolitan display of the cultures of the world, which have been subsumed and transformed by the metropolis into its mere sub-cultures – among them, Caribbean carnivals and Jamaican 'troubadour-polemisists' (7), Jewish ceremonies of the blessing of the bread, and various degrees of simulacra of the Viennese *Kaffehous* (44). All compete for bids in New York as a casino (4) or a race (212), trading in cultural currencies. Both consumer and consumed (his British accent, for instance, is a marketable commodity), Solanka becomes a critical flâneur in an attempt to distance himself from the city by reading it and pointing out its flaws, frivolities, excesses, and ignorance. While residual traces of his Third World roots can be discerned in occasional observations – India, China, Africa, and most of South America 'would have killed for the street merchandise of Manhattan' (6) – Solanka has effectively suppressed his Indian past like Saladin in *The Satanic Verses*. His critique of New York is served from the elitist and moralizing standpoint of an 'old-world' (4) Cambridge scholar, 'trained to the old European subtleties' (44), capable of distinguishing between Greek and Mesopotamian metaphors (otherwise clashing in buildings' architectural forms and inscriptions) and explaining his own jokes' cultural references ('Pythian verse,' the reader is told, 'is poetry written in the dactylic hexameter', 43).

As the novel progresses, however, New York is revealed as the global epicentre of the world's, as well as America's, fury. Its celebrated status in American national mythology as the gateway to the land of freedom, opportunity, and success and the key to the American dream ironically attracts and fosters the world's hostility towards America, a hostility both locally derived and globally circulated. Fury – 'sexual, Oedipal, political, magical, brutal' (30) – operates as a tectonic force, simultaneously driving or creative *and* destructive, an existential condition, a liminal state and a momentary lapse of consciousness. As a metaphor, fury is strongly reminiscent of shame in Rushdie's early novel of the same title in that both 'conditions' are at once the cause and effect of themselves, feeding off themselves and gaining in potency until they reach epidemic proportions. Whereas shame/shamelessness is more narrowly critiqued as associated with the political and social brutalities of Pakistan's early history, in the later novel, fury is a world-shaping force. *Fury* engages in tracing the ways in which specific genealogies and trajectories of fury – American as well as postcolonial, post-communist, nationalist, ethnic or indigenous, crisscross, overlap and inform each other.

In the life story of its protagonist, the novel traces a diasporic trajectory of fury which involves an interurban journey. Professor Malik Solanka, a graduate of, and, later, a historian of ideas at King's College Cambridge, has resigned his tenured position as a result of his growing disillusionment with academic life's 'narrowness, infighting and ultimate provincialism' (14) in the late 1980s. Inspired by a visit to Amsterdam's Rijksmuseum, where he observes with fascination and uncanny alarm a display of seventeenth-century dollhouses – 'meticulously period-furnished' (15), but uninhabited, as if 'some strange cataclysm [had occurred] in which property had remained undamaged while all breathing creatures had been destroyed' (15–16) – Solanka embarks on a compensatory creative project, the design of a series of 'Great Mind' dolls modelled after key figures in the European history of ideas, including Socrates, Galileo, Machiavelli, and Kierkegaard. After his move to London with his wife, Eleanor Masters, he develops a late-night series of history-of-philosophy programmes for the BBC in which his philosopher-dolls are interviewed by a 'smart, sassy, unafraid' time-travelling 'knowledge-seeker' female doll, named Little Brain or 'L.B.' (16–17). Hugely popular, *The Adventures of Little Brain* is soon hijacked by a BBC 'concept group' known as the Little Brains Trust (97) that projects L.B. into a lucrative superstardom, in the process degrading her to a 'monster of tawdry celebrity' (98), the very negation of her creator's principles and original intention. Enraged, Solanka has observed his doll's growth out of his control into an unstoppable phenomenon – an actress, a video game, a cover girl, and an autobiographer whose memoirs are classed as non-fiction – but has remained incapable of refusing the 'dirty money' (100). In an attempt to distance himself from the emancipated L.B. whose now seemingly unscripted career is otherwise fuelled by the growth of the culture industry and its new religion of fame (24), Solanka has fled to New York. His flight is also motivated by his self-loathing, both a result of his creation's and his own corruption and of an incident in which, during one of his moments of fury, he has contemplated the murder of his unsuspecting, sleeping wife and son.

His rage against the L.B. mania builds up on an earlier, childhood anger suppressed in the memory of Bombay as the city of his emasculation. No longer the maternal body of 'Wombay' that it is in *The Ground, Fury*'s Bombay is confined to domestic space where the carnivalesque inversions of fatherhood in *Midnight's Children* are replaced by a forced inversion of gender roles. Malik has been raised as a girl, at the insistence of his step-father, who has also repeatedly abused him sexually until the intervention of a neighbour, Mr. Venkat. The trauma of this abuse is further augmented by the departure of Mr. Venkat, Malik's symbolic surrogate father, as part of his *sanyasi* metamorphosis. In a gesture of sarcastic self-flagellation, fifty-five-year-old Solanka would define himself as a '*sanyasi* in New York', where both New York, as a city boiling with money (3) and obsessed with material possessions, and Solanka himself, who has flown business-class to JFK, landed in a familiar city speaking a familiar language, and retained his credit card, are the 'vulgar and inept' (81) negation of the *sanyasi*'s journey towards the divine.

In New York, Solanka's accumulated migrant fury and guilt, however, become productively involved with those of Eastern European Mila Milo and those of Indo-Lilliputian Neela Mahendra. Criticisms of the novel which accused Rushdie of a lack of political position tended to associate him with his protagonist. Indeed, Solanka appears to fall short of a distinct political cause and to adopt, instead, those of other migrants, where such 'borrowings' take place on a characteristically romantic/erotic level as strategies of mutual seduction.

Mila, with whom Solanka enters into a self-admittedly Oedipal relationship, is a descendant, on her father's side, of Serbian nationalist anger and culpability in the context of the Balkan crisis. As in Solanka's story, rage feeds on rage. Ethnic tensions suppressed under communism in Yugoslavia, a country itself a product of a forced union in the aftermath of World War I, erupted in its violent break-up in the early 1990s, after the collapse of the Soviet Union. Mila's father, Milosevic, has abridged his surname to 'Milo' in an attempt to dissociate himself from 'the other' Milošević, 'the fascist gangster pig'. Yet, while he agrees with 'the analysis of what Milosevic was doing in Croatia and was going to do in Bosnia', Milo has become increasingly concerned with the resulting 'demonization of the Serbs' (113). Perry Anderson points out that while 'human rights' was the 'battle-cry' in the Balkan War, the NATO campaign against Yugoslavia was both 'uplifting in its removal of Milošević' and 'valuable as a demonstration of American command in Europe' (9; 13). Motivated by his desire to act as 'the moral conscience of the place' (113), Mila's father returns from New York 'into the fury' of Belgrade and becomes its victim. This interplay of anger, guilt and violence is governed by the recurrent and inevitable transformation of defensive into offensive fury and of its victims into its agents in an endless vicious cycle: '[v]iolent action is unclear to most of those who get caught up in it. Experience is fragmentary; cause and effect, why and how, are torn apart. Only sequence exists' (252).

This pattern of violence also manifests itself in the geopolitical configurations in *Shalimar*. Tectonically speaking, the novel is reminiscent of the erosive sub-narratives of Islam in *The Satanic Verses*. America's 'relationship' with India has contributed to the creation of Shalimar, the international terrorist, who then 'surfaces' in Los Angeles, bent on retribution.

Urban signs signal, similarly to those in *The Ground beneath Her Feet*, the existence of subterranean instability and an imminent eruption on the site of the American metropolis, which is situated, as the text emphasizes, in an 'earthquake zone' (SC, 334). Before Shalimar's assassination of Max Ophuls, Los Angeles is 'all treachery, all deception, a quick-change, quicksand metropolis, hiding its nature, guarded and secret in spite of all its apparent nakedness'; the city appears to stimulate 'the forces of destruction' as they no longer need 'the shelter of dark' (SC, 5). An ambassador for counterterrorism supporting terror activities, Max Ophuls is himself 'a Himalaya', caused by 'the smashing together of great forces, by a clash of worlds' and the 'collision in him [is] still taking place' (SC, 20–1). He praises Los Angeles' earthquakes for their majesty and its landslides for their 'reproof of human vanity' (SC, 22). An 'occult servant of American geopolitical interest', Max enigmatically speaks, in a television talk-show, of a certain mysterious, subterranean 'lizard people', who 'supposedly dwell in tunnels below Los Angeles' (SC, 27; 335). As a result of his life on the borderline between the world's visible realities and invisible dealings, his hands are stained by both 'the world's visible and invisible blood' (SC, 335).

In the earlier novel, fury's 'cycle' is mirrored in the coup-countercoup developments in Lilliput-Blefuscu, echoes of the first stage of which make their way into New York through Neela Mahendra and become 'available' for Solanka's appropriation. Before we examine these developments, however, it is necessary to trace a series of analogous, local, New York eruptions of fury whose cumulative effect shapes, to a certain extent, Solanka's involvement with the world outside the city. African–American Jack Rhinehart, the elite S&M ('Single and Male') club with which he becomes involved, and a South-Asian taxi driver Solanka comes across all mobilize the suppressed fury of their past, thus wittingly or unwittingly transforming themselves from its victims into its perpetrators.

Solanka's friend Rhinehart has reinvented himself from a 'noted young radical journalist of colour with a distinguished record of investigating American racism' into 'simply, an American' (56–7). This transformation, echoing Fanon's diagnosis of a colonially-triggered pathology in the black man's donning of white masks, has generated in him a self-loathing rage (58) that, in turn, he attempts to redirect, firstly, into sexual conquests of the 'daughters of Paleface' (57) and, then, to his own demise, into a membership of the S&M secret society. The 'gilded young men' of the S&M club have articulated their own fury, 'born of what they who had so much, had never been able to acquire' – 'lessness, ordinariness' (202) – in the form of a possessiveness towards, and sadistic violence against, women. Their three young white female victims have been scalped, a technique that can itself be read as a perversely simulative reclamation of a Native American, masculine-coded fury, especially as the narrator's metaphor – the 'swish of the tomahawk' (155) – makes the connection explicit. The condemnation of the murderers ironically echoes the demonization of Native Americans precisely through the stereotyping of such practices as scalping and their appropriation as a justification for colonial expansion. The novel readily evokes further colonial labels of alterity, specifically, of savagery: voodoo, in connection with the pervasive (self-)dollification of New York women, and cannibalism, in an 'indigenous' Lilliput-Blefuscu context but one which is referred to, once again, in New York. The fact that these practices are mimicked as erotic fantasies points to the tectonic nature of the process in which discursive weapons from the arsenal of old colonial powers are disinterred and performed, on a subliminal, déjà-vu level, as the successful seductions of contemporary America. Before the S&M murderers are exposed, New York is haunted by the image of a killer wearing a Panama hat – an image which terrorizes the Panama-hat-wearing Solanka, but also one with which he identifies and with which the reader is invited to identify him for a considerable portion of the narrative. In this respect, to find Rushdie guilty, through his protagonist, of espousing an imperialist cosmopolitan cause, is to follow or, more precisely, to be teased into following, a line of interrogation of the text that it has already prescribed. The Panama hat as a signifier of a simulated and commodifed South-American Third World controlled by American economic and military might (in the U.S. purchase of the rights to build the Panama Canal in 1903, its long-standing control of it and its invasion of Panama in 1989) is a strong case in point. The journey of the hat, from the hands of its Ecuadorian weavers, through those of the gold-seekers crossing the Isthmus of Panama on their way to California and those of the construction crews of the Panama Canal, into New York haberdasheries (Miller 2000) and onto Solanka's head, once again demonstrates the way in which New York receives and appropriates cultural forms, in the process vanquishing their histories. Although Solanka symbolically wears this signifier and recognizes his corruption in it, his self-suspicion eventually disperses and the status quo is restored in the classical detective vein. New York is capable of capitalizing on its own crises, and, indeed, they even appear functional in sustaining its underlying uniformity through the promotion of sub-cultural niche identities. Violence born out of fury causes only ripples on the urban surface and is quickly subsumed by the city's flows. The story of the S&M club dissipates into 'the society scandal of the summer' (200).

Such serial eruptions and abatements of fury punctuate New York and articulate its tectonic rhythms. This is further demonstrated in Solanka's double encounter with a young Muslim, South Asian taxi driver, Ali Majnu. Solanka's two rides in his taxi are virtually indistinguishable from each other as, on both occasions, Majnu's anti-American and anti-Semite anger is expressed in the same form, as a vehement outburst of verbal road rage in an 'explosive, village-accented Urdu' (65). He swears 'victorious jihad' (65) and 'holy wrath' (175) against Manhattan's Tenth Avenue which, Solanka surmises, 'was perhaps being blamed . . . for the tribulations of the Muslim world' in the course of a staggering American-led Middle East Peace process (65–6). Rushdie's stereotypical representation of a Third World Muslim taxi driver as either 'Indian or Pakistani' and 'no doubt out of some misguided collectivist spirit of paranoiac pan-Islamic solidarity' (66), has provoked the criticisms of reviewers of the novel. Amitava Kumar observes that as a 'bigoted prophet on wheels, screaming deliverance', Majnu is expected to stand for 'the whole of Islam', thus bearing the 'brown man's burden' in having to 'answer for more than one is' (2001, 34). It should further be noted that Rushdie seems to be pitting, through his protagonist, an urban West against a 'village-accented' Islam, implicitly defending the former against the upheavals of the latter, especially as Solanka is introduced to the reader as a 'born-and-bred metropolitan of the countryside-is-for-cows persuasion' (6). Majnu's subsequent renunciations of both his anathemazing outpour ('I am not aware') and Islam ('I don't even go to the mosque', 66), however, complicate this interpretation. On the one hand, they seem to depoliticize his fury ('It's just words') and even to place him in a servile, mimic-man position, as he 'needily' pleads with Solanka: 'God bless America, okay?' (66). On the other hand, this plea can be seen as a self-defensive posture intended to conceal a subconscious aggression Majnu continues to harbour. This is certainly a reading the text supports as in Majnu's periodic anti-American tirades Solanka recognizes his own red-mist moments when a 'terrorist anger' (67) overcomes him. Majnu is a distant echo of Maulana Dawood in *Shame*: the notorious 'local divine' of Q./Quetta who rides 'around town on a motor-scooter donated by the Angrez sahibs, threatening the citizens with damnation' (S, 42). Both novels project an idea of the circular motion or fluidity of shame/fury which structure cities.

The tectonic Third World rhythms of New York in *Fury* operate rather like what Benedict Anderson (1983) has theorized as the horizontal sense of *meanwhile*, shared by the members of a modern nation as an imagined community. After Majnu's second reappearance, the reader is assured, to paraphrase Anderson, that somewhere out there in Manhattan, he continues to move along, incessantly cursing the city and 'awaiting his next reappearance in the plot' (33), his existence mirroring the periodic newspaper reports of the Panama-hat killer. These counter-rhythms, in other words, are at this stage still claimed by, and largely contained in, a characteristically modern consciousness of a national secular temporality shared by all New Yorkers, punctuated by Majnu's prefiguring intimations of divine time ('Islam will cleanse this street'; 'Islam will purify this whole city', 65). Majnu's next reappearance, motivated by 'terrorist anger', would be as Shalimar in Los Angeles in another, but related, plot, as we suggested earlier.

Fury, however, continues to operate, slowly abrading not only New York but the whole world, leaving 'craters' in cities, deserts, nations and the heart (129). Everybody, according to Mila, is 'quaking inside, behind their façade' (115). Although the novel contextualizes individual trajectories of fury, however, they are in danger of merging into one another. The New York S&M murders, for instance, are reminiscent of the London Granny Ripper murders in *The Satanic Verses*, specifically in the attempted scapegoating of a black man (here, Rhinehart) for crimes committed by white men of societal standing (the 'Metropolitan police', a phrase with Foucauldian undertones of policed identities as part of a metropolitan/civilizing project in this context, as we saw in the earlier novel). Race, as Rhinehart learns 'the hard way', is still an issue (151). In both cases, however, the black victims are shown to be implicated through their own propensity for violence. Fury, like globalization, can be a homogenizing force, driven by the cultivation of its own excesses and profiting from its incessant reproduction of lines of division.

Crucially, the global pervasiveness of fury relies on another ambiguous, travelling and universalizing trope – in discourses of racism, of liberal secularism, and of the globalization of capital – tolerance. Wendy Brown (2006) explores how tolerance, celebrated as a 'beacon of multicultural justice and civic peace' and a 'supplement of liberal equality and freedom' in Western discourses masks or naturalizes its own normative reproduction of the self-other opposition, where the free, civilized Western self has been articulated as the subject while the fundamentalist, barbaric other has been seen as an object of tolerance in an extraordinarily broad variety of contexts since the mid-1980s. Tolerance, she argues, 'is not the problem', but the 'call for tolerance', its invocation and the 'attempt to instantiate' it are 'signs of identity production and identity management in the context of orders of stratification or marginalization in which the production, the management and the context themselves are disavowed' (Brown 2006, 14).

Global commercial expansion, as we noted earlier, is also 'capable' of tolerance. The notion of '*glocommodification*' has been coined to refer to 'global commodification combining structural uniformity with symbolic diversity', where Domino's Pizza, for instance, seemingly tolerates, while in fact harnessing and profiting from, cultural difference by offering falafels in Israel (Ram 2004, 11–31).

In the novel, tolerance is invoked as a quality both necessitating and necessitated by fury. The murder of the 'wildest' and last of the three female victims, Saskia 'Sky' Schuyler, has been a response to her own 'sexual fury', but one directed inwards, in the form of 'masochistic excesses' and 'highest levels of tolerance' (201–2). Symbolically, only the 'Sky' is the limit of her ambition, intelligence, social standing, and sexual experimentation, where her 'limits' include a third-party tolerance for violence against others – she has known about the previous two murders and is 'crazily aroused' by them (202).

Tolerance becomes, in this way, the site of convergence of the novel's tectonic and specular urban configurations, where the slippage between positions of masochistic and sadistic tolerance parallels that between the positions of object and subject of fury. Fury and tolerance, the novel suggests, operate as erotically solicited submissions to the seductions performed by neoliberal discourse, both on the site of the western metropolis, as a characteristic expression of that discourse, and globally. In the context of Sky's murder, fury and tolerance expose uneven gender power relations (Sky is symbolically punished for her gender-transgressing sexual fury), but they also position her and her murderers – as victims/ perpetrators of hegemonic seductions – within larger, economic and political configurations. The American Dream, as a magnetic national ideology, is flaunted and seduces on a global scale. If fury has the revolutionary potential to explosively reveal the mechanisms of neoliberal seduction, it can also ironically become the very expression of this seduction. In being held together under the rubric of anti-Americanism, the world's multiple genealogies of fury lose their historical and political value like Panama hats: 'Even anti-Americanism,' Solanka proffers, is 'Americanism in disguise' (88).

The role of New York in these processes is also ambiguous. On the one hand, the narrative performs a recurrent slippage from a critique of the city to a critique of America, where the relationship between the two ranges from one of various analogies to a straightforward identification. Thus New York and America act as partners in a seduction strategy, where the city compensates for the way America 'insults the rest of the planet' by fostering lust (6); or, they have both re-invented themselves as Rome/the Roman Empire, with the world as its provinces (86–8); or, New York is a creation and faithful follower of America the deity (44). On the other hand, however, New York figures as yet another victim of America's 'omnivorous power' (44), seeking to break free, or as its disillusioned spouse, seeking divorce, with American seductions coded feminine. In one of the many stories Solanka overhears in the streets of Manhattan, a man describes his ambivalent relationship with his ex-wife expressed in his hesitation of whether to hit or kiss her. '[F]or wife,' Solanka interprets, 'read America' (89). The motif of a desired but denied divorce or separation recurs in the novel. It is mirrored in the persistent refusal of Rhinehart's white wife to grant him divorce and in the repetitive, desperate pleas of Solanka's wife for his return to his family. New York, then, a city which otherwise carries the cosmopolitan potential of Bombay – granting a 'sense of being crowded by other people's stories' (89) – appears to be both held in check by an institutionalized pact with America and caught up in the play of its seductions. As such, it is a city without hope of deliverance – a Gotham without a Batman and a Metropolis without a Superman (87).

In *Shalimar*, the relations between India and America acquire a distinctly Oedipal shape in the case of Max's relationship with his daughter, or, in an allegorical sense, a narcissistic shape in the case of America's games with the products of its own power in South Asia. Max is India's 'mountain-father' and she is his 'mountaineer': he holds 'her hands in his and up she came until she was straddling his shoulders, her groin against his neck' (SC, 21). Western cities, specifically Los Angeles and Paris in this novel, figure most explicitly as temptresses to which Max is both irresistibly drawn and which he scorns: for him an 'open city' is like 'a naked whore, lying invitingly back and turning every trick'. Los Angeles, an 'erotic capital of the obscure stratagem', knows 'precisely how to arouse and heighten our metropolitan desires' (SC, 22). Similarly, Paris is to be distrusted, since this 'innocent-uninnocent' city is 'a prostitute', 'too beautiful' but 'flaunting its beauty as if begging to be scarred' (SC, 140).

The invocation of feminine seduction as a strategy of hegemonic control is reminiscent of Jean Baudrillard's thought. In his study, *Seduction*, he explores this phenomenon as a play of appearances and a form of soft deception that represents 'mastery over the symbolic universe' (1990, 70). While he advocates seduction as alternative to production, he acknowledges (if sarcastically) that whereas 'once [the masses] had to endure domination under the threat of violence, now they must accept it by dint of seduction' (ibid. 175). Baudrillard's (1989) and Rushdie's assessment of America as a seduction is in its ability to simulate and live utopia, specifically the utopia of the American Dream, as if it were real. In *Fury*, Solanka's New York approximates the French theorist's conceptualizations of consumer society caught up in the spectacle of simulacra and technology. As in Baudrillard's analysis, simulation's seduction pervades social relations and defines them – as 'Seduce me./Let me seduce you.' – when 'all the stakes have been withdrawn' (1990, 175). Solanka has arrived in America to be erased and devoured as a conscious submission/consent to seduction/hegemony, but also as a self-inflicted punishment, motivated by a sense of guilt and self-loathing. His submission to Mila's, and then Neela's, seductions is marked by the same sense.

Moving, in a parasitic manner, from Mila to Neela, the protagonist appropriates, or is seduced, by what could be described as their *raison-d'êtres*, what gives them their identities and political concerns and governs their actions. This is reflected in their respective New York apartments – the focal point of Mila's is the MacPowerbook (176), while Neela's insists upon India 'in the overemphasized manner of diaspora' (208). Mila is the leader of the 'most fashion-forward geek posse in New York' (118), who live a double life. On the one hand, they are the creative artists of Webspyder.net who design websites for celebrities, lucrative for both parties. On the other, they possess the technological expertise, and it is implied, the political ambition, of cyber-pirates, capable of hitting Bill Gates (or 'the Evil Emperor') with a virus (118). In Manuel Castells' terms (2001), they belong, at once, to the entrepreneurial and the hacker layers of Internet culture, where, in this case, the former is effectively the negation of the principle of the latter. Mila, too, echoes the libertarian hacker slogan ('Information wants to be free', Bell 2007, 86) when she teaches Solanka about the evolved concept of authorship as a result of the development of the Internet – 'it's so much more cooperative. . . . You're still the magician, but let everyone else play with the wands sometimes', while assuring him, 'the financial upside is very, very strong (178). More indicatively of cyberculture's vulnerability to seduction, even as it romanticizes itself, Mila suggests to Solanka that, on the Internet, he would be the 'absolute monarch' (178) of his creations rather than losing control, as in the case of the story of Little Brain.

Neela Mahendra, a successful television producer in New York, is a descendant of Indian *girmityas* or indentured labourers, transported to the South Pacific two-island country of Lilliput-Blefuscu to work on its sugar plantations in the nineteenth century. The Swiftian Lilliput-Blefuscu, with its capital city of Mildendo, has otherwise been acknowledged as a 'transparent stand-in for Fiji' (Bruillette 141), a comparatively young British colony and thus one of the last to import Indian bonded servants (Mishra 2005, 17), but where the importation of indentured labour has, nevertheless, radically transformed the country's demography, in combination with divisive colonial policies which institutionalized racial difference between the Fijians and the Indo-Fijians (Emde 2005, 390–1). In the novel, Mildendo-born Neela is a fourth-generation member of Lilliput-Blefuscu's Indo-Lilliputian ('Indo-Lilly') ethnic group, in dispute with the 'indigenous' Elbee (L. B./Lilliput-Blefuscu) community over the issue of land ownership, a right constitutionally denied to Indo-Lillies (158).

As Neela tells her 'back-story' to Solanka in New York, over three Cosmo-politan cocktails, she admits that her roots are pulling at her and causing her to suffer from the 'guilt of relief' (157). While a loyal supporter of the Indo-Lilly cause, she is thus also a consumer of a stylized cosmopolitanism that is further caricatured in her lack of a sense of direction. As she 'never knew where anything was', her 'favourite stores, preferred restaurants and nightclubs . . . could have been anywhere' (159). Rishona Zimring reads Neela in light of her cosmopolitan drinking practices, as a 'tragic exemplar of an idealized global community' (2010, p. 10), yet this parodic reduction of her political commitments has wider implications, as we shall see, in pre-figuring the direction in which the Indo-Lilly resistance develops. Further, in Neela's universally-uncontested beauty, her glamour-style affiliation with cosmopolitanism, and her planned documentary on the Indo-Lilly resis-tance, Rushdie offers a satirical mirror of a particular variety of the Third World-born cosmopolitan celebrity, that of the Miss Universe contestant (a gentle poke at his then wife but also at his own variety of global chic, that of the cosmopolitan postcolonial intellectual). Lara Dutta, Miss Universe 2000, Bangalore-born and a student at Bombay University, reportedly listed as her hobbies 'rock-climbing, para-gliding, and bungee-jumping', while her 'career goal' was 'to become a documentary film-maker' (Metcalf *et al.*, 2002, 282).

With Neela's political inspiration and Mila's technical media support, Solanka embarks on a new creative project and the artistic sublimation of his own fury. He authors the story of *The Puppet Kings*, a hybrid master narrative of a post-apocalyptic world. This narrative invites a catoptric reading in its mirror-relation to the colonial and postcolonial histories of Lilliput-Blefuscu/Fiji – a location that reflects back on New York as its/the world's antipodes. As a result of a global ecological disaster on the planet Galileo-1, its northern Rijk civilization (allusive, simultaneously, of Amsterdam's Rijksmuseum, Fiji's history of Dutch exploration, and of British colonialism) is threatened. Its master cybernetist, Professor Akasz

Kronos (Professor Solanka's virtual analogue) moves his operations, as the Rijk lands drown, into the 'primitive but independent nation of Baburia, at the Galilean antipodes' (162), where he creates the Puppet-King cyborgs to defend Baburia from a possible assault by Rijk refugees. After winning for him the 'Battle of the Antipodes' against the incoming Rijk, however, the Puppets take on an independent existence and, becoming aware of their disenfranchisement, rebel against their increasingly tyrannical creator. Gaining power as Peekay (P. K./Puppet Kings) revolutionaries, they force Kronos into hiding (reminiscent, here, of Rushdie's position after the announcement of the fatwa) and inform Baburia's leader Mogol that from now on Peekays and Baburians are to live on their twin islands as equals. This, we understand, is not a declaration of peace but of a challenge, as the revolutionaries' last words are: 'Let the fittest survive' (167).

Clearly modelled after the plight of the Indo-Lillies, the Puppet Kings story is launched globally on the PlanetGalileo.com website and marketed through a 'wide range of *PK merchandise* [italics indicating a hyperlink] available for INSTANT shipping NOW. All major credit cards accepted' (168). In New York, therefore, diasporic hybridity (in Solanka's symbolic fusion of Neela's, Mila's, and his own fury) becomes available for commercial appropriation. As a Kronos/Titan/Gulliver figure, Solanka self-admittedly aligns himself with the master civilization of the global North, but this imagination – of North–South power relations – offers him (and Rushdie, as it would appear) a self-introspection of guilt.

Now developing in parallel with the Puppet Kings' proliferating virtual life that they have inspired, political events on Lilliput-Blefuscu take an unexpected turn and brim into New York. Two parallel demonstrations of, respectively, the newly-formed revolutionary FILB ('Free Indian Lilliput-Blefuscu') movement, and of the indigenous Elbees take place in the American city. While the former gathers migrant supporters of Indo-Lilliputian origin, it begins as a 'poor affair' and ends as a 'brawl'. The latter, 'less well attended', self-disperses. Equally unsuccessful, the two demonstrations degrade further, into a FILB-Elbee 'scuffle'. The only 'evidence' they leave in New York City 'of the force of a gathering fury on the far side of the world' are drying bloodstains on Washington Square (192–3). In accompanying Neela to the FILB protest demonstration, Solanka is motivated by jealousy rather than sympathy for the cause of a fellow member of the Indian diaspora – in his opinion, she has paid 'too much attention' to Babur, the designated leader of the Indo-Lilly revolutionaries (192).

As in *The Satanic Verses*, Rushdie remains sceptical towards self-appointed icons of resistance and towards the ability of collective popular protest 'to reclaim and remake' – a tendency John McLeod diagnoses in relation to the earlier novel's representation of urban riots as Rushdie's sanctioning of 'popular violence' by portraying it as a 'misguided attempt to move from the position of the oppressed to that of the persecutor' (2004, 156). While Rushdie's unease about popular protest could be traced back to Jawaharlal Nehru's idea of civil violence as a 'sign of political immaturity', alien to democratic politics (Chakrabarty 2007, 36–7), it is also informed by the devastating effects of Hindu–Muslim antagonisms in India. Mildendo reflects the inter-communal violence of *The Moor's Last Sigh*'s Bombay in *Fury*'s explicit comparison of Babur with the leader of the Shiv Sena, Bal Thackeray (227) and in the events of the counter-coup and its aftermath. It is not surprising, when seen in light of this context, that the counter-coup led by Babur in Lilliput-Blefuscu only turns back on itself the aggression of the persecutor by borrowing its most intense articulation, the coup led by the indigenous Elbee merchant, Skyresh Bolgolam. Bolgolam, 'accompanied by two hundred armed ruffians', marches into the Lilliputian Parliament and takes hostage of most of its Indo-Lilly members as well as the country's president, Golbasto Gue. The coup is described as 'spectacularly unnecessary', as Bolgolam has already achieved a reversal of the president's reforms towards equal electoral and property rights for Indo-Lillies (215–16). The response of Babur's revolutionaries, the FRM/'Fremen' (FILB radicals), however, is directly informed by Solanka's master-story of the Puppet Kings. The Fremen have come to identify with the P. K. plight for equal rights – one they have themselves inspired in the first place – that have been denied by Baburia's ruler, Mogol. The counter-coup, therefore, begins with a raid on Mildendo's toy stores, with the Fremen making off with Kronosian Cyborg masks and costumes. Later, when Bolgolam has been captured and the city occupied by the forces of Babur, himself now wearing a 'Commander Akasz' mask, it appears as if Mildendo has been literally conquered by Solanka's characters.

The relationship between New York and Mildendo is thus constituted through an intensive traffic of tectonic – cumulative, causative, explosive – and catoptric – reflective, creative and transformative – movements. The antipodean developments have been both the original and the translations of Solanka's ideas, fuelling eruptions in both cities. The coups are, for instance, both prefigured in the parallel Lilliputian and Indo-Lilliputian demonstrations in New York and staged there on a smaller scale. These eruptions do not appear to differ radically in the effects they have in the two locations – the slogan of the Fremen/P.K. revolution – 'Let the fittest survive' – is emptied only of the specificity of its fraught political significance when it takes to New York's streets. There, it is worn on T-shirts as the motto of the 'gym generation' (224), with echoes of a newly inflected Social Darwinism.

While Bruillette sees the novel as an exploration of the processes in which 'images and their origins become radically separate, as cultural products are used to sell or promote political ideologies' (139), Teverson examines the ways in which cultural forms can be both homogenized into brand names and contesting of such homogenization, situating Rushdie in-between the 'demands of the global market and the imperatives of local self-expression' (194). Indeed, *Fury* can be read as a casebook of globalization's contradictory currents, specifically as a complication, or even interrogation, of the thesis that the local is a product or a victim of the global. New York 'shapes', or assists in, the emergence of a global-narrative creator, in the figure of Solanka, who 'produces' and benefits from the local, Mildendo/Lilliput-Blefuscu history through the creation of the Puppet Kings. Yet this creator is himself worldly, the outcome of diaspora. The revolutionary Indo-Lillies are also the product of elsewhere, involving another location – India – and the globalizing forces of British colonialism. In appropriating the Puppet Kings narrative, the Fremen are re-claiming their own by fixing or localizing it. Localisms and globalisms appear to feed off each other in a cycle of identificatory/liberatory-essentialist/hegemonic appropriations, without a start or an end point.

A significant detail, however, that has escaped critical attention to the novel, is the fictionality of the counter-coup in Lilliput-Blefuscu when seen in its reference to the postcolonial history of Fiji. While the Fijian coup of 2000 is easily recognizable in the novel's Elbee-led coup (with bankrupt businessman George Speight in the role of Bolgolam), a counter, Indo-Fijian coup has not taken place. In this sense, *Fury* belongs to the specific catoptric genealogy in Rushdie's urban writing, as we established in the Introduction, characterized by the delineation of an axis of 'real' cities – Bombay, London, New York, Mexico City, and Los Angeles – which exist in parallel with phantasmal, usually dystopian places that often simultaneously contain coded references to 'real' ones. The relationship between the two is complicated through intricate patterns of mirroring that reconfigure both, as we have seen in relation to Jahilia in *The Satanic Verses*, for instance. In relation to *Fury*, however, this asymmetry raises an important question – why can cities such as Bombay, London and New York afford the luxury of referring to a positive (in the sense of undeniably existing, if critiqued) political geography outside the novels and to the material lives of its inhabitants while others can only allude to or 'borrow' locations from such a geography? *Fury* can be read as science fiction that anticipates the future of Fiji by projecting on it the history of India and providing a warning about what may happen. In imposing a corrupted counter-coup on his exploration of Indian diaspora in Fiji, Rushdie seems to enter the role of his self-critiqued protagonist. Solanka, like Rushdie, emerges as a global author who produces sign-posts of things to come by providing 'the old material [with] a fresh, contemporary twist' (190–1). Thus when the protagonist arrives in Mildendo, in search of Neela, he has a 'strong sense of déjà-vu': the city reminds him of 'Chandni Chowk, Old Delhi's troubled heart' (240). In Rushdie's modernized Swiftian analogy, Lilliput-Blefuscu appears a paradigmatic, and thus abstract or stereotypical, Third World country. Its name bears the trauma of its history of colonial exploration and reminds of its diminutive scale within the larger geopolitical operations of Europe/ global capitalism, a body (Gulliver's/Solanka's) coarsely obtrusive in an already embattled community. As in *Gulliver's Travels*, Lilliput-Blefuscu's internal politics continues to be reduced to petty differences over the ways of breaking a soft-boiled egg (157). In a column on Fiji, published in the wake of the 2000 coup, Rushdie presents the conflict between Fijians and Indo-Fijians as an episode in 'one of the great sagas' of the Indian diaspora, where migrant Indians' newly-racialized land 'owns them as once their old land did', urging that the 'British should be responsible for the Indians they brought to Fiji' (SATL, 341–3). In the novel, however, Lilliput-Blefuscu's internal conflict is presented as one between Elbees as collectivists/words and Indo-Lillies as individualists/numbers (158) and, in this way, as merely a part of the global transition from 'the epoch of the analog' (or, 'the richness of language, of *analogy*') to 'the digital era', signalling 'the final victory of the numerate over the literate' (8), or of global capitalism over local histories. The Indo-Lilly individualism and numerical abilities are also a parodic reference to the British stereotype of Asians as good hard-working capitalists (IH, 138).

The journey to Lilliput-Blefuscu feels like 'a return to the past' (236). Its airport, anachronistically named 'aerodrome', is 'pigsty, decrepit, malodorous, with sweating walls and two-inch roaches crunching like nutshells underfoot' (237). The island of Blefuscu is a tragic and unstable tectonic formation, with rocks as 'icons of accumulated volcanic wrath, prophecies from the past of the eruption of Indo-Lilly fury' (239) which has spread to, and is about to erupt in, the capital Mildendo. There, 'civil war bubbl[es] just beneath the surface' (241), even after the counter-coup.

Lilliput-Blefuscu is represented as a country caught in 'a condition of perpetual revolution' (191), like Solanka's Baburia, and one that can be 'visited' by virtual 'tourists' to PlanetGalileo.com.

At the same time, however, this is clearly a reading that has, as we suggested earlier, already been prescribed by the novel and one through which Rushdie as Solanka offers an introspective journey into the afterlife of his emancipated/misappropriated creations as well as his admission of responsibility as an inevitable 'party to these events' (235). The Third World-born migrant author figure, compromised by First World liberal seductions is symbolically punished in Solanka's return to London after Neela's heroic self-sacrifice for his freedom. The novel ends with a symbolic illustration of this punishment – the protagonist jumping up and down on a children's bouncy castle in Hampstead Heath. Solanka has been exiled in London as a city of a simultaneously self-imposed limbo, withdrawal, regression or imprisonment and one that is indicative of his loss of control over the signification of his texts. The transformation of Mildendo into a war zone of perpetual counter-coups after the Fremen's appropriation of the Puppet Kings narrative is the exact inversion of London in *The Satanic Verses* where Saladin's devil's horns, as worn by the Brickhall community, symbolize the successful transformative potential of stories. In *Fury*, this reclamation is distorted and the novel's appeal is on an individual level. Neela and Solanka, like each of the Puppet Kings, face their Galilean moments, cross-roads decision points based on Solanka's Galileo doll's impersonation of the Italian philosopher's choice. On the one hand, the Galilean moments Kronos has embedded in his cyborgs' values are dictated by the binary codes that have digitized narrative possibilities in the master-story and reduced hybridity to a crude paradigm of (non-)/identification. On the other hand, the Galilean moment is a necessary either/or choice of admission or disavowal of truth and responsibility in a secular individualist world.

The Kronosian values – lightness, quickness, exactitude, visibility, multi-plicity and consistency (165) – are derived from Italo Calvino's *Six Memos for the Next Millennium* (1988), a posthumous collection of the 'American lectures' he had been invited to deliver at Harvard University. While Solanka describes the possibilities prescribed in the cyborgs' moral codes as 'multiple-choice options' in each case, they appear binary in his presentation of these options. Quickness can, for instance, be interpreted as either efficiency or ruthlessness, and exactitude as either precision or tyranny. I invoke these two values in particular as they figure prominently in the choices that the counter-coup's leader and supporters are called upon to make. Calvino's aesthetic 'combinatorics' seems to govern politicized, mirror alternatives in *Fury*: a movement of national liberation can easily turn itself upside down, from a legitimate resistance struggle into a corrupted, ruthless and tyrannical, force.

The idea of political choice is, however, demoted in this way to a moral distinction between good and bad. In rebelling against their creator's dualistic values, the Puppet Kings acquire the political significance of Donna Haraway's utopian post-human cyborgs by threatening such fundamental polarities through an irreducibility to an either/or choice. The 'illegitimate offspring of militarism, patriarchal capitalism, not to mention state socialism', the cyborgs are 'often increasingly unfaithful to their origins' and their fathers are ultimately 'inessential' (Haraway 1991, 151). Yet, in mirroring political life in Lilliput-Blefuscu, they possess a fundamental flaw, even before their (re-)appropriation by the Fremen – rather than offering, like Haraway's liminal cybernetic organisms, 'a way out of the maze of dualisms' and a 'powerful infidel heteroglossia' (181), they succeed in radically antagonizing life in Baburia.

The place of the city in this polarized world, informed by the digital/cybernetic metaphor, is explored in relation to the West's/Global North's antipodean imagination through the popular trope of apocalypse. In naming his phantasmal planet after Galileo, Solanka encodes a double bind in its emplotment and a polarity in its structure – features that bear significance to the idea of globality and the interactions between the global and the local in the world which contains New York and Mildendo. Galileo-1 exists in a catoptric relationship with this world as the two mirror each other with variations. Whereas only reports of the melting polar ice-caps reach New York in the form of a vague, distant threat, the dominant, Northern civilization of Galileo-1 is in immediate danger. This apocalyptic scenario plays upon late-twentieth and twenty-first-century ecological concerns and their attendant sense of a shared, global responsibility for the planet. Ironically, the natural disaster has selectively affected only the advanced North, leaving the 'primitive' southern Baburia intact. The irony should be seen in the context of what Huggan and Tiffin describe as the often irreconcilable polarity of the 'Northern environmentalisms of the rich (always potentially vainglorious and hypocritical) and the Southern environmentalisms of the poor (often genuinely heroic and authentic)' (2010, 2). The 'partial' apocalypse on Galielo-1 leads to a radical symbolic inversion of power relations in which the 'backward' antipodean world takes the upper hand over the technologically-superior North that is drowning, as it were, in its own environmental fears.

A similarly selective apocalypse is imagined in a more recent Hollywood film, Ronald Emmerich's *The Day after Tomorrow* (2004). There, a frozen Northern hemisphere (most iconically envisaged in New York's stalactite-adorned Statue of Liberty) is forced to seek relocation into and help from its southern neighbours after the sudden onset of an Ice Age. The U.S. population is evacuated into Mexico, which kindly welcomes refugees at the end of the film. While the film imagines a world united globally in the face of a rather carnivalesque, if tragic, natural disaster and asserts a U.S. humility in the context of an otherwise equally-shared (or, in other words, globally displaced) guilt, the fate of Galileo-1's post-apocalyptic antipodes replays old narratives of early colonial encounters and the luring of the 'natives' with trinkets. Kronos, leaseholder and invader, pays Mogol the 'high rent' of 'an annual pair of wooden shoes' for every Baburian (163). The wooden shoes, another Dutch reference, here more specifically evokes a commodified national symbol promoting the tourist industry as a parallel to Fiji's own significant tourist industry marketing the idea of a tropical paradise. The 'olde-worlde' quaintness of Lilliput-Blefuscu's aerodrome (237) is easily belied and exposed as a myth of cultural preservationism in contemporary discourses of globalization as 'the intrusion of [Western] modernity on timeless, traditional' cultures (Appiah 2006). After the invasion of Solanka's characters, Mildendo gains merely symbols and names for the already diasporized cause of the Fremen and thus merely mirrors the paradoxically neo-'indigenous articulation' of the Elbees. 'Indigenous articulations', as James Clifford terms them, are constructed 'in dialogue with local, national and global narratives where elements of these narratives are selectively combined' (2001, 398). In a speech, Speight invoked the global discourse of indigenous rites comparing the plight of the 'native' Fijians to those of the Maori, indigenous Australians and Native Americans (Emde, 396).

Solanka's imagination of an antipodean world in a global post-apocalyptic context gestures towards another, postcolonial sense of guilt. Graham Huggan notes that 'ecologically-related' postcolonial contributions have tended to focus on 'settler cultures' and to explore issues such as 'the use of territorial metaphor to reflect changing patterns of land use', 'the rival claim of Western property rights and native/indigenous title', and 'the entanglement of biological and cultural factors in providing the ideological basis for imperial rule' (2004, pp. 703–4). Such studies are often tempted by 'imperialist nostalgia', a 'closet ideology the practitioners of which are given to mourn what they themselves have helped destroy' (704). As a Gulliver figure and a First World-situated author appropriating the stories

of an antipodean Third World, Solanka is also, and self-admittedly, implicated in the polarization of Lilliput-Blefuscu.

Fury and *Shalimar the Clown* project and critique a world in which the
American metropolis, New York or Los Angeles, paradigmatic cities of the
global North, have inherited or re-appropriated older hegemonic practices.
New York, for instance, appears to have succeeded Amsterdam and London
as an imperial centre in affecting the fate of distant places around the globe.
It both contains the world in an imperial cosmopolitan manner, hailing
it into the American dream, and articulates it as its antipodes. The 'glocalist' seductions which figure in the novels, however, testify to the contradictory positioning of globalization in the contemporary world as an agent of
change. Rushdie is even-handed in his critique of a homogenizing globalism and nationalist, ethnic, or indigenous localist articulations which
emerge as a response to it. Globalization and localization appear not so
much in tension with each other but as interrelated processes which
produce each other as well as oppositional cultural forms and political
behaviours. A metaphor for glocalist seductions can be seen in the ambiguous trope of tightrope-walking employed in *Shalimar*, which points, at once,
to the miraculous possibility of walking on air and to those political acts of
tightrope-walking, the manipulative acrobatic tricks and dangerous balanc-
ing of hegemonic power.

Chapter 7

Mirrors-for-Cities: Florence and Fatehpur Sikri, or Machiavelli and 'the Prince' in *The Enchantress of Florence*

In *Don Quixote*, the curate at the eponymous hidalgo's village expresses his indignation at contemporary theatre's disrespect for the classical unities of drama. Comedies, he protests, can have their first act set in Europe, the second in Asia, and the third in Africa; and where there is a fourth one, 'the scene would have shifted to America, so that the fable would have travelled to all four divisions of the globe' (I, 414). This comment is no doubt tongue-in-cheek in the context of Cervantes' novel, given the transgressive nature of his own literary creation, its allusions to the New World, and its evocation of Spanish imperial adventure in the imaginative geographies of chivalric romance. Yet it also points to the cartographic imagination of his epoch and, specifically, its global consciousness, marked by hierarchies, origins, divisions into old and new, and chronologies of discovery. Developing ancient ideas of the geometry of the globe, cosmographers had divided the earth into four abstract quadrants, placing Europe in one, and defining three other continents in relation to it: one to its east, one to its south and one opposite it on the other side of the globe. In his famous *Mundus Novus* letter, Amerigo Vespucci claimed to have reached the fourth and last portion of the globe (Johnson 2006, 22).

The curate's observation, therefore, underscores the Renaissance practice of mapping new cartographies onto classical schemas and populating newly discovered lands with European fantasies in the increasingly larger theatre of European geopolitics. The listed continents appear separated not by seas and oceans but by structural boundaries posited by genre conventions, just as explorers had navigated classical cosmographical systems in terms of which discoveries were understood and to which they were added. While this innovative worldliness, if only a superficial tribute to updated cartographies, seems alien to the village curate's mind, the comedies he speaks of portray an expanding and yet fractured world which necessitates boundaries and in which Europe and Asia, for example, cannot be held within the same act. In Walter Cohen's view, *Don Quixote* reflects a Baroque attitude to geographical expansion, marked by reflexivity and scepticism that is paralleled in Montaigne's essays, Donne's poetry and Shakespeare's *Hamlet* (2004, 34). The curate's remark can thus also be seen as a reflection on the earlier, enthusiastically speculative attitude to imperial expansion as cultural expansion in the Renaissance and famously evinced in Thomas More's utopian imaginings (ibid., p. 10).

Set mainly in the century before the publication of Part I of *Don Quixote* (1605), but fictionalizing historical figures who were Cervantes' contemporaries, Rushdie's novel, *The Enchantress of Florence* (2008) revisits intercontinental boundaries as linking rather than dividing paradigms. It traverses Asia, Europe and the New World and features Mughal, Persian and Ottoman empires, Medicean regimes, Scottish, French and Italian pirates, the voyages of Columbus, Vespucci, and Magellan as well as historical figures as diverse as Akbar the Great, Vlad the Impaler, Niccolò Machiavelli and Elizabeth I. In its final chapter, the novel refers to the first map that included the name of America, part of Martin Waldseemüller's 1507 *Cosmographiae Introductio* (a textbook on cosmography): the 'Geography of the World According to the Tradition of Ptolemy and the Contributions of Amerigo Vespucci and Other People' (EF, 332).

The novel, then, has completed its cosmography in the last portion of the world which functions not so much as a setting as the horizon of sixteenth-century cartographic and artistic expectations. It is, in part, these expectations that Rushdie's characters will travel through and reshape. Like Don Quixote, Rushdie's itinerant protagonist Mogor dell'Amore weaves and lives through stories of enchantment, which also save his life, thus reiterating Rushdie's well-rehearsed motif of Scheherazadean survival through storytelling. Both novels are considerably indebted to the Italian poet Ludovico Ariosto's globe-traversing romance epic *Orlando Furioso* (1516, 1521, 1532) as well as to its predecessor, Matteo Boiardo's unfinished *Orlando Innamorato*, which was published posthumously in 1495 and of which the *Orlando Furioso* was intended as a continuation (Waldman 2008, xii–xiii).[5] In this way, the novel claims the impure, vernacular genealogies of romance that have been productively influenced, since the time of the crusades, by the cultures of the East and, particularly, by the *Thousand and One Nights*(Beer 1970, 6) and, like *Don Quixote*, offers a reflexive commentary on this genre, specifically the *Furioso*, by re-charting its epic Eurasian geographies. Also in the manner of Ariosto's *Orlando Furioso*, *The Enchantress* brings contemporary concerns to its historical explorations. The *Furioso* returns to the age of Charlemagne to stage a war between Christendom and the Saracens which reflected contemporary, sixteenth-century fears of Ottoman expansion into Europe as well as the intra-European imperial rivalry during the period (Cohen 2004, 8). In its intertextual engagement with the sixteenth century, *The Enchantress* seeks to posit alternatives to the neoliberal thesis of the contemporary relationship between East and West as a clash between Islam and the West and to the image of a sword-yielding Islam in its encounter with Hinduism on the site of what is now the Indian subcontinent.

The Enchantress is a novel about cities that bridge continents. Specifically, it is set during the period in which continents were 'taking shape' and becoming consolidated as cultural inventions at the height of the age of discovery, and when cities developed as 'nodal points' (Cowen 2007, 101) in flourishing networks of travel, trade and exploration that linked the entire world and projected an idea of it as 'Europe's oyster' (Cohen 2004, 6). The novel, however, charts its main interurban route in the opposite direction, from Asia to Europe, following dynastic genealogies, Silk Road trajectories and lines of Eastern imperial expansion – from Andizhan, 'the Mughals' original family seat in Ferghana' (EF, 3), through Samarkand, to the Safavid cities of Tabriz and Herat, then to Ottoman Stamboul, Vlad the Impaler's Wallachian capital of Targoviste, Genoa, and Florence. This route is marked by violent clashes between Mughal and Persian, Persian and Ottoman, and Ottoman and Byzantine empires. A cross-continental wave-like tectonic movement of migration, forcing and transformation begun in 'Asia' successively engages neighbouring regions and cultures until it spills over into 'Europe', in the process bringing both continents into being. The final stages of this movement trace the westward Ottoman expansion as a phenomenon forcefully employed in the invention of Europe through its identification with Christendom against the 'terrible Turk' (Marino 2007, 141). At the other side of this continental borderline in the making, the Ottoman Sultanate is engaged in a comparable geomorphic exercise. It rules through 'metamorphosis' – no longer the positive idea of a cross-cultural self-translation, but a violent process of conversion towards the production of Janissary slave-soldiers: 'We will take your finest offspring from you and we will transform them utterly. We will make them forget you and turn them into the force that keeps you under our heel'. Stripped of their Christianity, the captured boys are 'obliged to put on Islam like a new pair of pajamas' (EF, 179).

The novel's tectonic orientation, therefore, is in its concerns with the malleability of 'continental' thought, with the shifting sets of cultural, geomorphic and historiographical assumptions that found the imagination of continents, of the boundaries between them and of their histories and chronologies. It seeks to record and imagine less explored trajectories which brought continents together as well as those contingencies within early 'continental' thought that rejected intolerance and the denigration of cultural difference involving, instead, curiosity, experimentation and risk in the initial encounters of East and West. Catoptrically, as we shall see, these encounters are informed by a series of mutual *misrecognitions*, evoking the Lacanian notion of the development of the self-other relationship in a fictional direction, and presented here as both playful interactions and ones that open up a political potential.

Across the rift in the continental imagination, the novel brings into each other Renaissance Florence under the Medici in the late fifteenth and early sixteenth centuries and Fatehpur Sikri, the capital of the third Mughal emperor Akbar, founded in 1570 and abandoned fifteen years later (Isar *et al.*, 1981, 44). Historically, the Florence of Lorenzo de' Medici – Duke of Urbino and the 'new prince' to whom Machiavelli dedicates his now classic, controversial volume, *The Prince*[6] – predates Akbar's Fatehpur Sikri by about half a century, though Rushdie's Florentine storylines refer even further back in time, to the city of Machiavelli's youth that witnessed the rise and fall of the Dominican friar Girolamo Savonarola in the last two decades of the fifteenth century. Through Machiavelli's eyes, for instance, we see compared Savonarola's 'bonfire of the vanities' and his public burning at the stake in Florence's Piazza della Signoria.

At the other end of Rushdie's continuum, Mughal genealogies stretch back in time, several generations before Akbar, to the founder of the Timurid Empire in the fourteenth century, Timur Leng ('Tamerlane', 1336–1405) and the Mongol Genghis Khan (1167?–1227). Babur, Akbar's grandfather and the first Mughal emperor was a descendant of the former on his father's and of the latter on his mother's side (Metcalf *et al.*, 2002, 14). Mughal emperors persistently emphasized their lineage from Timur, in particular, and Genghis Khan as a way of legitimizing their power and obsessively sought control over Samarkand, Timur's capital city, which they saw as 'the cradle of the Mughals' (Berinstain 2002, 13–24). Babur made several attempts at acquiring the city, all with temporary success. In the novel, the eponymous Enchantress is taken captive at the end of one of these short-lived victories, when Samarkand is besieged and recaptured by the Uzbeks at the beginning of the sixteenth century (ibid., 20). Akbar also nurtured the idea of seizing the city, and the monumental tomb that he built near Delhi to his father, Humayun, evokes elements of the architecture of Samarkand (ibid., 48).

The story of the Enchantress serves as the main bridge over the distance in time and space between Florence and Fatehpur Sikri, or one of the many routes between the two cities, as it is also a story of transcontinental journeys. Over the course of the novel, the story is recounted to Akbar by Mogor dell'Amore, the central candidate for the role of the 'stranger in the city [who] has many things to say' from the second epigraph: a quotation from the Urdu-Persian poet, Mirza Ghalib. This epigraph is preceded by one from the Renaissance humanist Francesco Petrarch, so that from its very start, the book seeks to establish a notion of Eastern and Western narratives' parallelism and equal validity. As Keepers of Tales, the ladies at the Mughal court are consulted about the veracity of Mogor's account, which they eventually confirm, in the process also making corrections and contributions to it. Qara Köz ('Lady Black Eyes'), later Angelica and Enchantress of Florence, is 'the hidden princess' and sister of the Emperor Babur. Captured, as we saw, at the siege of Samarkand, she is then passed successively, as a spoil of war, from the hands of the Uzbek chief, 'Lord Wormwood' or Shaibani Khan to those of Shah Ismail of Persia and, finally, to those of Florentine Antonino Argalia (now Arcalia the Turk, a 'Janissary musketeer' fighting for Selim I) at the historical battle of Chaldiran (1514) which established a new border between the Ottoman and the Safavid empires. Renamed 'Angelica', she is taken to Florence, which initially falls under her spell but which later accuses her of bewitching Lorenzo II and causing his death. In the final leg of her journey, the Enchantress flees to the New World. The story circles back to its beginning with Mogor dell'Amore's arrival at Fatehpur Sikri and his claims to be Akbar's uncle, son of the princess Qara Köz and a 'Mughal of love'.

In this way, Akbar hears a version of his past, which is also the past of Florence and which has returned to him, having circumnavigated the globe, more than half a century later. He interrupts Mogor's story with comments, questions, supplements, criticisms and hypotheses, and draws comparisons between the Florentine republic and his own empire. In this exchange, Rushdie is indebted to Marco Polo's accounts to Kublai Khan in Italo Calvino's *Invisible Cities* (1972) but, more importantly, to a central idea in Renaissance humanism – the idea of a direct, dialogic exchange, across time, with the ancients. Thus Petrarch dramatized himself in conversation with 'Cicero': in a famous letter he wrote to the Roman orator he turned him into the reader of his own work. The authoritative voice of this Cicero praises Petrarch for his talent as a writer and scolds him for his political and moral shortcomings (Ascoli 2007, 438). Similarly, Machiavelli explains in a letter (1513) how he approaches, on a day-to-day basis, the writing of *The Prince* :

> In the evening . . . [a]s I go in I put off my everyday clothes, all soiled with mud and filth, and put on robes fit for a royal court; being thus suitably clad, I enter the company of the men of old, who receive me affection-ately . . . . I am not afraid to talk to them, and I ask them about the reasons for their actions and they of their great kindness give me a full answer. (1981, 35–6)

The novel appears to refer precisely to this well-known passage in 'Niccolò's habit to commune every evening with the mighty dead' (EF, 250). In his study of Machiavelli, John Pocock points out that the notion of a 'conversation between men in time' or the 'meeting of like minds' was seen as the highest form of human experience which served to socialize and politicize intellectual life in the Renaissance (1975, 61–2). If Machiavelli turned to the intellects of Rome like fellow thinkers, Rushdie's Akbar is dramatized in dialogue with Florentine thought and experience. The novel repoliticizes the Renaissance idea of discoursing with the past as a dialogic encounter between East and West in the form of two cities, yet notably these are the fragile Florentine republic and the capital of a stable and expanding empire. While Machiavelli places himself in the position of a dutiful student of ancient models of society and 'asks' for guidance, Akbar is motivated by his curiosity as well as being seduced by Mogor's storytelling craft. Mogor's story concerns him directly and has political consequences only if he chooses to believe it. In this encounter, Akbar is the dominant figure who allows himself to be entertained and informed. Whereas Sikri is the city of the novel's present, Florence functions as an archival city of historical traces which resurface in Sikri through Mogor's stories. A travelled, worldly, latter-day Machiavelli, Mogor councils the 'new prince', placing in this way his destiny, like the Florentine did, in his power of rhetorical persuasion.

Equally political is Rushdie's choice of 'authoritative' representatives of Florentine thought and experience – Niccolò ('il Machia') Machiavelli, Antonino Argalia and Agostino Vespucci (cousin of Amerigo). This trio, counterbalancing Akbar's oneness (though he muses on his royal 'plurality' and flirts with the idea of referring to himself in the first person singular), is ironically unified in the idea of displacement – whether as displacement from the city, from role expectations, or from a central part in an immediate historical context. Machiavelli, the political innovator, has no recourse to political power under the Medici regime. Argalia, the epic romance hero, is a soldier of fortune who switches sides and whose wanderings establish no myth of dynastic foundation. Agostino Vespucci, historically one of Machiavelli's former subordinate assistants during his employment at the Second Chancery of the Republic (Viroli 2005, x) is in fact doubly displaced – both from the 'real' Vespucci and from 'legitimate' fatherhood. As the Enchantress's ghost reveals to Akbar in the closing pages of the novel, Mogor is the product of the incestuous union between Vespucci and the daughter he has had with the Enchantress's maid and 'Mirror'. This conceit asserts the East–West interlinking in the genealogy of storytelling that is untraceable to an origin on its Eastern side and plural on its Western side. Named 'Niccolò Antonino Vespucci' (335), Mogor symbolically continues the line of a triumvirate of displaced Florentine fathers in a fairytale echo of the three mothers of Omar Khayyam in *Shame*.

Mirror Cities: The Paradoxes and Tautologies of Freedom

In his *Discourses on Livy* (1514–18), cited in the novel's bibliography, Machiavelli succinctly articulates what he perceives to be the double purpose of cities in a Florentine context inspired by the Roman example: 'a city that lives free has two ends – one to acquire, the other to maintain itself free' (cited in Hörnqvist 2004, 72). In its obvious contradiction, this statement reveals what Mikael Hörnqvist describes as Machiavelli's 'Janus-faced' republic, seeking liberty at home whilst pursing empire abroad – two radically opposed ends which become recognizably 'complementary' and 'interactive' in imperialist strategy. Hörnqvist argues that Machiavelli's work, specifically *The Prince* and the *Discourses*, should thus be viewed within the tradition of Florentine imperial republicanism, dating back to the fourteenth century. For the Florentine author, empire becomes 'an attribute of republican liberty, to be placed alongside justice, the common good and the equality of citizenship' (ibid., 74–5; 226). However, despite Florentine aspirations for 'imperial greatness and hegemonial rule over Tuscany, Italy, and, on occasions, even the entire world' (ibid., 42), Machiavelli would describe his native city as lacking the foundations needed for territorial growth and as the negative version of Roman greatness. Although modelled on the imperial mother city of Rome in civic humanist discourses, Florence had started as a Roman colony and as such, Machiavelli argued, it was unlikely to 'make great strides' (ibid., pp. 267–70).

During Machiavelli's lifetime, Italy witnessed a French (1494) and a
Spanish (1512) invasion (Viroli 2005, x–xii) and continued to be vulnerable
to their intervention. *The Enchantress* also indicates the precarious position
of Florence in the shifting alliances of the main players in Europe during
the period – an age of war as a game of musical chairs (251). Having served
the republic as a secretary to the Second Chancery (a post comparable to
an under-secretary for foreign affairs which involved numerous foreign
missions) for fourteen years, Machiavelli was dismissed from office, tortured
and exiled from Florence in 1513, the year after the dissolution of the
republic and the restoration of the Medici (Penman 1981, 4–6). As we saw
earlier, it is the Florence from which Machiavelli was exiled – a desired but
unattainable city – to which the novel refers. During this period, Machiavelli
was composing *The Prince*, a 'mirror-for-princes' piece dedicated to the new
ruler, Lorenzo, in the hope of winning his favour and securing its author a
post in the city's administration.

Conversely, Akbar's Fatehpur Sikri was the centre of an ever-expanding
empire, with dominions stretching south from Kabul in Afghanistan to
almost the whole of the Indo-Gangetic plain and in the process of further
extension to the south through matrimonial diplomacy in the submission
of the Hindu sovereigns of Rajasthan or through the conquest of the Islamic
kingdoms of Malwa and Gujarat (Isar *et al.*, 44; Berinstain 2002, 41). A
palatine 'City of Victory', it was raised on the site where Akbar's grandfather,
Babur, had built a Garden of Victory, in celebration of his invasion of India
in 1527 (Berinstain, 50). It thus proclaimed, at once, dynastic allegiance
and an ambition for innovation in that Akbar had broken with the Mughal
tradition by which the emperor should reside at Agra or Delhi (37). Akbar
was the first Mughal ruler who succeeded in unifying the territorial gains of
his conquests into a centralized whole (Crowe *et al.*, 1972, 68) by instituting
a political, military and religious system which he controlled (Berinstain,
37). He had emerged, politically, through his refusal to share power, with
his *vakil* (prime minister, ibid., 39) or with other nobles, at the age of
nineteen. Fatehpur Sikri reflects this ambition for singularity – a twentieth-
century Indian architect observes that while cities are usually the result of
the efforts of many generations, Sikri was 'the work of one man, in a single
phase of his life' and a 'frozen moment in history' (cited in Isar *et al.*, 46).
There are many speculations as to the reason why the city was abandoned
in 1585, and the novel explores what seems to be one of the dominant
hypotheses – a sudden crisis in its water supply (ibid., 44).

Rushdie's synchronous urban history thus seems to contrast vulnerable
Florence, under a nominally republican regime, a city whose main aim is to

maintain itself free, whilst paradoxically relying on the protection of France or Spain, and a stable, singular, and central Sikri, a living monument to imperial victory, reaping the benefits of territorial expansion and acquisition. The novel ironically decentres the imperial republican idea of the complicity of conquest abroad and freedom at home as the twin strategic dimensions of a city-state by offering two cities. Each of them is torn by contradictions that expose and indict the paradoxical tautologies of freedom. The forceful break-up of these tautologies can be described as tectonic in its effects, since it involves a displacement across continental boundaries and a reversal of East–West power relations, whilst in the process also allowing an interurban, transcontinental catoptric exchange. The two ends of the city are made to see each other in the pattern of a mirror reflected in another mirror. Rushdie's political target is Florence's rhetorical and Sikri's practical ambition for absolute power that is interrogated through their conversation across time. This ambition is diagnosed as their 'curse', showcased as 'the curse of the human race' (310–11) and, as I will argue, interrogated through what the novel posits as their parallel secularly-informed humanism.

The novel ironically demonstrates the process of the confluence of freedom as a desire and as a political weapon. This process is based on Machiavelli's division of people, appropriating his characteristically classificatory style, into two categories – those who desire freedom from oppression, or the people, and those who desire to command, or the great (Hörnqvist, 72). The Rana of Cooch Naheen epitomizes both categories and as such encapsulates Machiavelli's two ends of the city.

Reappearing from *Midnight's Children* (the Rani of Cooch Naheen, patron of the Free Islam Convocation's leader), this figure is here in an earlier (male) incarnation, as an 'upstart princeling' (32) of Kathiawar who rebels against and is suppressed by Akbar. Yet, whereas the Rana of Cooch Naheen is a 'feudal ruler absurdly fond of talking about freedom', for Akbar, the absurdity lies in the very concept of freedom. Not only does he belong to the pure category of the great, but he does so tautologically – an idea on which Rushdie ironically and indulgently expands in a series of puns. The emperor has been 'known since his childhood as Akbar, meaning 'the great', and later, in spite of the tautology of it, as Akbar the Great, the great, great one, great in his greatness, doubly great' (30). In Akbar, as Justin Neuman suggests, Rushdie demonstrates his fondness for hyperbole through a portrayal of 'the charming side of megalomania' (2008, 679). Yet beneath its charms lurks the tautology of freedom of the self as a microcosm of the city: 'Freedom from whom, and from what, the emperor harrumphed inwardly. Freedom was a children's fantasy, a game for women to play. No man was ever free' (32–3). In Machiavellian terms, Akbar has no reason to contemplate freedom precisely because he can afford it, being both its source and its vanishing point. The repetition in his name mirrors Machiavelli's circular argument, and in his thoughts Rushdie parodically prefigures poststructuralist notions of the inescapable control of ideology as the ideology of ideology.

The relations in which the idea of freedom is caught in Western discourses (specifically, the neoliberalism that the North, the U.S. and international organizations seek to impose globally today) are unsettled further through its transposition into the Mughal context. If in Western discourses of democracy, 'freedom' and 'oppression' have figured as antonyms, Erik Ohlander points out that this polarization is alien to Islamic languages such as Arabic, Persian or Urdu. There, the word 'justice' rather than 'freedom' is the semantic opposite of 'oppression' or 'tyranny' (2009, 238). He traces the etymology of this opposition, as alternative to the Western distinction, to pre-Islamic times, where 'oppression' denotes 'physical displacement' that 'justice' seeks to rectify and counterbalance. In the context of the *Qur'an* and medieval Islamic mirrors-for-princes, the pair is seen in terms of Islamic morality, where a transgression from divine prescriptions is rectified by 'acts of equilibrium' (ibid., 238). In his policies, Akbar is motivated by a similar desire for balance which also accounts for his reaction to the idea of freedom.

Freedom and equilibrium interact to inspire his experimental Tent of the New Worship, based on the historical 'Ibadat Khana': 'a place of disputation where everything could be said to everyone by anyone on any subject, including the non-existence of God and the abolition of kings' (36). The historical Ibadat Khana was set up by the thirty-three-year-old Akbar in 1575 as a 'centre for inquiry into religion and philosophy' (Eraly 2003, 187). While initially allowing only Muslims in the intention of providing them with a space for airing and resolving sectarian differences, Akbar opened the house, four years later, to members of all other faiths. Reportedly, the participants in the debates formed groups as based on their religious beliefs while the emperor 'came and went between them to discuss their arguments' (Berinstain, 68) but retained the privilege of being always right (Eraly, 189). His biographer, Abul Fazl explained the purpose of the Ibadat Khana discussions in terms of the role of the emperor as an interpreter of religious law (Rezavi 2008, 198).The location of the Ibadat Khana building has never been determined as it appears to have left no archaeological traces, though historical references to it after the abandonment of Sikri would suggest the debates may have been relocated (ibid., 168, 202). Rushdie takes up this opportunity to represent it as an essentially impermanent, shape-shifting, migrant or nomadic structure as well as, importantly, a miniature 'tent-city' (80) within the city of Fatehpur Sikri and symbolic of its ruler's spirit of tolerance. The polemic nature of the discussions, however, is likened to a marching army that sets up temporary camps in its advances (80), thus revealing a Machiavellian confluence of the ideas of territorial and ideological conquest in the emperor's thinking.

Whereas the Ibadat Khana debates had an unexpected result in weakening Akbar's faith in Islam (Eraly, 189), in the novel the discussions lead the emperor one step further. By questioning the idea of religion as tradition, based on its specific understanding as an 'eternal handing down' from one generation to the next, Akbar arrives at the atheist 'suspicion that men had made their gods and not the other way round' (83). The historical Akbar was increasingly drawn to Sufism, despite claims of being Islam's representative, and went as far as authoring a 'syncretic, regi-centric creed' known as *Din-e-Ilahi* ('Divine Faith') in which all religions were gathered 'in such a way that they be one and all at the same time' (Berinstein, 68–9) and to which all could subscribe whilst (idealistically) remaining faithful to their own religious convictions (Eraly, 202). In an interview, Rushdie translates the phrase as 'the religion of all the gods' (2008b, n. pag.), emphasizing Akbar's pantheist leanings.Eminently secular in orientation and based on reason, *Din-e-Ilahi* was never promulgated outside a narrow circle of intimates and left no followers. Like Fatehpur Sikri, it remains a singular, experimental moment in history. In the novel, Rushdie makes a passing reference to this 'creed' as Akbar's 'desire to find the one faith within all faiths' (314), whilst sidelining his mystical crises and ambitions to become a spiritual guide (68) in favour of secular national imaginings.

Although Rushdie's Akbar frequently entertains questions on the nature of religion, these serve to mobilize a vision of the city that mirrors Nehru's secular paradigm of India: 'In this place he would conjure a new world, a world beyond religion, region, rank, and tribe' (43). The little tent-city functions as a rehearsal ground for an experiment to be applied to the entire realm of his dominions. Distancing himself from his 'bloodthirsty ancestors', Akbar feels as a 'Hindustani' and dreams of 'a country' (33–34). He abandons his inherited languages, Chaghatai and Persian, and adopts instead 'the bastard mongrel speech of the army on the move, urdu, camp-language' (34). He institutes reforms in the empire's administrative and military system of governance by ensuring that no single ethnic or religious group forms a majority (312–13). He decrees that religious observance should be free of persecution (327). In all these innovations, Akbar seeks to conjure a world where 'all races, tribes, clans, faiths and nations' would form together 'the one grand Mughal synthesis' (317). Foreignness would also be permitted and Rushdie generously credits Mogor with the impetus behind Akbar's reforms: it is the foreigner who has proposed the fundamental changes.

To a large extent, however, this 'culture of inclusion' remains a vision inherently torn by contradictions and by Akbar's own doubts. He flirts with the possibility of making Mogor his honorary son, but rejects it as a 'weakness' and a 'sentimentality' (217). The embryonic idea of a country is overshadowed by the desire for a centralized empire, only strengthened through the pluralist reforms, and for absolute, universal rule in Akbar's visions of himself as a 'king of a world without frontiers or ideological limitations' (307) in which he has power over people's lives 'by right of conquest' (310). The Mughal synthesis ironically synthesizes Machiavelli's two ends of the city in Akbar's ability to quell difference with his fist (310). The little tent-city experiment leads to a discord 'so intemperate' as to make the emperor wonder if 'freedom [is] indeed the road to unity' (80). All of Akbar's intellectual pursuits are made possible by the fact of his empire's stability and military successes in the first place. His chroniclers, Abdul Qadir Badauni, the critic, and Abul Fazl, the sycophant, both note the 'leisure' in which his conquests and victories allowed him to indulge (Rezavi, 196). As the centre of Akbar's universe, Fatehpur Sikri reflects his imperial cosmopolitanism, containing a collection of 'the most beautiful women [of] the world' in his harem as well as 'foreigners, pomaded exotics, weather-beaten merchants, [and] narrow-faced priests out of the West' (43; 47) who can be summoned for Akbar's entertainment and the satiation of his, respectively, erotic, philosophical and religious curiosity on a par.

As an innovator, Akbar is the mirror image of the 'new prince' to whom Machiavelli addresses his political advice, and the Florentine's maxims, stratagems and philosophical inquiries are projected into Sikri via the medium of interlinked dreams. In the process, they undergo catoptric transformations. Both Machiavelli and Akbar reject tyranny and both do so ideologically. As an apologist for the Italian city-state, Machiavelli championed liberty against tyranny where tyranny was understood as an abrogation of the principle of the double purpose of the city, specifically, as a confluence which ignores the principle of the geographical divergence of aims. Tyranny is the result of 'men's desire to dominate turned inward' (Hörnqvist, 74). In order to avoid being a tyrant, the skilful statesman should not attempt to suppress his desire for power, but should rather channel it outwards in the service of imperial conquest and subjugation (ibid.). In the novel, the idea of tyranny involves questions to do with cruelty and love. 'Should I be a cruel tyrant,' asks Akbar in the role of an Oriental padishah who appears in Machiavelli's dream as counselled by a Mogor figure in the role of an 'Italian Pasha' (189). For Rushdie's Machiavelli, Argalia's defection to the Ottoman side constitutes the worst crime, not because it involves a conversion to Islam, but because it implies an 'inward' turn 'against his own kind' (187). The dialogic scenario of Machiavelli's Florentine mirror-for-princes, however, is refracted both through the Ottoman context, in which the metamorphosed Argalia-come-Arcalia serves the Sultan, and the Mughal context, in which Mogor counsels Akbar. In the place of tyranny, Machiavelli recommends the more palatable use of fear – 'turned inward' on one's own people – as a political strategy. Fear is also to replace the ruler's ambition for the love of his people, since it is 'fickle' (189). At the other end of the dream channel, however, the vain advisee Akbar desires both power and love, and attempts to negotiate a middle ground. As a result, he rejects tyranny and hatred, and embraces fear, as advised, but under a different guise – not as the opposite of love but as its complementary force. The evocation of the Ottoman context in this transcontinental dream 'writes back' to Machiavelli's reassertion of the medieval scholastic dichotomy between European freedom and Asian despotism (Marino, 158) by revealing them as each other's mirror counterparts. The Florentine contrasted the governments of France and 'the Turk', claiming the territories of the latter would be more difficult to conquer because his people 'are all his slaves and bound to him', but easier to hold, once conquered. Conversely, France would be easy to conquer but difficult to hold (Machiavelli 2008, 17). The episode also responds to the broader Orientalist paradigm of Eastern or Islamic despotism that includes the Mughal context in the triptych view of Indian history we discussed in relation to *The Moor's Last Sigh*. In *The Enchantress*, 'Eastern despotism' has a European guide. Just like the French kingdom appears to be only the symmetric inversion of the Ottoman sultanate, the roles assigned to Stamboul and Sikri reflect back the image of Florence. In Machiavelli's 'dark mirror' (286), the novel suggests, imperial republicanism is a mere catoptric variant of tyranny. 'Inward' and 'outward' become interchangeable in the cross-continental dream encounter.

Contrapuntal Cities: Secular Humanist Imaginings

The rehabilitation of the two cities is invested in a catoptric imagining which involves the interplay of Renaissance Florence's secular humanist discourse and Akbar's policies of tolerance and inclusivity, his notion of a Mughal synthesis, his philosophical/theological openness of mind, and his disillusionment with God. Humanism, Rushdie argues in an interview, is not culturally specific but has variations everywhere (2008b, n. pag.). Akbar arrives at the idea of a 'religion of man' in which man is the engine of history and to whom temples should be dedicated (83; 307). The disputes at the tent-city as well as Mogor's daring disagreement with the emperor lead him to suspect that 'discord, difference, disobedience, disagreement, irreverence, iconoclasm, impudence, even insolence might be the offspring of the good' and that religion can be 'rethought' or even 'discarded' (310–318). The Florentine crowds in Mogor's stories lead him to ponder the modernist quandary of what it means to be a man in the crowd, whether the crowd enhances or erases 'one's sense of selfhood' until he sees himself in the composite role of a modern flâneur and Haroun al-Rashid wandering the streets of Baghdad to see how his citizens live (141).

The interurban parallel offers Rushdie a rehearsal ground for well-tested ideas of dialogicity, hybridity, plurality and secularism. Bradley and Tate discuss the text as representative of what they term the 'New Atheist novel' – a literary response which positions itself critically in relation to contemporary religious mobilizations. They comment that, in *The Enchantress*, 'religious voices are permitted to speak' (2010, 14) within the utopian space of the novel genre, so that 'questions about God can be explored without the advent of aggression'. In the place of a 'violent clash of civilizations', they argue, Rushdie offers the notion of a 'quarrel over God' as a 'courteous, if heartfelt, disagreement of principle' (ibid., 94).

The 'quarrel over God', however, mediates more prominently in this novel not between East and West, as in the case of *The Satanic Verses*, but between narrower sectarian differences within the East. Difference is celebrated in the tent-city debates between the Water Drinkers and the Wine Lovers or *manqul* and *ma'qul* groups (79), supporting, respectively, divinely versus humanly inspired knowledge (Malik 2008, 5–6). Conversely, difference is diagnosed as a sectarian polarization in the Sunni-Shiite conflict as a quarrel over the power of different varieties of potato witchcraft – between the 'Sunni potato witches of the east Khazar Sea' and 'their Shiite sisters in the west' (212). This quarrel between witches is shown to have determined the outcome of the battle of Chaldiran, so that while the clash between empires appears not a matter of a heartfelt disagreement, it is historically/mythically traced to one. Whereas in the magical realist economy of the text, sectarian division parallels the split of magic into witchcraft and enchantment, such an analogy and its attendant feminization could easily be misconstrued outside this economy, as the Rushdie Affair has shown.

The novel seeks to posit a local rather than imported form of secularism – one that has arisen from Akbar's experience of a multi-religious, multi-cultural, multi-ethnic empire, and, at the same time, one that listens to the voice of its Florentine liberal republican counterpart. Neelam Srivastava (2008) identifies a form of 'radical secularism' in Rushdie's work – one which seeks to counter its Nehruvian or 'rationalist' variety. Rationalist secular policy after Partition, polarized the private and the public spheres as the realms of, respectively, religious belief and reason, whilst reducing the former to affect and subordinating it to the latter. Rushdie's work recuperates, she argues, an Indian secularism that is 'intended differently from how it is conceived in Western political thought; not as an anti-religious state but as a non-sectarian one', guaranteeing a 'basic symmetry of treatment to all religions' (18–22).

In Sikri, Rushdie locates a nascent, if historically isolated, form of Indian secularism that will be drowned in sectarian violence centuries later. In Akbar's vision, the future is a 'dry hostile antagonistic place' where people 'hate their neighbours and smash their places of worship and kill one another' in the 'quarrel over God' (347). In this sense, it is not that the debates at the tent-city permit *religious* voices to speak, but rather that they allow *secular* voices. The development is in the opposite direction to which Bradley and Tate see it. The world of Sikri is not imagined within the parameters of secularism as equated with the contemporary Western state, tolerant of religious voices, whilst concealing an anti-Muslim bias. Political and religious tolerance precedes and feeds into a secular vision, and as the novel suggests, it has Eastern origins unparalleled in the West at the time.

The novel's Florence is just emerging from the uncompromising moral reforms of the Dominican friar, Girolamo Savonarola, and their damage to the city's worldliness, a worldliness symbolically destroyed in the burning of mirrors at the bonfire of the vanities and replaced with the unequivocal mirror reflecting Florence as the New Jerusalem (Milner 2006, 99). The reference to Machiavelli's torture under the reinstated Medici regime also contributes to a Western negation of tolerance. The novel's epistolary encounter between the contemporaries Akbar and Elizabeth I is even more telling. As Paul Stevens (2004) notes, in 1563, seven years into his rule, Akbar initiated a policy of toleration by revoking the tax on Hindu pilgrims. At the same time, Elizabeth embarked on a policy of 'rigorous and increasingly brutal religious uniformity'. The comparison is also invoked in Lord Tennyson's poem, 'Akbar's Dream', celebrating the Ibadat Khana and

Akbar's 'tolerance of religions and abhorrence of religious persecution [which] put our Tudors to shame' (101).

As we suggested earlier, however, Florence is recuperated as one of the cities that gave rise to humanist rhetoric, a rhetoric that finds its Eastern counterpart in Sikri. Akbar is placed, as we saw, in the role of a humanist rhetorician, drawing lessons from the Florentine past, which is also his own. Before the appearance of Mogor, he dreams of the 'joys of discourse' with an interlocutor who is his equal and with whom he can 'speak freely, teaching and learning' (35). In this conversation, the Florentine piazza and the Ibadat Khana reflect each other as potentially liberatory urban spaces. The piazza, as a central space of Rushdie's Renaissance Florence and a theatre of history, mediates against the commonplaces of an elitist High Renaissance. The impermanence and vulnerability of the little tent-city mirrors the theatricality and volatility of the Florentine piazza, marked by an ever adaptable civic scenography in rituals and festivities, but also executions (Strocchia 2006). In both, control can be resisted, but equally, discord can turn into aggression. The Florentine crowd lives in an 'ecstasy that hover[s] on the edge of violence' (263). It can easily transform from 'a crowd of individual sovereign entities' into a 'mob' (301–2). As the Scottish Lord Hauksbank points out to Mogor, although Florence has imagined into being the 'highest of sovereigns, the individual human self', this sovereign is 'forever at the mercy of many insurgents', such as fear, isolation or pride (17).

The notion of humanism that the novel celebrates in the interurban dialogue of East and West echoes Edward Said's understanding of the term as contrapuntal critique of canonical humanism: 'not a way of consolidating and affirming what "we" have always known' but a 'means of questioning, upsetting and reformulating . . . commodified, packaged, uncontroversial, and uncritically codified certainties' (2004, 27–8). Thus the novel places its critique in a worldly context of co-existence and mutual reflexivity, where humanism is not an exclusively Western practice and where it did not originate in Renaissance Florence. As Said argues, it has cosmopolitan roots in the Sicily, Tunis and Baghdad of some two hundred years earlier (ibid., 54). Unlike Said's anti-essentialist and anti-totalizing criticism, however, the novel's humanism tends towards a re-mystification of its universal values. Argalia, for instance, proffers that 'Florence was everywhere and everywhere was Florence' (265). In an interview, Rushdie comments that human nature is 'the great constant' (2008b, n.pag.).

To a certain extent, perhaps, the text responds to Akbar's universalist ambitions, paradoxically both in terms of power and of toleration. Stevens suggests that the emperor's 'imagined community' was defined in increasingly universal rather than national terms, quoting the *Akbar-nama* where Abul Fazl interprets Akbar's reforms as 'the foundation of the arrangement of mankind' in 'the administration of the world' (102). The novel notes Akbar's reformist and his biographer's historiographic attempts to assert the emperor's universal rule in terms of temporality. Akbar replaced the Muslim era of *Hegira* with the Persian *Ilahi* era (Berinstain, 47), beginning with his own accession (Eraly, 213). In line with this departure from Islamic temporality, Abul Fazl delineated historical time as uninterrupted, and flowing not from Mohammed, but from Adam to Akbar, thus asserting the emperor's status as a universal rather than a Muslim ruler (Mukhia 2009, 4). For Stevens, Akbar's policies of toleration were inspired both by his political universalism and by a 'genuinely religious desire for synthesis' (102). Such hyperbolical imaginings appeal to Rushdie's sense of parody. Akbar's 'greatness' develops in relation to Machiavelli's theorizations of magnificence in the figure of the ideal new prince. At the same time, this interplay pushes Akbar towards a more explicitly secular humanist vision.

Another catoptric analogy signals the end of this vision and the two cities' enchantment with each other in the parallel drought of Florence's river Arno and the Sikri lake. In Florence, the event is construed as an omen which precipitates the Enchantress's expulsion from the city. In Sikri, the calamity is far more devastating, leading to the evacuation of the whole population. There the drought is associated with the departure of Mogor, following his fall from favour with the emperor and his son Jahangir's attempt on the foreigner's life. While, for Machiavelli, Arno is symbolic of *Fortuna*, the irrational, uncontrollable and often pernicious force of 'unlegitimated contingency', which shapes history and which the new prince must subdue (Pocock, 156–8), the juxtaposition suggests that the end of the interurban dialogue has been caused by a common, human fault, the rejection of the other or the negation of tolerance. Whereas for Akbar, the 'subtleties of water' are replaced by the 'banality of solid ground' (86) in a vision of a divisive hostile future, the remorseful Florentine crowd withdraws, restored to its consciousness.

Interurban Romance: Renaissances, Wandering and Misrecognitions

For a reviewer of the novel, the synchronicity of Florence and Sikri is a difficult, if not impossible conceit. Even though he acknowledges Rushdie's repudiation of linear and Eurocentric Renaissance histories, Neuman is puzzled by the text's 'parallel realities in which the seeds of secular humanism flower not once but twice', arguing that the Renaissance as the 'rediscovery of science, philosophy, and aesthetics of antiquity and the rebirth of Europe [. . .] cannot describe an Islamic culture that never lost Hellenism in the first place' (675–7). Conversely, in their edited volume, *Other Renaissances* (2006), Schildgen *et al.,* urge for an understanding of the 'Renaissance' as a travelling idea which acquires different manifestations in different geographical contexts and as a 'transcultural phenomenon rather than one that has originated and is owned by the West' (6–9). This formulation of the Renaissance idea responds, more specifically, to the suppression of those 'Other Renaissances' that did not culminate in a modernity (Andrews 2006, 9–10) and the collection examines a fifteenth-sixteenth century Ottoman Renaissance and a late eighteenth-century Indian Renaissance, among others. In interviews, Rushdie suggests that an artistic Renaissance took place in India as evinced in Mughal art, architecture and music. The figures of court artists Dashwanth and Tansen are mobilized in the novel's, respectively, pictorial and musical imagining of Mughal India.

Neuman's concern seems to be with the broad application of the notion of 'Renaissance' to a variety of contexts, thus stripping it of its historical specificity, which would lead to its devaluation. Such an anxiety indeed reveals a Eurocentric defensiveness of the term's singularity perceived to be under threat in the novel as well as of continental cultural boundaries and of stereotypes of the East. Neuman boxes out the East into a separate 'act' like the play ridiculed in *Don Quixote.* He further seems to ignore the nature of 'the Renaissance' as an invention, a creative and violent *misrecognition,* in the Lacanian and Althusserian senses of the term, through which the Western subject will be hailed into modernity. At the same time, however, the comment evinces the problematics of figuring the complex ways in which East and West co-existed during the period – both *before* the ideological consolidation of a European superiority and, from a contemporary perspective, in an awareness of its *future* immanence. In this awareness, critical studies which seek to recuperate both East and West from their always already recognized positions necessarily employ a strategic comparativism. A recent collection on 'Renaissance Empires', for instance, appears to be adopting the term 'Renaissance' as a Western temporal marker to designate co-temporal phenomena in the East in order to differentiate between Eastern and Western empires by the 'capitalist effects' of the latter (Greer *et al.,* 2007, 3). A comparative history is complicated by the fact that Western studies of imperialism, as Rajan and Sauer point out, often tend to treat imperialism as a Western invention, whereas 'most empires before Columbus were not of Western origin' (2004, 5). Stevens takes issue with Hardt and Negri's distinction between patrimonial empires and national empire states, where the former gives way to the latter through a process of displacement of sovereignty from the monarch to the people. Popular sovereignty and religious toleration, as we saw, were more obvious characteristics of the old patrimonial empire of Akbar than of Elizabethan England (101).

Rather than merely inviting comparisons between East and West, Rushdie's novel draws on the dialogicity of the genre in order to stage a dynamic interurban conversation, as we have seen. In the process, it interrogates the immanence of a European 'rebirth' through the 'othering' of the East by mobilizing the fluidity, contingency and mutual misrecognition in the early encounters of East and West during the age of discovery. Having established, through Mogor's travelled eyes, the superiority of Sikri over the cities of the West, London as well as Florence, Venice and Rome, the novel unsettles this hierarchy. The encounter between the worlds of East and West begins with a fraudulent letter and a misnomer. Rather than the 'real' letter from Elizabeth I, Akbar hears Mogor's version, serving his own agenda, in which he is misrecognized as 'Lord Zelabdim Echebar, King of Cambaya' (72). The misnomers amuse rather than anger him and he gradually imagines into being a similarly fraudulent other by the name of 'Rani Zelabat Gloriana Pehlavi' (73) with whom he falls in love. East and West, the novel suggests, have necessarily made each other up. This early indirect and imaginatively speculative encounter opens up the possibility of their romance. Akbar sends a series of love letters to the fictional English Queen, but she never receives them. The romance between India and England remains one-sided and Florence displaces London in the East–West enchantment.

The novel revisits romance as the genre which offers precedents of cross-cultural enchantment without necessarily historicizing or denigrating cultural difference and which has allowed self-reflexive commentary on the ways it can be employed. Neuman's 'recognition' of Mughal India as a monolithically Islamic culture stuck in Hellenistic times echoes early Orientalist thought in the Renaissance notion of historicity as time travel, where the past figures as a foreign country. Seventeenth-century England would medievalize India as its own recent past (Stevens, 96–9). The novel intervenes at a time prior to such consolidations of tectonic scope and significance, situating the Florentine Renaissance as a common East–West storytelling past, thus installing and subverting the transferral of spatial into temporal distance in a historiographically metafictional mode.

In offering a romance story between East and West that is also a journey of the East into the West, the novel is indebted to Boiardo's *Orlando Innamorato* and Ariosto's *Orlando Furioso*, where Angelica, princess of Cathay, arrives at Charlemagne's court with her brother Argalia. While the latter work ends on the triumphant victory of Christianity over the Saracens, where Orlando is healed of his love for the Eastern princess, the novel's romantic hero Argalia dies defending Angelica from the Florentine crowds in a world of pagan enchantment and disenchantment. As we noted, Argalia is dissociated from his namesake's purely Eastern origins and is given affiliative freedom here. He is a Florentine but shares his 'orphan status' with the Prophet of Islam and wonders how 'the face we see in the mirror [can] be our foe' (172). In bringing the princess into his home city, he hopes she will forge a union between 'the great cultures of Europe and the West' (276). In his reworking of Ariosto's text, Rushdie builds on the romantic genre's interplay of cultural and romantic affiliations, but here enchantment rather than disenchantment is posited as the 'cure', an alternative to the conceptualization of the East–West encounter as a clash of civilizations. In Fredric Jameson's understanding, the romance form is characterized by a 'dialectical self-consciousness' in simultaneously positing an enemy to the self and questioning his construction as evil when 'what is responsible for his being so characterized is quite simply the identity of his conduct with mine, which he reflects as in a mirror image' (1981, 118).

Whereas one of the major criticisms that have been aimed at the genre is that it seduces the reader (Beer 1970, 14), the novel self-admittedly seeks to seduce the reader into its utopian East–West interurban romance. It playfully draws on what became a tradition of misrecognition in European journeys of discovery and on the mutual enchantment of the genres of romance and travel writing during the period. The progress of European exploration mirrored, as Barbara Fuchs (2001, 18–19) points out, the wanderings of the romantic hero and his incidental discoveries, in the 'perverse refusal of the landscape to furnish the exact object of desire'. Explorers set off for El Dorado but discovered Bolivia; they sought the Fountain of Youth but found Florida. In the novel, 'they did not find India' but 'a further west'; islands 'metamorphosed into continents' and continents 'proved to be mere islands' (330). If in the *Furioso*, the term 'Cathay' (Angelica's homeland) refers both to a broad Far East and to 'India' (588), in *The Enchantress*, as he approaches Sikri, Mogor expects to find an emperor not unlike the mythical Prester John, an elusive Oriental potentate and a Western fantasy in which he rules an India often undistinguished from Ethiopia (Figueira 2004, 76). Following Columbus' 'mistake', the

Enchantress attempts to 'enchant into being' an elusive passage to India 'through the landmasses of *Mundus Novus* into the Gangetic Sea' (333), but arrives instead 'in the pages of a story' (335), the cartographic story of Waldseemüller's *Cosmographiae Introductio.* Mogor brings her story back, but to Sikri, not the place she left. He is not her descendant, but that of her Mirror. These endless displacements, digressions, and misrecognitions provocatively re-employ the conceptual and geomorphic indeterminacies in East's and West's imagination of each other and of their self-image. The heroine is an enchantress of Sikri as well as of Florence.

In a postcolonial context, misrecognition responds to the violent recognition or fixation of the colonized subject described by Fanon by allowing rather than 'denying the play of difference' (Bhabha 1994, 107). Misrecognitions can be remedied or disclaimed – Akbar protests against the identification of the New World's inhabitants as 'Indians' (329). But they can also interrogate 'originary' identifications – Akbar's grandfather Babur seeks Samarkand but arrives in Hindustan. The novel's world takes on the shape of the imagined cartography of romance in which the solidity of recognitions is eroded by the fictionality of misrecognitions. Romantic cartography functions not as the background against which the interurban dialogue is set, but as their 'mirror stage' which conditions their multiple 're-worldings' in relation to, and through, each other. If Gayatri Spivak's term 'worlding' (1985, 128) suggests the othering exercise through which the category of the Third World is articulated, in the context of this novel and Rushdie's work in general, worlding is re-fashioned as a constant re-worlding in which epistemic and ontological recognitions can be rethought and contested as versions of world. Romance, in Jameson's view, centralizes 'worldness' in this phenomenological sense (1981, 112). In the form's temporal orientation, mediating between past and present, he finds a 'salvational historicity' in moments of crisis or contingency (ibid., 148). Rushdie's choice of the form can therefore be seen in relation to the contemporary urgency of an East–West dialogue, as well as of a Sunni-Shiite dialogue towards a process of a positive reworlding.

The Enchantress of Cities: Syntheses and Sp(l)itting Images

As the title of the novel indicates, the woman-city interface is central to the development of its urban configurations, perhaps more so than in any other of Rushdie's works. As the title also indicates, however, women are often assigned symbolic roles in relation to cities. The text's specular dynamics seeks to dissociate women from the artistic idealizations and cartographic embodiments of the Renaissance; but this strategy often involves their re-mythologizing. In Florence, the Enchantress becomes the city's 'special face, its new symbol of itself' as a place of peace and self-sacrifice (275; 286). As a wilful traveller, she is an emblem of routes over roots. As a story, she personifies romance's capacity for a narrative – as against a national or a biological – production, re-production and multiplication. To a certain extent, she remains a Renaissance art object – high-born, beautiful, allegorical – but reminds us of the violence of cartographic representation – she magically sinks into the atlas en route to the New World.

The Enchantress's strategic re-inscription into new symbolic codes involves an interplay of specular and tectonic configurations. The novel replaces the myth of the Rape of Europa with the Asian Enchantress's abduction by the Uzbek Lord, abduction/seduction by the Persian Shah and her falling in love and her voluntary departure with Florentine Argalia. She forges interurban and transcontinental connections, thus displacing the Phoenician princess and the foundational myth of Europe, but travels in this way the same journey: from mortality to cultural memory, from the individual to the iconic. This journey is invested with the promise of migration/diaspora over stasis/locality, geomorphic dynamics over continental fixity and boundedness, and enchantment over conflict. The new Eurasian continent she moulds into being is an unstable entity with indefinite, ever-shifting contours which takes the form of an inter-urban route.

One of the ways in which the novel unsettles her mythological status is by endowing her with a temporary existential crisis during which her 'sovereign self' is sketched in conflict with her love as selflessness and she questions her choice of leaving behind her 'natural world' (256). This crisis serves a diasporic decentring of origins – she chooses the self as 'trying to become' (280) because to be a Mughal, she surmizes, is 'to roam', 'to scavenge', 'to be lost' (257). A more powerful antidote to her idealization and to her romantic expectations is the novel's ironic demystification of her magic. The Enchantress is capable of 'overdoing it' (281) – her power of enchantment over Florence, and later the passage to India through the New World, fails her because she has 'overexerted' herself. Fostering a global community is an impossible feat and the world splits into old and new chronologies.

Her status as an emblematic unifying mother figure of the new Eurasian continent is further destabilized in her barrenness and displaced, instead, through numerous specular projections into the generation of new story threads. Her 'Mirrors' multiply. The nameless slave girl Mirror is her shadow self, whose daughter mothers Mogor, making the journey 'back' to Sikri possible. Her sister, the princess Khanzada, chooses to return home to Andizhan, and thus stands for the opposite of the Enchantress's choice. Khanzada's journey, however, is marginalized, signalling a dead-end story. Angélique, Argalia's 'memory palace' is also bounced across the world, but as a concubine. Raped, stripped of her identity, and transformed into a mnemonic repository of others' stories, she kills herself, but only after releasing into the world the tale of Argalia's adventures. The shadow self of the Enchantress as Angelica, she serves as a sobering reminder of the dangers of the self's journey. In Florence, the Enchantress temporarily becomes 'Simonetta Due', the successor/reincarnation of the first Simonetta (Cattaneo Vespucci), a Florentine cult and Platonic beloved of Guiliano de Medici (Garrard 2003, 36–7), when the Duke's magic mirror reflects her image.

While such Menippean multiplications of alternative stories and selves celebrate plurality and impurity in the specular construction of cities, they also often tend towards schematicity – a feature which has been symptomatic of Rushdie's treatment of women as urban and cultural codes. Stephanie Johnson, for instance, takes issue with Rushdie's employment of Sheherazade as a cipher. In his work, the Sheherazadean storytelling formula, 'one thousand + one (+ one . . .)', recurrently signifies the infinity of metamorphosis, positing the 'necessity of story playing on story *ad infinitum* against the evil of historic and mythological monologisms', but at the same time abstracts Sheherazade from the 'substance' of the *Thousand and One Nights* (2005, 118–20). In *The Enchantress*, Sikri and Florence are brought together through the markedly schematic reciprocity of their hedonistic cultures. Both cities feature landmark brothels, each of which is represented by prostitutes whose nicknames are translations of each other across the interurban divide. Sikri's Hatyapul brothel, the House of Skanda, is named after the Hindu god of war; Florence's Macciana brothel, the House of Mars, is named after the Roman equivalent. Skanda's Skeleton and Mattress mirror Florence's Skandal, a 'skeletal structure', and La Matterassina, 'the giantess' (147). Inverted mirrors of each other, the two sets of prostitutes mark the boundaries of fluctuation of the female form conflated with that of the city as its 'two extremes' – 'the unyielding dominance of bone' and 'the flesh that engulfed' (61) – and, as such, are intended to encompass it in its entirety.

The Florentine brothels counterbalance, as in *The Satanic Verses*, against monolithic constructions of the message of religion; this time, Christianity. During the rise of Savonarola's cult of the Weepers, when the Florentine brothels are closed, 'the stink of religious sanctimony' fills the air (148).

The Sikri brothel mediates against Akbar's centralization of power, as symbolized in his harem. In another echo of *The Satanic Verses*, the brothel mirrors the harem. For the Skanda prostitutes, making love is like '*fighting a battle*', whereas the concubines in Akbar's harem are boxed in cubicles like '*an army of love*' (153–4, original emphasis). The two cities' hedonistic culture, then, can offer a subversive alternative to the status quo, as a safety valve from both secular and religious power, but it can also duplicate the regime in structure, principle and assertiveness, as the names of the brothels suggest, as well as reproducing its internal/sectarian or interpretative polarizations. At the other extreme of the specular spectrum, the novel attends to the violence of synthesis in the masculine imagination of the female form as an analogy of the city. In Akbar's harem, a replica of his vision of Mughal synthesis, Mogor sees all of the emperor's women as well as the ones he has known and their stories merge into one '*composite Concubine*' (156, original emphasis). As the Florentine opposite number of the Sikri harem, the 'memory palace' Angélique houses a 'brothel' of memories. The memory palace and the harem can be mobilized as collective/metonymic urban paradigms and structured into specific orders of knowledge that serve their 'designers'.

   The novel evokes the iconography of rape to point to the effects of such epistemological violence as well as to the adaptability of its signification. Rape is construed as an ambiguous political act to which different agents may lay claim. The Enchantress's Florentine Mirrors – Simonetta, the married 'woman of virtue', and Angélique, a victim of rape – are reminiscent of Machiavelli's Lucrezia, the central female figure in his play, *La Mandragola/ The Mandrake* (1518). The play revolves around the devising and implementation of a seduction strategy. Callimaco, a young Florentine merchant, enlists the help of the scheming 'parasite' Ligurio to bed the beautiful and virtuous Lucrezia, married to a rich but naïve Florentine lawyer, Nicia. Machiavelli refashions the foundational myth of the Roman Republic – the rape of Lucretia. In the place of the chaste Roman matron and martyr, symbol of Rome's civic virtue and integrity (Martinez, 13), he offers the shrewd Florentine Lucrezia, who is eventually co-opted in her own seduction and the conspiratorial deception of her husband. In the Florentine political context, Lucrezia has been seen as a 'moral casualty', reminiscent of the city of Florence – one which has been allowed/allowed herself to 'come under the control of the Francophile Lorenzo di Medici (Callimaco) while the Florentine Gonfalonier Solderini (Nicia) remained the nominal head of state' (di Maria, 141). Machiavelli's Lucrezia has been read, variously, as a symbol of the 'corrupted civic body of the early cinquecento Florence' (Martinez, 9), whose submission was both fateful and orchestrated, or as a capable virtuoso, in the Machiavellian sense, 'able to wrest back control of her destiny from the whims of changing fortune' (Barber, 459).

In the novel, the composite figure of the Enchantress and her Mirrors once again unsettles the foundational iconography of rape, while partaking in its dynamic. She serves as a symbol of urban renewal through travel, which involves her co-option into larger scripts, but also her own use of manipulation and negotiation in a strategic effort to survive. Her story, like that of Europa and Lucretia, is told/plotted by others, to the extent that she appears as imaginary as Akbar's wife, Jodha, another one of her Mirrors. These multiple reflections and deflections of the figure of the Enchantress participate in the novel's project of a feminized/feminist variant of the mirror-for-princes genre. 'La Specchia', we are told, is the 'feminine' of the Italian masculine noun for 'mirror' and the story of the Enchantress challenges the authority of this masculinist mirror, specifically the combination of the qualities forming the idea of male virtue as the embodiment of civic excellence in Machiavelli's *The Prince*: 'general ability', 'military valour', 'technical expertise', 'unscrupulous political one-up-manship' (Penman, 16) and an 'active intelligence seeking to dominate' (Pocock, 37) as well as the rhetorical prowess instrumental in covert political persuasion. The Enchantress's life rather than her voice is intended to offer a corrective mirror to Florentine *Realpolitik*, humanist disenchantment, and historiographic and geomorphic fixities. At the same time, however, she closely approximates Machiavelli's notion of *Fortuna*, derived from the pagan goddess, a feminine, irrational and unpredictable force which can reward the prince for his virtue or vindictively betray him when he lacks it. Her symbol is the wheel, by which men are raised to power and fame and then abruptly cast down by changes they cannot foresee (Pocock, 37–8). Rushdie's Enchantress is a worldly/cosmopolitan, global/universal, unique and yet multiple, superhuman agent of history who commands the male heroes' fortune, remoulding continents, directing the outcomes of battles and enchanting cities while she can. As such, she belongs to a mythical, messianic urban matrix and can hardly offer a positive mirror for women.

In its broad interplay of tectonic, catoptric and specular configurations, *The Enchantress of Florence*'s mirror-for-cities seeks to posit the ideas of simultaneity and mutual visibility in a rejection of the past as alterity and of a rhetoric of Western expertise or reformist intervention. The humanist notion of dialogue across time enables East and West to be each other's contemporaries with a shared past. Their ideologies, Machiavelli's imperial republicanism and Akbar's universal hegemony, are pitted against each other, or made to see each other, as we noted.

In bringing the two cities together across a vast geographical expanse, the novel seems to rehearse a notion of globalization as a planet-shrinker, though set in the time of a global circulation of narratives, before the dawn of capitalism. European mercantilism, as Neuman notes, seems to have been largely omitted from Rushdie's Renaissance world. Yet, the duplicity of imperial republicanism in Machiavelli's two ends of the city parallels the tensions in contemporary notions of globalization, whether seen in its 'split personality' as, at once, a continuing decolonization and a new and powerful form of colonialism, or in its 'dialectical nature' as both heterogenizing and homogenizing (Cooppan 2005, 84–5; 94). In a similar vein, Hörnqvist traces the implications of Machiavelli's theory beyond the Florentine context, to an elusive contemporary force related to a notion of globalization as a mask of imperialism aiming to conquer the world in the name of freedom (290). Outside political discourses, Machiavelli's writing, specifically *The Prince*, has become a global commodity. Tellingly, his thought has been appropriated, for instance, by studies in business management, marketing and corporate strategy. One of these studies borrows the same humanist paradigm of a conversation across time in order to stage an 'imaginary interview' with a 'Harvard Business School-educated Niccolò Machiavelli', a descendant of the author of *The Prince*, who counsels the readers of *Business Horizons* on the success of business enterprise 'as his ancestor would see it' (Parkhouse 1990, 3). The danger of romanticizing the figure of Machiavelli as a humanist guide, even in response to his long-standing demonization, is apparent in the convergence of capitalist and imperialist expansion. The position of Florence and Fatehpur Sikri at the shifting intersection of multiple alignments and counter-alignments – in relation to freedom and tyranny, enchantment and disenchantment – is thus both liberatory and precarious. In the dialogue between the two cities, however, the novel urgently affirms the coevality of East and West against notions of the journey East as time-travel to the past. Whereas for Paul Gilroy, the cosmopolitan challenge today is of 'being in the same present' (2004, 74), for Doreen Massey, this is 'precisely the challenge of space, the full recognition of coeval others' (2007, 216).

Afterword

Urban Thresholds: The Respectorate of I and the Insultana of the Otter Way

Rushdie's most recent book, *Luka and the Fire of Life* (2010), traces the journey of the eponymous young protagonist into the magic world of the stories of his father, Rashid Khalifa, the Rushdie figure familiar from the author's earlier children's fiction, *Haroun and the Sea of Stories* (1990). Luka, as the title suggests, is on a quest for the healing Fire of Life with which he will be able to revive his dying father. His journey, structured like a computer game, complete with successive levels of difficulty and 'cheats' that speed him on his way, takes him to the city-like land of the Respectorate of I, his first obstacle and, yet, it is playfully implied, the easiest to overcome.

This episode stages a recognizable technique of Rushdie's oeuvre, the interplay of violent, reflective and seductively provocative strategies in the remaking of cities that I have been discussing throughout this book. The Respectorate, a paradigmatic Foucauldian disciplinary regime, inhabited and policed by Rats, is reminiscent, in its punned name, of *prefecture* (a territory under an administrative, legal or military and, often, provincial over-lordship in the ancient Roman world but with many contemporary 'derivatives', such as the French 'police prefectures' or the English 'school prefects'). The Rats, who see themselves as guardians of identity, self-enforce the rights and boundaries of the 'I' to the point of absurdity: 'That you say you are offended,' squeaks the Border Rat, 'insults me mortally' (71). The neighbouring twin city/realm of Disrespectorate, otherwise inhabited by Otters, launches a full-blown air strike on the Rats, bombing them with rotten eggs and 'disinfecting' itching powder, until it chases out the Rat police. Liberated, the ordinary citizens of Respectorate tear down its prison walls. Notably, the Otters have been led to success by their young and beautiful queen, the Insultana, a 'sharp-tongued abuser' who 'respects nobody and nothing' (77–78). In Rushdie's consistent satirical assaults on tyranny, fundamentalism, censorship or a sanitized political correctness, women are the most powerful enemy of hegemonic mystifications.

A satirist by trade, British author and cartoonist Martin Rowson defends precisely what Rushdie's Insultana embodies, the 'power of offence'. He sees this power as an integral part of politics and the most effective transgression of a commonsensical 'ur-morality'. Offence should not be deployed, however, he urges, for its own sake but as a way of 'comforting the afflicted and afflicting the comfortable' and 'in reaction to something itself more offensive' (2009, 142–157). In Rushdie's Respectorate, however, we cannot help recognizing a trope for his life under the fatwa which curtailed his 'power of offence'. His continued interest in the life-sustaining power of story in *Luka* is further accompanied by an anxiety about the after-life of his fictions which can easily become 'tantalizing political commodities for various consumer groups' (Brouillette 2007a, 82). *Fury's* Galilean choice between conformity (the Respectorate way) and truth (the Otter way) is also echoed here in what seems to be Rushdie's defense of the novelist's truth-telling duty ('two and two make four, not five', sing the Otters, 79). Finally, that Rushdie sees himself as an Insultana in the sense of a liberator of cities is particularly ironic, given the fact that he holds, among his many awards and accolades, the honour of The Freedom of the City in (strangely) Mexico City, Strasbourg and El Paso. Rushdie's persona aside, however, his satirical arsenal leads, in novels such as *The Enchantress*, in particular, to a certain romanticization of transgression as the definitive power of story. There, catoptric urban configurations acquire a schematically tendentious form with respect to travel and, to an extent, religion (whether Islam/ Hinduism or Christianity). Rather than positing a dialogue between proponents and opponents of travel or religion, the novel frequently stages one between stasis extremists and stasis transgressors, religious extremists and religion transgressors. Without doubt, varieties in-between these two positions are offered, but they remain temporary deviations from the norm that are licensed by, and move along, the pre-established continuum. Unsurprisingly, the dialogue arrives at a pre-destined resolution.

In an interesting recent discussion, Arthur Bradley and Andrew Tate explore and critique similar contemporary secular mobilizations in the form of what they have termed the 'New Atheist novel': a new hybrid genre whose leading practitioners include Ian McEwan, Martin Amis, Philip Pullman and Rushdie. *The Satanic Verses*, they argue, is the 'first' New Atheist novel. This genre seeks to position itself as a response to 'the so-called return of the religious in the supposedly secular West' (3) and, more specifically, to the rise of American Christian fundamentalism and of Islamic extremism. In critiquing the solipsism of religious extremism, however, New Atheist novelists ironically posit a new *mythos* of humanist piety in defending the 'morality of the novelistic imagination' (1–13). New Atheist novels, they point out, offer, in fact, a classically metaphysical or even theological story in its own right by valorizing the novel as a free utopian space and assigning it the redemptive role traditionally associated with God (107–11). Rushdie's work in general can be seen as an attempt to dramatize historical instances of the encounter between secular and religious discourses. In the best case, this process works towards the articulation of something new but, in the worst case, towards the tendentious schematicity that I discussed above.

This study, then, has foregrounded and investigated the location of Rushdie's cities at the dynamic intersections of colonial, postcolonial and global contexts. Each of these contexts contaminates, illuminates, or interrogates the others, often resulting in contesting geographical and historical configurations. Most prominently, colonial, postcolonial and global urban cartographies overlap in the trope of the globe. In *Midnight's Children*, one of Saleem Sinai's childhood possessions is a tin globe, which eventually loses its stand and breaks into two 'cheap metal hemispheres' along the line of the Equator. Saleem puts the globe together again with Scotch Tape and begins to use it as a football, clanking the 'tin sphere around the Estate, secure in the knowledge that the world [is] still in one piece (although held together by adhesive tape) and also at [his] feet', until his sister, annoyed with the noise he is making, crushes the globe 'under her furious heels' (MC, 266–7). This episode is reminiscent of the comic, self-involved way in which Charlie Chaplin, in his famous role as the Great Dictator (1940), performs a gymnastic dance with an inflatable globe, spinning it on his fingertip, gently patting it up into the air, waiting for it to land on various parts of his body, and then sending it back up with an effortlessly swift flick of his hand, his foot or his buttocks. The difference between Chaplin's and Rushdie's characters is, of course, marked. Global perspectives are polarized. In the hands of Chaplin's Adenoid Hynkel, the world is an easily destructible toy, yet it also mirrors the Führer's inflated, and therefore deflatable, ego. In contrast, Rushdie's Saleem has been caught, as have his family, city and country, in the global games of the British Empire, as the legend of the tin globe suggests. His is a battered world, perpetually coming apart along the imaginary lines of countless parallels and meridians and ironically splitting into its *hemi*-spheres, terms that at once hold together and fragment the fiction of the globe. The contemporary rhetoric of the globe, of the global and of globalization continues to split along discursive Equators, breeding modern-day perspectives that mirror those of Saleem and Hynkel: perspectives which play with the curious trope of the globe, flirting with what Peter Hulme describes as its assumed 'perfection, completion, and universality', its paradoxical evasion of scrutiny (2005, 51). Yet, 'globality', as Rushdie's characters know, is inseparable from imperial projects. A recurrent idea in this book has been the interplay of the old and the new cities or ages of a city: an idea through which urban histories and geographies are continuously reconfigured, even in the face of new global projects or perspectives. The globe is destroyed by Saleem's sister, an irreverent Insultana.

The dynamic, interdisciplinary critical paradigms employed here – the tectonic, the catoptric and the specular – have pointed to the possible urban futures Rushdie envisions by illuminating radically new urban meanings. This book has engaged with the ways in which the city re-invents itself and challenges hegemonic discourses: spatially and temporally, through travel, materially and discursively, intertextually, geographically (cartographically) and historically, in ways auditory (musical) and visual, in and through geopolitical interactions, conflicts and geo-morphic shifts, through light reflections and mirror effects, and in and through the dynamics of subjectivity and understandings of gender and sexuality. Urban con-figurations in Rushdie's novels have the ability to unsettle and even explode tectonic monoliths, to refract and re-cast hegemonic cartographical and historiographical models, to destabilize the lingering impulse to gender notions of the land or the nation and, most of all, to cross-pollinate and self-proliferate, thus remaining open to their own future re-visioning.

Jacques Derrida offers a similar concept of cities as 'threshold' zones of encounter or convergence in his essay, 'The Generations of a City', based on the Czech capital, Prague (1997, 19). Writing in 1992, three years after the fall of the Berlin Wall, Derrida had in mind a city in transition, one that had newly acquired its freedom and that sought to rebuild itself in a way that reflected that freedom. He arrives at the idea of Prague's threshold condition through a poststructuralist pun on the city's name (the Czech word *prah* means 'threshold'). But one could argue that all cities partake of this condition of perpetual re-definition and transformation, where this very instability is what constitutes both a potential for resistance and a continuing vulnerability. Bombay, as we saw, underwent a similar transition at Independence but was redefined, and indeed renamed 'Mumbai', with the rise of the Hindu right. This latter change, at once an act of resistance against the colonial origin of 'Bombay' and an exclusive re-formulation, has become a veritable threshold moment in the history of the city, which has plunged it into a dark age. While the generations of the city in Derrida's essay stand for the communities of people who inhabit and construct their city, his use of the term *generation* could be interpreted as a conscious indication not only of the successive ways in which the city has been transformed, but also of the perpetual recreation, innovation or proliferation of cities. As we have seen, Rushdie's novels continuously generate, in this way, new cities out of old ones, where the moment of the threshold both separates and bridges the old and new ages of a city.

Beyond the remit of this book and the very broad and porous cultural limits of Rushdie's urban cartographies, the tectonic, the catoptric and the specular offer resources for investigating the reconfigurational politics of literature's geographical and historical imagination. The catoptric, in particular, has a far wider potential both as a critical paradigm and as a literary motif that is constantly mutating to penetrate hegemonic boundaries and to adapt to new cultural conditions. Like the mirror, it persistently invites reflection(s) and the passage beyond barriers and old selves.

Notes

1. The opening credits of the film are followed by a statement of authenticity. The High Islamic Congress of the Shiat in Lebanon, the viewer is told, has approved the 'accuracy' and 'fidelity' of the film.
2. For instance, a *massovik* is a person who organizes meetings for the *masses* or collective trips.
3. In *The Ground*, the party responsible for the change of the name of Bombay to Mumbai is only ever referred to as 'the MA party'. Presumably, this is an allusion to Mumbai's Axis, which figures prominently in Rushdie's *The Moor's Last Sigh* (see Chapter 4).
4. Yet, in *Jasmine*, the experience of entering America is also compared to a passage through a revolving door or an ascent on an escalator. 'How could something be always open and at the same time closed?', the heroine wonders, 'How could something be always moving and always still?' (1990, 103). These retrospective images of the postcolonial migrant's passage into the West conceptualize America as a consumerist space, an institution, or a higher floor. Characteristic of both metaphors is a circular movement, or the illusion of movement – they are tropes that stand for the constant recycling of inside space through the controlled absorption of outside space.
5. For affinities between *Orlando* and *Don Quixote* see David Quint (1993).
6. *The Prince* was completed in 1513 and published posthumously in 1532.

Bibliography

Ackroyd, Peter (2000), *London: The Biography*, London: Chatto & Windus.

Ahmad, Aijaz (1992), *In Theory: Classes, Nations, Literatures*, London: Verso.

Akkad, Moustapha (dir.) ([1976] 2003), *The Message: The Story of Islam*, Filmco International Productions, DVD, Anchor Bay Entertainment.

Ali, Monica (2003), *Brick Lane*, London: Doubleday.

Amiran, Eyal (2002), 'Salman Rushdie', in Bertens, Hans and Natoli, Joseph (eds) *Postmodernism: The Key Figures*, Oxford: Blackwell, 287–291.

Anderson, Benedict (1983), *Imagined Communities: Reflections on the Origin and Spread of Nationalism*, London: Verso.

Anderson, Miranda (2007), *The Book of the Mirror: An Interdisciplinary Collection Exploring the Cultural History of the Mirror*, Cambridge: Scholars Press.

Anderson, Perry (2002), 'Force and consent', *New Left Review* 17: 5–30.

Andrews, Walter (2006), 'Suppressed Renaissance: Q: When Is a Renaissance Not a Renaissance? A: When It Is the Ottoman Renaissance!', in Schildgen, Brenda D., Zhou, Gang, and Gilman, Sander L. (eds). (2006), *Other Renaissances: A New Approach to World Literature*, New York: Palgrave Macmillan, 17–34.

Appadurai, Arjun (2000), 'Spectral housing and urban cleansing: notes on millennial Mumbai', *Public Culture* 12(3): 627–651.

Appiah, Kwame Anthony (2006), 'The case for contamination', *New York Times Magazine*, 1 January. (www.nytimes.com/2006/01/01/magazine/01cosmopolitan.html?scp = 1&sq = Kwame%20Anthony%20Appiah%20January%201%20 2006&st = cse, accessed 10 April 2011).

The Arabian Nights (the *Thousand and One Nights*) ([c. 1500] 1992), Husain Haddawy (trans.), London: Everyman's Library.

Aravamudan, Srinivas (1994), 'Being God's postman is no fun, yaar: Salman Rushdie's *The Satanic Verses*', in Fletcher, D. M. (ed.), *Reading Rushdie: Perspectives on the Fiction of Salman Rushdie*, Amsterdam: Rodopi, 187–208.

Ariosto, Ludovico ([1532] 2008), *Orlando Furioso*, Guido Waldman (trans.), Oxford: Oxford University Press.

Ascoli, Albert Russell (2007), 'Worthy of faith? Authors and readers in early modernity', in Martin, John Jeffries (ed.), *The Renaissance World*, London: Routledge, 435–451.

Baker, Stephen (2000), '"You must remember this": Salman Rushdie's *The Moor's Last Sigh*', *Journal of Commonwealth Literature* 35(1): 43–54.

Barratt, Andrew (1987), *Between Two Worlds: A Critical Introduction to The Master and Margarita*, Oxford: Clarendon Press.

Barthes, Roland ([1957] 1993), *Mythologies*, Anette Lavers (trans.), London: Vintage.

Bassnett, Susan and Trivedi, Harish (1999), 'Introduction: of colonies, cannibals and vernaculars', in Bassnett, Susan and Trivedi, Harish (eds) *Post-colonial Translation: Theory and Practice*, London: Routledge, 1–18.

Baudrillard, Jean ([1986] 1989), *America*, Chris Turner (trans.), London: Verso.

— ([1979] 1990), *Seduction*, Brian Singer (trans.), Montréal: New World Perspectives.

Bayeu, Francisco (1763), *Surrender of Granada*, Private collection; exh. Museo Camon Aznar, Saragossa.

Beer, Gillian (1970), *The Romance*, London: Methuen.

Bell, David (2007), *Cyberculture Theorists: Manuel Castells and Donna Haraway*, London: Routledge.

Belliappa, Mukund (2008), 'Bombay writing: are you experienced?', *Antioch Review* 66(2): 345–362.

Benjamin, Walter (2001), 'The task of the translator', Harry Zohn (trans.) in Venuti, Lawrence (ed.) *The Translation Studies Reader*, London: Routledge, 15–23.

Berinstain, Valérie (2002), *Mughal India: Splendours of the Peacock Throne*, London: Thames & Hudson.

Bhabha, Homi K. (1990), 'Novel metropolis', *New Statesman and Society* 16 (February): 16–18.

— (1994), *The Location of Culture*, London: Routledge.

Bhattacharya, Neeladri (2008), 'Predicaments of secular histories', *Public Culture* 20(1): 57–73.

Birns, Nicholas (1993), 'The Trojan myth: postmodern reverberations', *Exemplaria* 5(1): 45–78.

Boehmer, Elleke (2007), 'Postcolonial writing and terror', *Wasafiri* 22(2): 4–7.

Borges, Jorge Luis (2001), 'The translators of the *Thousand and One Nights*', Esther Allen (trans.) in Venuti, Lawrence (ed.) *The Translation Studies Reader*, London: Routledge, 34–48.

Bouchard, Norma (1997), 'Whose "excess of wonder" is it anyway? Reading Umberto Eco's tangle of hermetic and pragmatic semiosis in *The Island of the Day Before*', in Capozzi, Rocco (ed.) *Reading Eco: An Anthology*, Bloomington, IN: Indiana University Press, 350–361.

Bradley, Arthur and Tate, Andrew (2010), *The New Atheist Novel: Philosophy, Fiction and Polemic After 9/11*, London: Continuum.

Bray, Xavier (1996), 'Francisco Bayeu, Saragossa', Exhibition Review, *The Burlington Magazine* 138 (1120): 479–481.

Brennan, Timothy (1989), *Salman Rushdie and the Third World: Myths of the Nation*, London: Macmillan.

Brouillette, Sarah (2005), 'Authorship as crisis in Salman Rushdie's *Fury*', *Journal of Commonwealth Literature* 40(1): 137–156.

— (2007a), *Postcolonial Writers in the Global Literary Marketplace*, Basingstoke: Palgrave Macmillan.

— (2007b), 'South Asian literature and global publishing', *Wasafiri* 22(3): 34–38.

— (2010), 'The creative class and Gautam Malkani's *Londonstani*', *Critique* 51(1): 1–17.

Brown, Wendy (2006), *Regulating Aversion: Tolerance in the Age of Identity and Empire*, Princeton, NJ: Princeton University Press.

Brundage, Burr C. (1979), *The Fifth Sun: Aztec Gods, Aztec World*, Austin, TX: University of Texas Press.

Bulgakov, Mikhail ([1966] 1996), *The Master and Margarita*, Michael Glenny (trans.), London: The Harvill Press.

Calvino, Italo (1988), *Six Memos for the Next Millennium*, Cambridge, MA: Harvard University Press.

— ([1972] 1997), *Invisible Cities*, William Weaver (trans.), London: Vintage.

Capozzi, Rocco (1996), 'Metaphors and intertextuality in Eco's neo-Baroque narrative machine: *The Island of the Day Before*', *Rivista di Studi Italiani* 14(4): 165–189.

Carroll, Lewis ([1865] 1996), *Alice's Adventures in Wonderland in the Complete Illustrated Lewis Carroll*, Ware: Wordsworth Editions, 15–120.

— ([1896] 1996), *Through the Looking-Glass and What Alice Found There*, in *The Complete Illustrated Lewis Carroll*, Ware: Wordsworth Editions, 126–250.

Castells, Manuel (2001), *The Internet Galaxy: Reflections on the Internet, Business and Society*, Oxford: Oxford University Press.

Castro, María A. (2010), 'Separation and displacement in Francisco Pradilla's Orientalist paintings: *La Rendición de Granada* (1882) and *El Suspiro del Moro* (1892)', in López-Calvo, Ignacio (ed.) *One World Periphery Reads the Other: Knowing the 'Oriental' in the Americas and the Iberian Peninsula*, Newcastle upon Tyne: Cambridge Scholars, 244–256.

de Certeau, Michel (1988), *The Practice of Everyday Life*, Steven Randall (trans.), Berkeley, Los Angeles, London: University of California Press.

Cervantes, Miguel de ([1605–15] 1998), *Don Quixote*, Tobias Smollett (trans.), Ware: Wordsworth Editions.

Di Cesare, Mario A. (1975), *The Altar and the City: A Reading of Virgil's Aeneid*, New York and London: Columbia University Press.

Chakrabarty, Dipesh (2007), '"In the name of politics": democracy and the power of the multitude in India', *Public Culture* 19(1): 35–57.

Chambers, Claire and Faqir, Fadia (2010), 'Keynote: interview', unpublished paper, Postcolonialism and Islam (16–17 April), University of Sunderland.

Chandavarkar, Rajnarayan (2009), *History, Culture and the Indian City*, Cambridge: Cambridge University Press.

Chandra, Vikram (1995), *Red Earth and Pouring Rain*, London: Faber.

— (1997), *Love and Longing in Bombay*, London: Faber.

— (2006), *Sacred Games*, London: Faber.

Chaplin, Charlie (dir.) (1940), *The Great Dictator*, United Artists.

Chardin, Jean-Jacques (1989), 'What the "decadents" see in the mirror: the catoptric system in British fin-de-siècle poetry', *Cycnos* 5: 123–131.

Clifford, James (1991), 'The transit lounge of culture', *Times Literary Supplement* 3 (May): 7–8.

— (1997), *Routes: Travel and Translation in the Late Twentieth Century*, Cambridge, MA and London: Harvard University Press.

— (2001), 'Indigenous articulations', *Contemporary Pacific* 13(2): 468–490.

Cohen, Walter (2004), 'The literature of empire in the Renaissance', *Modern Philology* 102(1): 1–34.

Cook, Rufus (1997), 'Cultural displacement and narrative duplicity', *Centennial Review* 41(2): 205–216.

Cooppan, Vilashini (2005), 'The ruins of empire: the national and global politics of America's return to Rome', in Loomba, Ania , Kaul, Suvir, Bunzl, Matti, Burton, Antoinette and Esty, Jed (eds), *Postcolonial Studies and Beyond*, London: Duke University Press, 80–100.

— (2009), *Worlds Within: National Narratives and Global Connections in Postcolonial Writing*, Stanford, CA: Stanford University Press.

Cowen, Alexander (2007), 'Cities, towns, and new forms of culture', in Martin, John Jeffries (ed.), *The Renaissance World*, London: Routledge,101–117.

Crowe, Sylvia and Haywood, Sheila (1972), *The Gardens of Mughal India*, London: Thames & Hudson.

Cundy, Catherine (1997), *Salman Rushdie*, Manchester: Manchester University Press.

Dee, Jon (2003), 'After midnight: the novel in the 1980s and 1990s', in Mehrotra, Arvind Krishna (ed.) *A History of Indian Literature in English*, London: Hurst, 318–336.

Derrida, Jacques (1997), 'Pokoleniata na edin grad' ('The generations of a city'), *Leteratura* 17: 19–21.

Desai, Anita ([1988] 1998), *Baumgartner's Bombay*, London: Vintage.

Desai, Kiran ([2006] 2007), *The Inheritance of Loss*, London: Penguin.

Devi, Mahasweta (1995), *Imaginary Maps*, Gayatri C. Spivak (trans.), London: Routledge.

Dharwadker, Vinay (2001), 'Cosmopolitanism in its time and place', in Dharwadker, Vinay (ed.) *Cosmopolitan Geographies: New Locations in Literature and Culture*, New York and London: Routledge, 1–14.

Dickens, Charles ([1865] 1997), *Our Mutual Friend*, London: Penguin.

Didur, Jill (2011), 'Cultivating community: counterlandscaping in Kiran Desai's *The Inheritance of Loss*', in DeLoughrey, Elizabeth and Handley, George B. (eds) *Postcolonial Ecologies: Literatures of the Environment*, New York: Oxford University Press, 43–61.

Eco, Umberto (1986), 'Mirrors', in Bonissae, Paul, Herzfeld, Michael and Posner, Roland (eds) *Iconicity: Essays on the Nature of Culture*, (trans. not cited), Tüblingen: Stauffenburg-Verlag, 215–237.

— (1995), *The Island of the Day Before*, William Weaver (trans.), London: Secker and Warburg.

Emde, Sina (2005), 'Feared rumours and rumours of fear: the politicisation of ethnicity during the Fiji coup in May 2000', *Oceania* 75(4): 387–402.

Emmerich, Ronald (dir.) (2004), *The Day after Tomorrow*, Twentieth Century Fox.

Enoch, J. M. (2007), 'Archaeological optics: the very first known mirrors and lenses', *Journal of Modern Optics* 54(9): 1221–1239.

Eraly, Abraham (2003), *The Mughal Throne: The Saga of India's Great Emperors*, London: Weidenfeld & Nicolson.

Falconer, Rachel (2001), 'Bouncing down to the underworld: classical katabasis in *The Ground Beneath Her Feet*', *Twentieth Century Literature* 47(4): 467–509.

Federico, Sylvia (1997), 'A fourteenth-century erotics of politics: London as a feminine new Troy', *Studies in the Age of Chaucer* 19: 121–155.

Figueira, Dorothy (2004), 'Civilization and the problem of race: Portuguese and Italian travel narratives to India', in Rajan, Balachandra and Sauer, Elizabeth (eds), *Imperialisms: Historical and Literary Investigations, 1500-1900*, London: Palgrave Macmillan, 75–92.

Fischer, Michael M. J. and Abedi, Mehdi (1990), 'Bombay Talkies, the word and the world: Salman Rushdie's *The Satanic Verses*', *Cultural Anthropology* 5(2): 107–159.

Fletcher, D. M. (ed.) (1994), *Reading Rushdie: Perspectives on the Fiction of Salman Rushdie*, Amsterdam: Rodopi.

Fletcher, Richard (1989), *The Quest for El Cid*, London: Hutchinson.

— (1994), *Moorish Spain*, London: Phoenix.

Fokkema, Douwe and Bertens, Hans (eds) (1989), *Approaching Postmodernism*, Amsterdam/Philadelphia: John Benjamin.

Foucault, Michel ([1984] 1998), 'Different spaces', in Faubion, James D. (ed.) *Essential Works of Foucault 1954–1984*, Vol. 2, Robert Hurley (trans.), London: Penguin, 175–185.

— ([1969] 2001), *The Archaeology of Knowledge*, A. M. Sheridan Smith (trans.), London: Routledge.

— ([1966] 2002), *The Order of Things: An Archaeology of the Human Sciences*, (trans. not cited), London: Routledge.

Frampton, Kenneth (1996), *Studies in Tectonic Culture: The Poetics of Construction in Nineteenth and Twentieth Century Architecture*, Cambridge, MA and London: MIT Press.

Fuchs, Barbara (2001), *Mimesis and Empire: The New World, Islam and European Identities*, Cambridge: Cambridge University Press.

Gangar, Amrit ([1995], 2003), 'Films from the city of dreams', in Patel, Sujata and Thorner, Alice Thorner, *Bombay: Mosaic of Modern Culture*, New Delhi: Oxford University Press, 210–224.

Ganti, Tejaswini (2004), *Bollywood: A Guide to Popular Hindi Cinema*, New York and London: Routledge.

Garrard, Greg (2004), *Ecocriticism*, London: Routledge.

Garrard, Mary D. (2003), 'Who was Ginerva de' Benci? Leonardo's portrait and its sitter recontextualized', *Artibus et Historiae* 27(53): 23–56.

Gasché, Rodolphe (1986), *The Tain of the Mirror: Derrida and the Philosophy of Reflection*, Cambridge, MA and London: Harvard University Press.

Ghamari-Tabrizi, Behrooz, Bonakdarian, Mansour, Rahimieh, Nasrin, Sadri, Ahmad and Abrahamian, Ervand (2009), 'Editors' introduction', *Radical History Review* 105 (Fall): 1–12.

Ghosh, Amitav (1988), *The Shadow Lines*, London: John Murray.

Ghosh, Aparisim (1998), 'Cricket in no man's land', *Time South Pacific* 23 November (http://www.studentnews.cnn.com/ASIANOW/time/asia/magazine/1998/981123/ghosh_essay1.html, accessed 15 May 2004).

Gilliat-Ray, Sophie (2010), *Muslims in Britain: An Introduction*, Cambridge: Cambridge University Press.

Gilroy, Paul (2004), *After Empire: Melancholia or Convivial Culture?*, London: Routledge.

Glotfelty, Cheryll (1996), 'Introduction: literary studies in an age of environmental crisis', in Glotfelty, Cheryll and Fromm, Harold (eds) *The Ecocriticism Reader: Landmarks in Literary Ecology*, Athens: University of Georgia Press, xv–xxxvii.

Gogol, N. V. ([1842] 1998), *Dead Souls*, Christopher English (trans.), Oxford: Oxford University Press.

Gopal, Priyamvada (2007), 'Sir Salman's long journey', *The Guardian* 18 June (http://www.guardian.co.uk/commentisfree/2007/jun/18/comment.books-comment, accessed 4 April 2011).

— (2009), *The Indian English Novel: Nation, History and Narration*, Oxford: Oxford University Press.

Gopalan, Lalitha (2002), *Cinema of Interruptions: Action Genres in Contemporary Indian Cinema*, London: British Film Institute.

Gordin, Michael D, Tilley, Helen and Prakash, Gyan (eds) (2010), 'Introduction: Utopia and dystopia beyond space and time', in Gordin, Michael D. *et al.* (eds) *Utopia/Dystopia: Conditions of Historical Possibility*, Princeton, NJ: Princeton University Press, 1–17.

Gordon, Jan B. (1987), 'The *Alice* books and the metaphors of Victorian childhood', in Bloom, Harold (ed.) *Lewis Carroll. Modern Critical Views*, New York: Chelsea House Publishers, 17–30.

Graham-Brown, Sarah (2003), 'The seen, the unseen and the imagined: private and public lives', in Lewis, Reina and Mills, Sara (eds) *Feminist Postcolonial Theory: A Reader*, Edinburgh: Edinburgh UP, 502–519.

Greer, Margaret R., Mignolo, Walter D. and Quilligan, Maureen (2007), 'Introduction', in Greer, Margaret *et al.* (eds) *Rereading the Black Legend: The Discourses of Religious and Racial Difference in the Renaissance Empires*, Chicago, IL: University of Chicago Press, 1–26.

Gurnah, Abdulrazak (ed.) (2007), *The Cambridge Companion to Salman Rushdie*, Cambridge: Cambridge University Press.

Hansen, Thomas Blom (2002), *Wages of Violence: Naming and Identity in Postcolonial Bombay*, Princeton, NJ: Princeton University Press.

— (2008), 'Reflections on Salman Rushdie's Bombay', in Varshney, Ashutosh (ed.) *Midnight's Diaspora: Critical Encounters with Salman Rushdie*, Ann Arbor: University of Michigan Press, 91–111.

Haraway, Donna J. (1991), *Simians, Cyborgs, Women: The Reinvention of Nature*, London: Free Association Books.

Hardt, Michael and Negri, Antonio (2000), *Empire*, Cambridge, MA: Harvard University Press.

Hariharan, Githa ([1999] 2000), *When Dreams Travel*, London: Picador.

Herbert, Caroline (2008), '"No longer a memoirist but a voyeur": photographing and narrating Bombay in Salman Rushdie's *The Ground Beneath Her Feet*', *Journal of Postcolonial Writing* 44(2): 139–150.

— (2011), 'Lyric maps and the legacies of 1971 in Kamila Shamsie's *Kartography*', *Journal of Postcolonial Writing* 47(2): 159–172.

Herwitz, Daniel (2004), 'Reclaiming the past and early modern Indian art', *Third Text* 18(3): 213–228.

Holsen, James and Appadurai, Arjun (1996), 'Cities and citizenship', *Public Culture* 8(2): 187–204.

Hörnqvist, Mikael (2004), *Machiavelli and Empire*, Cambridge: Cambridge University Press.

Howard, Robert Glenn (2005), 'The double bind of the Protestant Reformation: the birth of fundamentalism and the necessity of pluralism', *Journal of Church and State* 47(1): 91–108.

Huggan, Graham (1989), 'Decolonizing the map: post-colonialism, post-structuralism and the cartographic connection', *ARIEL* 20(4): 115–132.

— (2004), '"Greening" postcolonialism: ecocritical perspectives', *Modern Fiction Studies* 50(3): 701–733.

Huggan, Graham and Tiffin, Helen (2010), *Postcolonial Ecocriticism: Literature, Animals, Environment*, London: Routledge.

Hulme, Peter (2005), 'Beyond the straits: postcolonial studies and beyond', in Loomba, Ania, Kaul, Suvir, Bunzl, Matti, Burton, Antoinette and Esty, Jed (eds), *Postcolonial Studies and Beyond*, London: Duke University Press, 41–61.

Hunt, Maurice (2003), 'Shakespeare's Venetian paradigm: stereotyping and sadism in *The Merchant of Venice* and *Othello*', *Papers on Language and Literature* 39(2): 162–184.

Huntington, Samuel P. (1993), 'The clash of civilizations?', *Foreign Affairs* 72(3): 22–49.

Hutcheon, Linda ([1988] 1996), *A Poetics of Postmodernism: History, Theory, Fiction*, London: Routledge.

Irigaray, Luce (1985), *Speculum of the Other Woman*, Gillian C. Gill (trans.), Ithaca, NY: Cornell University Press.

Isar, Renée and Isar, Raj (1981), 'Akbar at Fatehpur Sikri', *History Today* 31(1): 44–48.

Jacobs, Jane M. ([1996] 2002), *Edge of Empire: Postcolonialism and the City*, London: Routledge.

Jameson, Fredric ([1981] 1996), *The Political Unconscious: Narrative as a Socially Symbolic Act*, London: Routledge.

Johnson, Christine R. (2006), 'Renaissance German cosmographers and the naming of America', *Past and Present* 191: 2–43.

Jones, Stephanie (2005), 'Emboldening Dinarzad: the *Thousand and One Nights* in contemporary fiction', in Wen-chin Quyang and van Gelder, Geert Jan (eds) *New Perspectives on Arabian Nights*, London: Routledge, 115–133.

Jussawalla, Feroza (1996), 'Rushdie's *Dastan-e-Dilruba: The Satanic Verses* as Rushdie's love letter to Islam', *Diacritics* 26(1): 50–73.

Kabir, Ananya Jahanara (2002), 'Subjectivities, memories, loss: of pigskin bags, silver spittoons, and the partition of India', *Interventions* 4(2): 245–264.

— (2011), 'Deep topographies in the fiction of Uzma Aslam Khan', *Journal of Postcolonial Writing* 47(2): 173–185.

Kaplan, Caren (1996), *Questions of Travel: Postmodern Discourses of Displacement*, Durham, NC: Duke University Press.

Kapoor, Raj (dir.) ([1955] 2002), *Shree 420*, DVD, Yash Raj Films International Ltd.

Kapur, Geeta (1978), *Contemporary Indian Artists*, New Delhi: Vikas.

Kapur, Geeta and Rajadhyaksha, Ashish (2001), 'Bombay/Mumbai 1992–2001', in Blazwick, Iwona (ed.) *Century City: Art and Culture in the Modern Metropolis*, London: Tate, 16–39.

Kapur, Shekar (dir.) (1987), *Mr India*, Perf. Amil Kapur, Sridevi, Amrish Puri.

Karmi, Ghada (1996), 'Woman, Islam and patriarchialism', in Yamani, Mai (ed.) *Feminism and Islam: Legal and Literary Perspectives*, Reading: Ithaca Press, 69–85.

Keown, Michelle, Murphy, David and Procter, James (2009), 'Introduction: theorizing postcolonial diasporas', in Keown, Michelle, Murphy, David and Procter,

James (eds) *Comparing Postcolonial Diasporas*, Basingstoke: Palgrave Macmillan, 1–18.

King, Bruce (2011), 'Kamila Shmasie's novels of history, exile and desire', *Journal of Postcolonial Writing* 47(2): 147–158.

Kipling, Rudyard ([1888] 1965), 'On the city wall', in *Soldiers Three and Other Stories*, London: Macmillan, 322–355.

Kortenaar, Neil Ten (1997), 'Postcolonial ekphrasis: Salman Rushdie gives the finger back to the empire', *Contemporary Literature* 38(2): 232–259.

Kosambi, Meera ([1995] 2003), 'British Bombay and Marathi Mumbai: some nineteenth century perceptions', in Patel, Sujata and Alice Thorner, *Bombay: Mosaic of Modern Culture*, New Delhi: Oxford University Press, 3–24.

Kumar, Amitava (2001), 'The bend in their rivers', *The Nation* 26 (November): 32–38.

— (2002), *Bombay, London, New York*, London: Routledge.

Kumar, R. Siva (1999), 'Modern Indian art: A brief overview', *Art Journal* 58(3): 14–21.

Kuortti, Joel (2007), '*The Satanic Verses*: "To be born again, first you have to die"', in Gurnah, Abdulrazak (ed.), *The Cambridge Companion to Salman Rushdie*, Cambridge: Cambridge University Press, 125–138.

Kureishi, Hanif (1990), *The Buddha of Suburbia*, London: Faber.

— (2009), *Something to Tell You*, London: Faber.

LaBossiere, Camille R. (1983), 'Compass of the catoptric past: John Glassco, translator', *Canadian Poetry* 13: 32–42.

Lacan, Jacques ([1949] 2004), 'The Mirror Stage as formative of the function of the *I*', in *Écrits: A Selection*, Alan Sheridan (trans.), London: Routledge, 1–8.

LeCuyer, Annette (2001), *Radical Tectonics*, London: Thames & Hudson.

Lindberg, David C. (1976), *Theories of Vision from Al-Kindi to Kepler*, London: University of Chicago Press.

Loomba, Ania, Kaul, Suvir, Bunzl, Matti, Burton, Antoinette and Esty, Jed (eds) (2005a), *Postcolonial Studies and Beyond*, London: Duke University Press.

— (2005b), 'Beyond what? An introduction', in Loomba, Ania, Kaul, Suvir, Bunzl, Matti, Burton, Antoinette and Esty, Jed (eds), *Postcolonial Studies and Beyond*, London: Duke University Press, 1–38.

Machiavelli, Niccolò ([1513] 1981), 'Letter to Francesco Vettori, 10 December 1513', in Penman, Bruce (trans. and ed.) *Niccolò Machiavelli: The Prince and Other Political Writings*, London: Dent, 33–37.

— ([1519?] 1985), *La Mandragola/The Mandrake*, in *The Comedies of Machiavelli: The Woman from Andros, The Mandrake, Clizia*, bilingual ed., David Sices and James B. Atkinson (trans.), Cambridge: Hackett Publishing, 154–275.

— ([1532] 2008), *The Prince*, Peter Bondanella (trans.), Oxford: Oxford University Press.

Malik, Jamal (2008), 'Introduction', in Malik, Jamal (ed.) *Madrasas in South Asia: Teaching Terror?* London: Routledge, 1–22.

Marino, John A. (2007), 'The invention of Europe', in Martin, John Jeffries (ed.), *The Renaissance World*, London: Routledge, 140–165.

Martin, John Jeffries (ed.) (2007), *The Renaissance World*, London: Routeldge.

Martinez, Ronald L. (1983), 'The pharmacy of Machiavelli: Roman Lucretia in *Mandragola*', *Renaissance Drama* 14: 1–43.

Marzolph, Ulrich and van Leewuven, Richard (eds) (2004), *The Arabian Nights Encyclopedia*, Vol. 2, Santa Barbara, CA: ABS-CLIO.

Masselos, Jim ([1995] 2003), 'Migration and urban identity: Bombay's famine refugees in the nineteenth century', in Patel, Sujata and Alice Thorner, *Bombay: Mosaic of Modern Culture*, New Delhi: Oxford University Press, 25–58.

Massey, Doreen (1994), *Space, Place and Gender*, Cambridge: Polity Press.

— (2005), *For Space*, London: Sage.

— (2007), *World City*, Cambridge: Polity Press.

Massey, Doreen and Jess, Pat (eds) (1995), *A Place in the World? Places, Cultures and Globalisation*, Oxford: Oxford University Press.

Mazumdar, Ranjani (2007), *Bombay Cinema: An Archive of the City*, Minneapolis, MN: University of Minnesota Press.

McClintock, Anne (1995), *Imperial Leather: Race, Gender and Sexuality in the Colonial Contest*, London: Routledge.

McLeod, John (2004), *Postcolonial London: Rewriting the Metropolis*, London: Routledge.

Mehrotra, Arvind Krishna (2003), 'Introduction', in Mehrotra, Arvind Krishna (ed.) *A History of Indian Literature in English*, London: Hurst, 1–26.

Mehta, Suketu (2005), *Maximum City: Bombay Lost and Found*, London: Review.

Melchoir-Bonnet, Sabine (2001), *The Mirror: A History*, Katharine H. Jewett (trans.), London: Routledge.

Mernissi, Fatima (2003), 'The memory of spatial boundaries', in Lewis, Reina and Mills, Sara (eds) *Feminist Postcolonial Theory: A Reader*, Edinburgh: Edinburgh University Press, 489–501.

Meserve, Margaret (2008), *Empires of Islam in Renaissance Historical Thought*, Cambridge, MA: Harvard University Press.

Metcalf, Barbara D., and Metcalf, Thomas R. (2002), *A Concise History of India*, Cambridge: Cambridge University Press.

Miller, Tom (2000), 'The crown of Montecristi', *Natural History* 109(5): 54–64.

Milner, Stephen J. (2006), 'The Florentine Piazza della Signoria as practiced place', in Crum, Roger G. and Paoletti, John T. (eds) *Renaissance Florence: A Social History*, Cambridge: Cambridge University Press, 83–103.

Mishra, Sudesh (2005), 'Time and *girmit*', *Social Text* 82, 23(1): 15–36.

Mishra, Vijay (1989), 'The texts of "Mother India"', *Kunapipi* 11(1): 119–137.

— (2002), *Bollywood Cinema: Temples of Desire*, London: Routledge.

Mistry, Rohinton (1987), *Tales from Firozsha Baag*, London: Faber.

— (1991), *Such a Long Journey*, London: Faber.

— (1996), *A Fine Balance*, London: Faber.

— (2002), *Family Matters*, London: Faber.

Mohamed, Khalid (dir.) (2000), *Fiza*, Trans UK, DVD.

Mondal, Anshuman (2007), '*The Ground Beneath Her Feet and Fury*: the reinvention of location', in Gurnah, Abdulrazak (ed.), *The Cambridge Companion to Salman Rushdie*, Cambridge: Cambridge University Press, 169–183.

Moore, Lindsey (2010), 'The enchantress of Florence', *The Literary Encyclopedia* 20 August (http://www.litencyc.com/php/sworks.php?rec = true&UID = 23534, accessed 1 February 2011).

Moore-Gilbert, Bart (1996), '"The Bhabhal of Tongues": reading Kipling, reading Bhabha', in Bart Moore-Gilbert (ed.) *Writing India 1757–1990: The Literature of British India*, Manchester: Manchester University Press, 111–138.

— (2009), *Postcolonial Life-Writing: Culture, Politics and Self-Representation*, London: Routledge.

Morton, Stephen (2008), *Salman Rushdie: Fictions of Postcolonial Modernity*, Basingstoke: Palgrave Macmillan.

Moss, Laura (1998), '"Forget those damnfool realists!": Salman Rushdie's self-parody as the magic realist's "last sigh"', *ARIEL* 29(4): 121–139.

Mukherjee, Bharati (1990), *Jasmine*, London: Virago.

Mukhia, Harbans (2009), 'Time in Abu'l Fazl's historiography', *Studies in History* 25(10): 1–12.

Murray, Alex (2004), 'Jack the Ripper, the dialectic of enlightenment and the search for spiritual deliverance in *White Chapell, Scarlet Tracings*', *Critical Survey* 16(1): 52–66.

Musil, Robert ([1930] 1995), *The Man Without Qualities*, Sophie Wilkins (trans.), London: Picador.

Nadler, Steven (2003), *Rembrandt's Jews*, Chicago, IL: University of Chicago Press.

Nagarkar, Kiran (1995), *Ravan and Eddie*, London: Viking.

Nandy, Ashis (2005), 'The idea of South Asia: a personal note on post-Bandung blues', *Inter-Asia Cultural Studies* 6(4): 541–545.

— (2010), 'An ambiguous journey to the city: a dialogue with Ashis Nandy', *Pratilipi* March–June (http://pratilipi.in/2010/06/an-ambiguous-journey-to-the-city-a-dialogue-with-ashis-nandy/, accessed 12 May 2011).

Neuman, Justin (2008), 'The fictive origins of secular humanism: on Rushdie's *The Enchantress of Florence*', *Criticism* 50(4): 675–682.

Newell, Stephanie (2009), 'Postcolonial masculinities and the politics of visibility', *Journal of Postcolonial Writing* 45(3): 243–250.

Nicholls, Brendon (2007), 'Reading "Pakistan" in Salman Rushdie's *Shame*', in Gurnah, Abdulrazak (ed.), *The Cambridge Companion to Salman Rushdie*, Cambridge: Cambridge University Press, 109–121.

Nixon, Rob (2005), 'Environmentalism and postcolonialism', in Loomba, Ania, Kaul, Suvir, Bunzl, Matti, Burton, Antoinette and Esty, Jed (eds), *Postcolonial Studies and Beyond*, London: Duke University Press, 233–251.

O'Brien, Susie (2001), 'Articulating a world of difference: ecocriticism, postcolonialism and globalization', *Canadian Literature* (170/171): 140–158.

O'Connor, Erin (2002), 'Epitaph for the body politic', *Science as Culture* 11(3): 405–414.

Ohlander, Erik (2009), 'Enacting justice, ensuring salvation: the trope of the "just ruler" in some medieval Islamic mirrors for princes', *The Muslim World* 99(2): 237–252.

Otis, Laura (1999), *Membranes: Metaphors of Invasion in Nineteenth-Century Literature, Science, and Politics*, Baltimore, MD: John Hopkins University Press.

Ovid ([8 AD] 1998), *Metamorphoses*, A. D. Melville (trans.), Oxford: Oxford University Press.

Parry, Benita (1988), 'The content and discontents of Kipling's imperialism', *New Formations* 6 (Winter): 49–64.

Patel, Sujata and Thorner, Alice (1995), *Bombay: Mosaic of Modern Culture*, New Delhi: Oxford University Press.

Penman, Bruce (1981), 'Introduction', in Penman, Bruce (trans. and ed.) *Niccolò Machiavelli: The Prince and Other Political Writings*, London: Dent, 1–22.

Peters, F. E. (2003), *Islam: A Guide for Jews and Christians*, Oxford: Princeton University Press.

Petersen, Wolfgang (dir.) (2004), *Troy*, Helena Productions Ltd.

Pike, David L. (2002), 'Modernist space and the transformation of underground London', in Gilbert, Pamela K. (ed.) *Imagined Londons*, Albany, NY: State University of New York Press, 101–119.

Pocock, John Greville Agard (1975), *The Machiavellian Moment: Florentine Political Thought and the Atlantic Republican Tradition*, Princeton, NJ: Princeton University Press.

(Popov, Alek) Попов, Алек (2001), *Мисия Лондон (Mission London)*, Sofia: Zvezdan.

Pradilla, Francisco (1882), *Surrender of Granada*, Palacio del Senado, Madrid.

— (1892), *Sigh of the Moor*, Rodriguez Bauzá private collection (*in situ*), Madrid.

Prakash, Gyan (2010), *Mumbai Fables*, Princeton, NJ: Princeton University Press.

(Protohristova, Kleo) Протохристова, Клео (1996), *През огледалото в загадката: литературни и метадискурсивни аспекти на огледалната метафора* (*Per Speculum in Aenigmate: Literary and Metadiscursive Aspects of the Mirror Metaphor*), Shumen: Gluks (my trans. of Bulgarian title).

Proudfoot, Richard, Thompson, Ann and Kastan, David S. (eds) (1998), *The Arden Shakespeare. Complete Works*, Walton-on-Thames: Thomas Nelson and Sons.

Punter, David (2000), *Postcolonial Imaginings: Fictions of a New World Order*, Edinburgh: Edinburgh University Press.

Quint, David (1993), *Epic and Empire: Politics and Generic Form from Virgil to Milton*, Princeton, NJ: Princeton University Press.

Rajan, Balachandra and Sauer, Elizabeth (2004), 'Introduction: Imperialisms: early modern to premodernist', in Rajan, Balachandra and Sauer, Elizabeth (eds), *Imperialisms: Historical and Literary Investigations, 1500-1900*, London: Palgrave Macmillan, 1–11.

Ram, Uri (2004), 'Glocommodification: how the global consumes the local – McDonald's in Israel', *Current Sociology* 52(1): 11–31.

Ramanujan, Attipat Krishnaswami (1999), *The Collected Essays of A. K. Ramanujan*, Oxford: Oxford University Press.

Ranasinha, Ruvani (2007a), 'The fatwa and its aftermath', in Gurnah, Abdulrazak (ed.), *The Cambridge Companion to Salman Rushdie*, Cambridge: Cambridge University Press, 45–59.

— (2007b), *South Asian Writers in Twentieth-Century Britain: Culture in Translation*, Oxford: Clarendon Press.

Reder, Michael R. (ed.) (2000), *Conversations with Salman Rushdie*, Jackson, MS: University of Mississippi Press.

Rezavi, Syed Ali Nadeem (2008), 'Religious disputations and imperial ideology: the purpose and location of Akbar's *Ibadatkhana*', *Studies in History* 24(2): 195–209.

Robbins, Emmet (1982), 'Famous Orpheus', in Warden, John (ed.) *Orpheus: The Metamorphosis of a Myth*, Toronto: University of Toronto Press, 3–23.

Rowson, Martin (2009), 'The art of offence', *Index on Censorship* 38(1): 140–164.

Rushdie, Salman ([1999] 1991), *Haroun and the Sea of Stories*, London: Granta.

— (1992), *The Wizard of Oz*, London: British Film Institute.

— ([1991] 1992), *Imaginary Homelands: Essays and Criticism 1981–91*, London: Granta.

— ([1994] 1995), *East, West*, London: Vintage.

— ([1981] 1995), *Midnight's Children*, London: Vintage.

— ([1983] 1995) *Shame*, London: Vintage.

— ([1995] 1996), *The Moor's Last Sigh*, London: Vintage.

— (1996), 'Interview. Salman Rushdie talks to the London Consortium about *The Satanic Verses*', Collin MacCabe, *Critical Enquiry* 38(2): 51–70.

— (1997), 'Introduction', in Rushdie, Salman and West, Elizabeth (eds) *Mirrorwork: Fifty Years of Indian Writing 1947–1997*, London: Vintage, vii–xx.

— ([1988] 1998), *The Satanic Verses*, London: Vintage.

— ([1999] 2000), *The Ground Beneath Her Feet*, London: Vintage.

— (2001), *Fury*, London: Jonathan Cape.

— (2002), *Step Across This Line: Collected Non-Fiction 1992–2002*, London: Jonathan Cape.

— (2005), *Shalimar the Clown*, London: Jonathan Cape.

— (2008a), *The Enchantress of Florence*, London: Jonathan Cape.

— (2008b), 'The political Rushdie: an interview by Ashutosh Varshney', in Varshney, Ashutosh. *Midnight*, 9–22.

— (2008c), 'Salman Rushdie spins a yarn: a conversation with James Mustich', *Barnes & Noble Review* 2 June (http://bnreview.barnesandnoble.com/t5/Interview/Salman-Rushdie-Spins-a-Yarn/ba-p/425, accessed 6 March 2011).

— (2010), *Luka and the Fire of Life*, London: Jonathan Cape.

Ruthven, Malise (2008), 'Naming the unnameable', *Index on Censorship* 37(4): 133–143.

Ryan, Simon (1996), *The Cartographic Eye: How Explorers Saw Australia*, Cambridge: Cambridge University Press.

Said, Edward W. (2004), *Humanism and Democratic Criticism*, New York: Columbia University Press.

Sandhu, Sukhdev (2003), *London Calling: How Black and Asian Writers Imagined a City*, London: Harper Collins.

Sawhney, Sabina and Sawhney, Simona (2001), 'Reading Rushdie after September 11, 2001', *Twentieth Century Literature* 47(4): 431–443.

Scanlan, Margaret (2010), 'Migrating from terror: the postcolonial novel after September 11', *Journal of Postcolonial Writing* 46(3–4): 266–278.

Schildgen, Brenda D., Zhou, Gang and Gilman, Sander L. (eds) (2006), *Other Renaissances: A New Approach to World Literature*, New York: Palgrave Macmillan.

Scott, Ridley (dir.) (2000), *Gladiator*, DreamWorks.

Sealy, I. Allan ([1988] 1990), *The Trotter-Nama*, London: Penguin.

Sergeant, David (2009), 'Whispering to the converted: narrative communication in Rudyard Kipling's *Letters of Marque* and Indian fiction', *Modern Language Review* 104: 26–40.

Seyfert, Carl K., and Sirkin, Leslie A. (1979), *Earth History and Plate Tectonics: An Introduction to Historical Geology*, London: Harper & Row Publishers.

Shahani, Roshan G. (1995), 'Polyphonous voices in the city: Bombay's Indian-English fiction', in Patel, Sujata and Alice Thorner, *Bombay: Mosaic of Modern Culture*, New Delhi: Oxford University Press, 99–112.

Shakespeare, William ([1596?] 1998), *The Merchant of Venice* in Proudfoot , Richard, Thompson, Ann, and Kastan, David S. (eds), *The Arden Shakespeare. Complete Works*, Walton-on-Thames: Thomas Nelson and Sons, 829–856.

— ([1604?] 1998), *Othello* in Proudfoot , Richard, Thompson, Ann, and Kastan, David S. (eds), *The Arden Shakespeare. Complete Works*, Walton-on-Thames: Thomas Nelson and Sons, 939–975.

Shamsie, Kamila (1998), *In the City by the Sea*, London: Granta.

— (2000), *Salt and Saffron*, London: Bloomsbury.

— (2002), *Kartography*, London: Bloomsbury.

— ([2005] 2006), *Broken Verses*, London: Bloomsbury.

— (2009), *Burnt Shadows*, London: Bloomsbury.

Shamsie, Muneeza (2010), 'Pakistan: annual bibliography of commonwealth literature 2009', *Journal of Commonwealth Literature* 45(4): 641–658.

Sherer, Susan (1996), 'Secrecy and autonomy in Lewis Carroll', *Philosophy and Literature* 20(1): 1–19.

Slemon, Stephen (1988), 'Magic realism as post-colonial discourse', *Canadian Literature* 116: 9–24.

Spivak, Gayatri C. (1985), 'The Rani of Simur', in Barker, Francis, Hulme, Peter, Iversen, Margaret and Loxley, Diana (eds) *Europe and Its Others Vol. 1 Proceedings of the Essex Conference on the Sociology of Literature*, Colchester: University of Essex, 128–151.

— (1988), 'Can the Subaltern Speak?', in Nelson, Cary and Grossberg, Lawrence (eds) *Marxism and the Interpretation of Culture*, Urbana, IL: University of Illinois Press, 271–313.

— (1993), *Outside in the Teaching Machine*, New York and London: Routledge.

— (1996), 'Bonding in difference. Interview with Alfred Arteaga', in Landry, Donna and MacLean, Gerald (eds) *The Spivak Reader: Selected Works of Gayatri Chakravorty Spivak*, New York and London: Routledge, 15–28.

Srivastava, Neelam (2008), *Secularism in the Postcolonial Indian Novel: National and Cosmopolitan Narratives in English*, London: Routledge.

Stevens, Paul (2004), 'England in Moghul India: historicizing cultural difference and its discontents', in Rajan, Balachandra and Sauer, Elizabeth (eds), *Imperialisms: Historical and Literary Investigations, 1500-1900*, London: Palgrave Macmillan, 93–110.

Strocchia, Sharon T. (2006), 'Theatres of everyday life', in Crum, Roger G. and Paoletti, John T. (eds) *Renaissance Florence: A Social History*, Cambridge: Cambridge University Press, 55–80.

Suleri, Sara (1994), 'Contraband histories: Salman Rushdie and the embodiment of blasphemy', in Fletcher, D. M. (ed.), *Reading Rushdie: Perspectives on the Fiction of Salman Rushdie*, Amsterdam: Rodopi, 221–235.

— (2008), 'Rushdie beyond the veil', in Varshney, Ashutosh (ed.) *Midnight's Diaspora: Critical Encounters with Salman Rushdie*, Ann Arbor: University of Michigan Press, 112–121.

Suzuki, Mihoko (1989), *Metamorphoses of Helen: Authority, Difference and the Epic*, Ithaca and London: Cornell University Press.

Szulakowska, Ursula (2000), *The Alchemy of Light: Geometry and Optics in Late Renaissance Alchemical Illustration*, Leiden: Brill Academic Publishers.

Tambe, Ashwini (2006), 'Brothels as families: reflections on the history of Bombay's *kothas*', *International Feminist Journal of Politics* 8(2): 219–242.

— (2009), *Codes of Misconduct: The Regulation of Prostitution in Colonial Bombay*, Minneapolis, MN: University of Minnesota Press.

Taylor, Charles (2006), 'Religious mobilizations', *Public Culture* 18(2): 281–300.

Teverson, Andrew (2004), 'Salman Rushdie and Aijaz Ahmad: Satire, Ideology and *Shame*', *Journal of Commonwealth Literature* 39(2): 45–60.

— (2007), *Salman Rushdie*, Manchester: Manchester University Press.

Teyssot, Georges (2000), 'Baroque topographies', *Assemblage* 41 (April): 79.

Thorner, Alice ([1995] 2003), 'Bombay: diversity and exchange', in Patel, Sujata and Alice Thorner, *Bombay: Mosaic of Modern Culture*, New Delhi: Oxford University Press, xiii–xxxv.

Tomlinson, Janis (2010), 'Bayeu y Subias, Francisco (1734–95)', in Brigstocke, Hugh (ed.) *The Oxford Companion to Western Art*, Oxford: Oxford University Press (http://www.oxfordlineonline.com, accessed 9 December 2010).

Toor, Saadia (2005), 'A national culture for Pakistan: the political economy of a debate', *Inter-Asia Cultural Studies* 6(3): 318–340.

Trousdale, Rachel (2004), '"City of mongrel joy": Bombay and the Shiv Sena in *Midnight's Children* and *The Moor's Last Sigh*', *Journal of Commonwealth Literature* 39(2): 95–110.

Upstone, Sara (2006), 'The fulcrum of instability', *Wasafiri* 21(1): 34–38.

— (2009), *Spatial Politics in the Postcolonial Novel*, Farnham: Ashgate.

— (2010), *British Asian Fiction: Twenty-First-Century Voices*, Manchester: Manchester University Press.

Varma, Rashmi (2004), 'Provincializing the global city: from Bombay to Mumbai', *Social Text* 81(22.4): 65–89.

Varshney, Ashutosh (ed.) (2008), *Midnight's Diaspora: Critical Encounters with Salman Rushdie*, Ann Arbor, MI: University of Michigan Press.

Velazquez, Diego (1656), *Las Meninas*, Museo del Prado, Madrid.

Venuti, Lawrence (1996), 'Translation as a social practice: or, the violence of translation', *Translation Perspectives* 9: 195–213.

Virgil ([c. 42–29 BCE] 1983), *The Eclogues. The Georgics*, C. Day Lewis (trans.), Oxford: Oxford University Press.

— ([c. 19 BCE] 1997), *Aeneid*, John Dryden (trans.), Ware: Wordsworth Editions Ltd.

Viroli, Maurizio ([2005] 2008), 'Introduction', in Bondanella, Peter (ed.) *Niccolò Machiavelli. The Prince*, Oxford: Oxford University Press.

Waldman, Guido (2008), 'Introduction', in *Ludovico Ariosto. Orlando Furioso*, Guido Waldman (trans.), Oxford: Oxford University Press, vii–xvii.

Warner, Marina (1994), *Six Myths of Our Time: Managing Monsters*, London: Vintage.

— (2002), *Fantastic Metamorphoses, Other Worlds*, Oxford: Oxford University Press.

— (2006), *Phantasmagoria: Spirit Visions, Metaphors and Media into the Twenty-First Century*, Oxford: Oxford University Press.

Yeğenoğlu, Meyda (2003), 'Veiled fantasies: cultural and sexual difference in the discourse of orientalism', in Lewis, Reina and Mills, Sara (eds) *Feminist Postcolonial Theory: A Reader*, Edinburgh: Edinburgh University Press, 542–566.

Yeoh, B. S. A. (2005), 'The global cultural city? Spatial imagineering and politics in the (multi)cultural marketplaces of South-East Asia', *Urban Studies* 45(5/6): 945–958.

Young, Robert (1995), *Colonial Desire: Hybridity in Theory, Culture and Race*, London: Routledge.

Zimring, Rishona (2010), 'The passionate cosmopolitan in Salman Rushdie's *Fury*', *Journal of Postcolonial Writing* 46(1): 5–16.

Index